NOTES ON THE BOOK

OF NUMBERS

Notes on the Book of Numbers

C H MACKINTOSH

CHAPTER TWO
LONDON • ENGLAND

NOTES ON THE BOOK OF NUMBERS BY C. H. Mackintosh
UK ISBN 978 1 85307 223 9
Set of Six Notes on the Pentateuch ISBN 978 1 85307 219 2
This edition © Chapter Two 2007

The first edition of *Notes on the Book of Numbers* was first published in 1869 by publishers G. Morrish, 24 Warwick Lane, London. Several reprints followed. First single volume edition of *Notes on the Pentateuch* by Loizeaux Bros. USA 1972

Translated into Amharic, Arabic, Bulgarian, Chinese, Croatian, Czech, Danish, Dutch, Finnish, French, German, Greek, Hindi, Hungarian, Italian, Japanese, Korean, Norwegian, Polish, Portuguese, Romanian, Russian, Spanish and Swedish.

All rights reserved. No part of this publication may be reproduced or transmitted in any form or by any means, electronic or mechanical, including photocopying, recording, or storage in any information retrieval system, without written permission from Chapter Two.

CHAPTER TWO
Fountain House, Conduit Mews, London SE18 7AP, UK
www.chaptertwobooks.org.uk

Distributors:
- Bible, Book and Tract Depôt, 23 Santarosa Avenue, Ryde, NSW 2112, Australia
- The Bible House, Gateway Mall, 35 Tudor Street, Bridgetown, Barbados, WI
- Believers Bookshelf, 5205 Regional Road 81, Unit 3, Beamsville, ON, L0R 1B3, Canada
- Bible Treasury Bookstore, 46 Queen Street, Dartmouth, Nova Scotia, B2Y 1G1, Canada
- El-Ekhwa Library, 3 Anga Hanem Street, Shoubra, Cairo 11231, Egypt
- Bibles & Publications Chrétiennes, 30 rue Châteauvert, 26000 Valence, France
- CSV, An der Schloßfabrik 30, 42499 Hückeswagen, Germany
- Christian Literature Service, PO Box GP 20872, Accra, Ghana
- Christian Truth Bookroom, Paddisonpet, Tenali 522 201, Andhra Pradesh, India
- Words of Life Trust, 3 Chuim, Khar, Mumbai, 400 052, India
- Words of Truth, 38-P.D.A Lamphelpat, Imphal 795 004, Manipur, India
- Uit het Woord der Waarheid, Postbox 260, 7120AG Aalten, Netherlands
- Bible and Book Depot, Box 25119, Christchurch 5, New Zealand
- Christian Literature Depot, PO Box 436, Ijeshatedo, Surulere, Lagos, Nigeria
- Believers Bookshelf, PO Box 777, Shadewell Heights, Basseterre, St. Kitts, WI
- Grace & Truth Book-room, 87 Chausee Road, Castries, St. Lucia, WI
- Chapter Two S.A., Box 2234, Alberton 1450, South Africa
- Beröa Verlag, Zellerstrasse 61, 8038 Zürich, Switzerland
- Éditions Bibles et Littérature Chrétienne, La Foge C, Case Postale, 1816 Chailly-Montreux, Switzerland
- Chapter Two Bookshop, 199 Plumstead Common Road, London, SE18 2UJ, UK
- HoldFast Bible & Tract Depôt, 41 York Road, Tunbridge Wells, Kent, TN1 1JX, UK
- Words of Truth, PO Box 147, Belfast, BT8 4TT, Northern Ireland, UK
- Believers Bookshelf Inc., Box 261, Sunbury, PA 17801, USA

Printed in The Netherlands by Van der Perk Printers

PREFACE

Having read the proof sheets of the following "NOTES ON NUMBERS," I am prepared, so far, to write a preface. It is with no view of praising the book that I do so; but to shew my fellowship with the well-known author in all his labours. The book will speak for itself, and the reader must judge.

After twelve years of joint-editorship in the monthly issue of "THINGS NEW AND OLD," the reader will not be surprised at this mutual love of identification, in sending forth another volume of "NOTES." But for this, there is no reason why I should appear.

The wonderful sale of the three former volumes, and the desire that has been expressed, on all hands, for the fourth, bespeak for it a large circulation.

We will now glance for a moment at the *character* of the Book of Numbers. Fuller details will be found in the "NOTES."

It may be regarded as a divine history of the wanderings of the Israelites in the wilderness for about thirty-eight years and ten months, commencing with the first movement of the camp after the tabernacle was reared. And also, as a perpetual memorial of Jehovah's patient, tender, and unwearied care of His murmuring and rebellious people. It is emphatically a wilderness book, and characterized by journeyings, service, and all the vicissitudes of wilderness life. As such, it is deeply interesting, most instructive, and easily applied to the Christian in this present evil world. Compare Numbers 1 and 36:13, with Deuteronomy 1:3.

The first thing that attracts our attention, in reading the book, is sweet and precious to the heart beyond all expression – *God has His people numbered and gathered around Himself.* He dwelt in the camp – *"In the midst thereof I dwell."* Could love do more? Impossible! The twelve tribes guarded the tabernacle of the Lord. The Levites encamped directly around the court; and Moses, Aaron, and the priests, guarded the entrance whereby God was approached. The circumference of the camp, thus arranged, and all facing the tabernacle, is generally supposed to have been at least twelve miles. But that which gave unity, strength, and glory to the camp in the wilderness, was the presence of God in His tabernacle, as the centre of His chosen people. Blessed shadow of good things to come – of Christ as the centre, life, and glory of His church now!

Rather more than a year from the epoch of the Exodus, Jehovah commanded Moses to number the people that were able to bear arms, from twenty years old and upwards. The tribe of Levi, being exempt from military service, was numbered separately. But the complete number, *twelve*, was made up by the division of Joseph into Ephraim and Manasseh. Chapters 1, 2, 3.

Everything was now in its right place, and everyone knew for certain what he had to do, both when the cloud moved and when it rested. The tabernacle set up – the priests consecrated – the people numbered; they were now to leave Horeb. "The Lord spake unto us in Horeb, saying, Ye have dwelt long enough in this Mount." "And it came to pass on the twentieth day of the second month, in the second year, that the cloud was taken up from off the tabernacle of the testimony. And the children of Israel took their journeys out of the wilderness of Sinai; and the cloud rested in the wilderness of Paran." Deuteronomy 1:6; Numbers 10:11, 12.

The pillar of cloud by day, and the pillar of fire by night, guided all the movements of the camp (Numb. 9:17, 23). The moment the cloud ascended from the tabernacle, the silver trumpets sounded the alarm, and the whole camp was instantly in motion. Then Moses uttered the prayer, "Rise up, Lord, and let thine enemies be scattered: and let them that hate thee flee before thee." When the cloud rested, the whole camp rested, and every man knew his place and his work. And the Moses prayed, "Return, O Lord, unto the many thousands of Israel." Numbers 10:35, 36.

How imposing this camp must have been in the midst of the desert! Well might Balaam say, "How goodly are thy tents, O Jacob, and thy tabernacles, O Israel!" But its true loveliness is only seen by the eye of faith. It was the brightest spot in the world, though on the sand of the desert, and the richest in blessing. Far, far above all its other attractions is the knowledge that God Himself is there, thinking of everyone, and providing for their every need. Day by day, He spread a table for them in the wilderness; and gave then water from the flinty rock. The foot of the traveller was never swollen, and his raiment waxed not old those forty years. Deuteronomy 8:4.

There were upwards of six hundred thousand men above the age of twenty, besides the Levites, and women, and children, probably more than two millions altogether. But Jehovah gathered them all around Himself, as a father would gather his children, and covered them with the skirts of His cloud both by night and by day. "He spread a cloud for a covering; and fire to give light in the night" (Psalm 105:39). Thus was the Lord's family in the place of rest, peace, and blessing. The blood of the everlasting covenant had been sprinkled on the mercy-seat within the vail, and judgment had been executed on the sin offering outside the camp. Oh! that Israel had known! oh! that Israel had understood the lovingkindness of the Lord, and so put all their trust in Him! See Deuteronomy 32, 33.

In the position and service of the Levites there is always much that is interesting to the Christian. They were typical of the Church – or of the individual Christian – in service, just as the priests were typical of the Church in worship. The fact of the Levites being taken for the service of the Lord, in place of the firstborn, gave them a very special character. They were firstfruits unto the Lord. Thus it is that the Church is as the firstfruits, holy to the Lord – "the church of the firstborn ones." James 1; Hebrews 12.

As the Levites thus became God's possession for service, and belonged wholly to Him, so it is with the Church. We are redeemed – we are not our own – we are bought with a price; therefore we are to glorify God in our bodies and in our spirits which are His. We are to serve the living God, in communion with Christ our great High Priest above. The calling of the Church, however, is a much higher thing than the position of the Levites; for she is one with Christ, and the Holy Ghost gives the capacity and the gift for Christian service.

In conclusion, we may safely affirm that there is no truth in Christianity of such importance, or such practical power, as the blessed truth of the Church's relationship to Christ. "For in him dwelleth all the fullness of the Godhead bodily. And ye are complete in him, which is the head of all principality and power" (Col. 2:9, 10). We can only be men of war, worshipping priests, serving Levites in the truest and highest sense, in the proportion that we live in the power of this great truth. We are joined to the Lord by the one Holy Spirit – our life is hid with Christ in God. May we be content to be the Lord's hidden ones as to this world, and only be seen and known as His servants, until He come, then shall we also appear with Him in glory.

May the Lord accompany with His own rich blessing, and clothe with His own divine power, this volume of "NOTES ON NUMBERS." And may He accept it as service to Himself, and use it for His glory; and to His name alone be undivided praise. Amen

A.M.
London, Dec. 1, 1869.

Chapters 1 & 2

PEDIGREE AND BANNERS

The Book of Numbers in the Pentateuch

We now enter upon the study of the fourth grand division of the Pentateuch, or five books of Moses; and we shall find the leading characteristic of this book quite as strongly marked as that of any of the three books which have already engaged our attention. In the Book of Genesis, after the record of creation, the deluge, and the Babel dispersion, we have God's election of the seed of Abraham. In the book of Exodus, we have redemption. Leviticus gives us priestly worship and communion. In Numbers we have the walk and warfare of the wilderness. Such are the prominent subjects of these most precious sections of inspiration, while, as might be expected, many other points of deepest interest are collaterally introduced. The Lord, in His great mercy, has led us through the study of Genesis, Exodus, and Leviticus; and we can reckon on Him, with confidence, to conduct as through the Book of Numbers. May His Spirit lead the thoughts, and guide the pen, so that not a sentence may be committed to writing that is not in strict accordance with His holy mind! May every page and every paragraph bear the stamp of His approval, and be, at once, conducive to His glory, and the permanent profit of the reader!

"And the Lord spake unto Moses *in the wilderness* of Sinai, in the tabernacle of the congregation, on the first day of the second month, in the second year after they were come out of the land of Egypt, saying, Take ye the sum of all the congregation of the children of Israel, after their families, by the house of their fathers, with the number of their names, every male by their polls; from twenty years old and upward, all that are *able to go forth to war* in Israel; thou and Aaron shall number them by their armies." Chap. 1:1-3.

Here we find ourselves, at once, "in the wilderness," where those only are to be taken account of who are "able to go forth to war." This is strongly marked. In the book of Genesis the seed of Israel were in the loins of their father Abraham. In the Book of Exodus they were in the brickkilns of Egypt. In Leviticus they were gathered round the tabernacle of the congregation. In Numbers they are seen in the wilderness. Then, again, in full keeping with the above, and in confirmation thereof, in Genesis we hearken to the call of God in election; in Exodus we gaze upon the blood of the Lamb in redemption; in Leviticus we are almost entirely occupied with the worship, and service of the sanctuary. But no sooner have we opened the book of Numbers than we read of men of war, of armies, of standards, of camps, and trumpets sounding alarm.

All this is highly characteristic, and marks off the book on which we are now entering as one of special interest, value, and importance to the Christian. Each book of the Bible, each section of the inspired canon, has its own distinct place and object. Each has its own niche assigned to it by its divine Author. We must not entertain, for a moment, the thought of instituting any comparison in point of intrinsic value, interest, and importance. All is divine, and therefore perfect. The Christian reader fully and heartily believes this. He reverently sets his seal to the truth of the plenary inspiration of holy scripture – of all scripture, and of the Pentateuch amongst the rest; nor is he to be moved, one hair's breadth, from this by the bold and impious attacks of infidels, ancient, medieval, or modern. Infidels and rationalists may traffic in their unhallowed reasonings. They may exhibit their enmity against the book and its Author; but the pious Christian rests, not withstanding all, in the simple and happy belief that "All scripture is given by inspiration of God."

But while we must utterly reject the idea of any comparison

as to authority and value, we may, with very much profit, compare the contents, design, and scope of the various books of the Bible. And the more profoundly we meditate upon these, the more forcibly shall we be struck with the exquisite beauty, infinite wisdom, and wonderful precision of the volume a whole, and of each distinct division thereof. The inspired writer never swerves from the direct object of the book, whatever that object may be. You will never find anything in any one book of the Bible which is not in the most perfect harmony with the main design of that book. To prove and illustrate this statement would lead us through the entire canon of holy scripture, and hence we shall not attempt it. The intelligent Christian does not need the proof, however much he might be interested in the illustration. He takes his stand upon the great fact that the Book, as a whole, and in all its parts, is from God; and his heart reposes in the conclusion, that in that whole, and in each of those parts, there is not a jot or a tittle which is not in every way worthy of the divine Author.

Hear the following words from the pen of one who expresses himself as "deeply convinced of the divine inspiration of the scriptures, given to us of God, and confirmed in this conviction by daily and growing discoveries of their fullness, depth, and perfectness, ever more sensible, through grace, of the admirable perfection of the parts, and the wonderful connection of the whole." "The scriptures," says this writer, "have a living source, and living power has pervaded their composition: hence their infiniteness of bearing, and the impossibility of separating any one part from the whole, because one God is the living centre from which all flows; one Christ the living centre round which all its truth circles, and to which it refers, though in various glory; and one Spirit the divine sap which carries its power from its source in God to the minutest branches of the all-uniting truth, testifying of the glory, the grace, and the truth of Him whom God sets forth as the object, and centre, and head of all that is in connection with Himself, of Him who is, withal, God over all, blessed for evermore . . . . The more – beginning from the utmost leaves and branches of this revelation of the mind of God, by which we have been reached when far from Him – we have traced it up towards its centre, and thence looked down again towards its extent and diversity, the more we learn its infiniteness, and our own feebleness of apprehension. We learn, blessed be God, this, that the love which is its source is found in unmingled perfectness and fullest display of those manifestations of it which have reached us even in our ruined state. The same perfect God of love is in it all. But the unfoldings of divine wisdom in the counsels in which God has displayed Himself remain ever to us a subject of research, in which every new discovery, by increasing our spiritual intelligence, makes the infiniteness of the whole, and the way in which it surpasses all our thoughts, only more and more clear to us."

It is truly refreshing to transcribe such lines from the pen of one who has been a profound student of scripture for forty years. They are of unspeakable value, at a moment when so many are ready to cast a slight upon the sacred volume. Not that we are, in any wise, dependent upon human testimony in forming our conclusions as to the divine origin of the Bible, inasmuch as these conclusions rest upon a foundation furnished by the Bible itself. God's word, as well as His work, speaks for itself; it carries its own credentials with it; it speaks to the heart; it reaches down to the great moral roots of our being; it penetrates the very innermost chambers of the soul; it shows us what we are; it speaks to us as no other book can speak; and, as the woman of Sychar argued that Jesus must be the Christ because He told her all things that ever she did, so may we say in reference to the Bible, It tells us all that ever we did, is not this the word of God? No doubt it is only by the Spirit's teaching that we can discern and appreciate the evidence and credentials with which holy scripture presents itself before us; but still it does speak for itself, and needs not human testimony to make it of value to the soul. We should no more think of having our faith in the Bible established upon man's testimony in its favour than we should think of having it shaken by his testimony against it.

It is of the very last possible importance, at all times, but more especially at a moment like the present, to have the heart and mind established in the grand truth of the divine authority of holy scripture – its plenary inspiration – its all-sufficiency for all purposes, for all people, at all times. There are two hostile influences abroad, namely, infidelity, on the one hand, and superstition, on the other. The former denies that God has spoken to us in His word. The latter admits that He has spoken, but it denies that we can understand what He says, save by the interpretation of the Church.

Now, while there are very many who recoil with horror from the impiety and audacity of infidelity, they do not see that superstition, just as completely, deprives them of the scriptures. For wherein, let us ask, lies the difference between denying that God has spoken, and denying that we can understand what He says? In either case, are we not deprived of the word of God? Unquestionably. If God cannot make me understand what He says – if He cannot give me the assurance that it is He Himself who speaks, I am, in no wise, better off than if He had not spoken at all. If God's word is not sufficient, without human interpretation, then it cannot be God's word at all. That which is insufficient is not God's word. We must admit either of two things, namely, that God has not spoken at all, or if He has spoken, His word is perfect. There is no neutral ground in reference to this question. Has God given us a revelation? Infidelity says, "No." superstition says, "Yes, but you cannot understand it without human authority." Thus are we, in the one case as well as in the other, deprived of the priceless treasure of God's own precious word; and thus, too, infidelity and superstition, though apparently so unlike, meet in the one point of depriving us of a divine revelation.

But, blessed be God, He has given us a revelation. He has spoken, and His word is able to reach the heart and the understanding also. God is able to give the certainty that it is He who speaks, and we do not want any human authority to intervene. We do not want a poor rush-light to enable us to see that the sun is shining. The beams of that glorious luminary are quite enough without any such miserable addition. All we want is to stand in the sunshine and we shall be convinced that the sun shines. If we retire into a vault or into a tunnel, we shall not feel his influence; and just so is it with regard to scripture, if we place ourselves beneath the chilling and darkening influences of superstition or infidelity, we shall not experience the genial and enlightening power of that divine revelation.

Belonging to the people of God

Having said thus much as to the divine volume as a whole, we shall now proceed to consider the contents of the section which lies open before us. In Numbers 1 we have the declaration of the *"pedigree;"* and in Numbers 2, the recognition of the *"standard."* "And Moses and Aaron took these men which are expressed by their names: and they assembled all the congregation together on the first day of the second month, and *they declared their pedigrees* after their families, by the house of their fathers; according to the number of the names, from twenty years old and upward, by their polls. As the Lord commanded Moses, so he numbered them in the wilderness of Sinai." Chap. 1:17-19.

Has this any voice for us? Does it convey any great spiritual lesson to our understanding? Assuredly it does. In the first place, it suggests this important question to the reader, "Can I declare my pedigree?" It is greatly to be feared there are hundreds, if not thousands, of professing Christians who are wholly incompetent to do so. They cannot say with clearness and decision, *"Now are* we the sons of God" (1 John 3:2). "Ye *are* all the children of God by faith in Christ Jesus." " And if ye are Christ's, then *are* ye Abraham's seed, and heirs according to the promise." (Gal. 3:26, 29) " For as many as are led by the Spirit of God, they *are* the sons of God. . . . The Spirit itself beareth witness with our spirit, that we *are* the sons of God." Rom. 8:14, 16.

This is the Christian's "pedigree," and it is his privilege to be able to "declare" it. He is born from above – born again – born of water and the spirit, i.e., by the word and by the Holy Ghost (compare, diligently, John 3:5; James 1:18; 1 Peter 1:23; Eph. 5:26). The believer traces his pedigree directly up to a risen Christ in glory. This is Christian genealogy. So far as our natural pedigree is concerned, if we trace it up to its *source*, and then declare it honestly, we must see and admit that we are sprung from a ruined stock. Ours is a fallen family. Our fortunes are gone; our very blood attainted; we are irrecoverably ruined; we can never regain our original position; our former *status* and the inheritance which belonged to it are irretrievably lost. A man may be able to trace his genealogical line throughout a race of nobles, of princes, or of kings; but is he is finally to "declare his pedigree," he cannot stop short of a fallen, ruined, outcast head. We must get to the *source* of a thing to know what it really is. It is thus God looks at and judges of things, and we must think with Him if we would think aright. His judgment of men and things must be dominant for ever. Man's judgment is only ephemeral, it lasts but for a day; and hence, according to faith's estimate, the estimate of sound sense, "It is a *small* thing to be judged of man's day" (1 Cor. 4:3). Oh! how small! Would that we felt more deeply how small a thing it is to be judged of man's judgment, or, as the margin reads it, of man's day! Would that we walked, habitually, in the real sense of the smallness thereof! It would impart a calm elevation and a holy dignity which would lift us above the influence of the scene through which we are passing. What is rank in this life? What importance can attach to a pedigree which, if honestly traced, and faithfully declared, is derived from a ruined stock? A man can only be proud of his birth when he stops short of his real origin: "born in sin and shapen in iniquity." Such is man's origin – such his birth. Who can think of being proud of such a birth, of such an origin? Who but one whose mind the god of this world hath blinded?

But how different with the Christian! His pedigree is

heavenly. His genealogical tree strikes its roots into the soil of the new creation. Death can never break the line, inasmuch as it is formed in resurrection. We cannot be too simple as to this. It is of the utmost importance that the reader should be thoroughly clear on this foundation point. We can easily see from this first chapter of Numbers, how essential it was that every member of the congregation of Israel should be able to declare his pedigree. Uncertainty, on this point, would have proved disastrous; it would have produced hopeless confusion. We can hardly imagine an Israelite, when called to declare his pedigree, expressing himself in the doubtful manner adopted by many Christians now-a-days. We cannot conceive his saying, "Well, I am not quite sure. Sometimes I cherish the hope that I am of the stock of Israel, but at other times, I am full of fear that I do not belong to the congregation of the Lord at all. I am all in uncertainty and darkness." Can we conceive such language? Assuredly not. Much less could we imagine anyone maintaining the monstrous notion that no one could possibly be sure as to whether he was a true Israelite or not until the day of judgment.

All such ideas and reasonings – all such doubts, fears, and questions, we may rest assured, were foreign to the mind of the Israelite. Every member of the congregation was called to declare his pedigree, ere taking his place in the ranks as a man of war. Each one was able to say, like Saul of Tarsus, "Circumcised the eighth day, of the stock of Israel," &c. All was settled and clear, and necessarily so if there was to be any real entrance upon the walk and warfare of the wilderness.

Now, may we not legitimately ask, "If a Jew could be certain as to his pedigree, why may not a Christian be certain as to his?" Reader, weigh this question, and if you are one of that large class of persons who are never able to arrive at the blessed certainty of their heavenly lineage, their spiritual birth, pause, we beseech you, and let us reason with you on this momentous point. It may be you are disposed to ask, "How can I be sure that I am, really and truly, a child of God, a member of Christ, born of the word and Spirit of God? I would give worlds, were they mine, to be certain as to this most weighty question."

Well, then, we would earnestly desire to help you in this matter. Indeed one special object before us in penning these "Notes" is to assist anxious souls, by answering, as the Lord may enable us, their questions, solving their difficulties, and removing the stumbling-blocks out of their way.

Wisdom is justified of all her children

And, first of all, let as point out one special feature which belongs to all the children of God, without exception. It is a very simple, but a very blessed feature. If we do not possess it, in some degree, it is most certain we are not of the heavenly race; but if we do possess it, it is just as certain that we are, and we may, therefore, without any difficulty or reserve, "declare our pedigree." Now what is this feature? what is this great family characteristic? Our Lord Jesus Christ supplies the answer. He tells us that "Wisdom is justified of *all* her children" (Luke 7:35; Matt. 11:19). All the children of Wisdom, from the days of Abel down to the present moment, have been marked by this great family trait. There is not so much as a single exception. All God's children – all the sons of Wisdom have always exhibited, in some degree, this moral feature – they have justified God.

Let the reader consider this. It may be he finds it hard to understand what is meant by justifying God; but a passage or two of holy scripture will, we trust, make it quite plain. We read in Luke 7 that "all the people that heard Jesus, and the publicans, *justified God,* being baptised with the baptism of John. But, the Pharisees and lawyers rejected the counsel of God against themselves, being not baptised of him" (ver. 29, 30). Here we have the two generations brought, as it were, face to face. The publicans justified God and condemned themselves. The Pharisees justified themselves and judged God. The former submitted to the baptism of John – the baptism of repentance. The latter refused that baptism – refused to repent – refused to humble and to judge themselves.

Here we have the two great classes into which the whole human family has been divided, from the days of Abel and Cain down to the present day; and here, too, we have the simplest possible test by which to try our "pedigree." Have we taken the place of self-condemnation? Have we bowed in true repentance before God? This is to justify God. The two things go together – yea, they are one and the same. The man who condemns himself justifies God; and the man who justifies God condemns himself. On the other hand, the man who justifies himself judges God; and the man who judges God justifies himself.

Thus it stands in every case. And be it observed, that the very moment we take the ground of repentance and self judgment, God takes the ground of a Justifier. God always justifies those who condemn themselves. All His children justify Him, and He justifies all His children. The moment David said, "I have sinned against the Lord," the answer was, "The Lord hath put away thy sin." Divine forgiveness follows, with the most intense rapidity, human confession.

Hence it follows that nothing can be more foolish than for any one to justify himself, inasmuch as God must be justified in His sayings, and overcome when He is judged (comp. Psalm 51:4; Rom. 3:4). God must have the upper hand in the end, and then all self justification shall be seen in its true light. The wisest thing therefore is to condemn ourselves. This is what all the children of Wisdom do. Nothing is more characteristic of the true members of Wisdom's family then the habit and spirit of self-judgment. Whereas, on the other hand, nothing so marks all those who are not of this family as a spirit of self-vindication.

These things are worthy of our most earnest attention. Nature will blame anything and everything, any one and every one but itself. But where grace is at work, there is ever a readiness to judge self, and take the lowly place. This is the true secret of blessing and peace. All God's children have stood on this blessed ground, exhibited this lovely moral trait, and reached this grand result. We cannot find so much as a single exception in the entire history of Wisdom's happy family; and we may safely say, that if the reader has been led, in truth and reality, to own himself lost – to condemn himself – to take the place of true repentance – then is he, in very deed, one of the children of Wisdom, and he may therefore, with boldness and decision, "declare his pedigree."

Knowing one's pedigree

We would urge this point at the outset. It is impossible for any one to recognise and rally round the proper "standard" unless he can declare his "pedigree." In short, it is impossible to take up a true position in the wilderness so long as there is any uncertainty as to this great question. How could an Israelite of old have taken his place in the assembly – how could he have stood in the ranks – how could he expect to make any progress through the wilderness, if he could not distinctly declare his pedigree? Impossible. Just so is it with Christians now. Progress in wilderness life – success in spiritual warfare, is out of the question if there be any uncertainty as to the spiritual pedigree. We must be able to say, "*We know* that we have passed from death unto life" – "*We know* that we are of God" – "We believe and are sure," ere there can be any real advance in the life and walk of a Christian.

Reader, say, can you declare your pedigree? Is this a thoroughly settled point with you? Are you clear as to this in the very depths of your soul? When you are all alone with God, is it a perfectly settled question between you and Him? Search and see. Make sure work of it. Do not slur the matter over. Build not upon mere profession. Say not "I am a member of such a church; I receive the Lord's supper; I hold such and such doctrines; I have been religiously brought up; I live a moral life; I have done nobody any harm; I read the Bible and say my prayers; I have family worship in my house; I give largely in the cause of philanthropy and religion." All this may be perfectly true of you, and yet you may not have a single pulse of divine life, a single ray of divine light. Not one of these things, not all of them put together, could be accepted as a declaration of spiritual pedigree. There must be the witness of the Spirit that you are a child of God, and this witness always accompanies simple faith in the Lord Jesus Christ. "He that believeth in the Son of God hath the witness in himself" (1 John 5:10). It is not, by any means, a question of looking into your own heart for evidences. It is not a building upon frames, feelings, and experiences. Nothing of the sort. It is a childlike faith in Christ. It is having eternal life in the Son of God. It is the imperishable record of the Holy Ghost. It is taking God at His word. "Verily, verily, I say unto you, He that heareth my word, and believeth on him that sent me, *hath* everlasting life, and shall not come into judgment (*krisin*), but *is passed* from death unto life." John 5:24.

Being ready for battle

This is the true way to declare your pedigree; and be assured of it, you must be able to declare it ere you can "go forth to war." We do not mean to say you cannot be saved without this. God forbid we should say any such thing. We believe there are hundreds of the true spiritual Israel who are not able to declare their pedigree. But we ask, Are such able to go forth to war? Are they vigorous military men? Far from it. They cannot even know what true conflict is; on the contrary, persons of this class mistake their doubts and fears, their dark and cloudy seasons, for true Christian conflict This is a most serious mistake; but alas! a very common one. We continually find a, low, dark, legal condition of soul defended on the ground of Christian conflict, whereas, according to the New Testament, true Christian conflict or warfare is carried on in a region where doubts and fears are unknown. It is when we stand in the clear daylight of God's full salvation – salvation in a risen Christ – that we really enter upon the warfare proper to us as Christians. Are we to suppose, for a moment, that our legal struggles, our culpable unbelief, our refusal to submit to the righteousness of God, our questionings and reasonings, can be viewed as Christian conflict? By no means. All these things must be regarded as conflict with God; whereas Christian conflict is carried on with Satan. "We wrestle not against flesh and blood, but against principalities, against powers, against the rulers of the darkness of this world, against wicked spirits in high places." Eph. 6:12.

This is Christian conflict. But can such conflict be waged by those who are continually doubting whether they are Christians or not? We do not believe it. Could we imagine an Israelite in conflict with Amalek in the wilderness, or with the Canaanites in the land of promise, while yet unable to "declare his pedigree" or recognise his "standard?" The thing is inconceivable. No, no; every member of the congregation, who was able to go forth to war was perfectly clear and settled as to those two points. Indeed he could not go forth if he were not so.

Three types of conflict

And, while on the important subject of Christian conflict, it may be well to call the reader's attention to the three portions of New Testament scripture in which we have three distinct characters of conflict presented, namely, Romans 7:7-24; Galatians 5:17; Ephesians 6:10-17. If the reader will just turn, for a moment, to the above scriptures, we shall seek to point out the true character of each.

In Romans 7:7-24 we have the struggle of a soul quickened but not emancipated – a regenerated soul under the law. The proof that we have before us, here, a quickened soul is found in such utterances as these, "That which I do, I allow not" – "to will is present with me" – *"I delight in the law of God after the inward man."* None but a regenerated soul could speak thus. The disallowance of the wrong, the *will* to do right, the inward delight in the law of God – all these are the distinct marks of the new life – the precious fruits of regeneration. No unconverted person could truthfully use such language.

But, on the other hand, the proofs that we have before us, in this scripture, a soul not fully emancipated, not in the joy of known deliverance, not in the full consciousness of victory, not in the assured possession of spiritual power – the plain proofs of all this we have in such utterances as the following, "I am carnal, sold under sin" – "what I would that do I not; but what I hate that do I" – "O wretched man that I am! who shall deliver me?" Now, we know that a Christian is not "carnal," but spiritual; he is not "sold under sin," but redeemed from its power; he is not a "wretched man" sighing for deliverance, but a happy man who knows himself delivered. He is not an impotent slave, unable to do the right thing, and ever compelled to do the wrong; he is a free man, endowed with power in the Holy Ghost, and able to say, "I can do *all* things through Christ that strengtheneth me." Philippians 4.

We cannot here attempt to enter upon a full exposition of this most important scripture; we merely offer a suggestion or two which may help the reader to seize its scope and import. We are fully aware that many Christians differ widely as to the interpretation of this chapter. Some deny that it presents the exercises of a quickened soul; others maintain that it sets forth the experiences proper to a Christian. We cannot accept either conclusion. We believe it exhibits to our view the exercises of a truly regenerated soul, but of a soul not set free by the knowledge of its union with a risen Christ, and the power of the Holy Ghost. Hundreds of Christians are actually in the seventh of Romans but their proper place is in the eighth. They are, as to their experience, under the law. They do not know themselves as sealed by the Holy Ghost. They are not in possession of full victory in a risen and glorified Christ. They have doubts and fears, and are ever disposed to cry out "O wretched man that I am! Who shall deliver me?" But is not a Christian delivered? Is he not saved? Is he not accepted in the Beloved? Is he not sealed by that Holy Spirit of promise? Is he not united to Christ? Ought he not to know and enjoy, and to confess all this? Unquestionably.

Well then he is no longer, as to his standing, in the seventh of Romans. It is his privilege to sing the song of victory at heaven's side of the empty tomb of Jesus, and to walk in the holy liberty wherewith Christ makes His people free. The seventh of Romans is not liberty at all, but bondage, except indeed at the very close, where the soul is able to say, "I thank God." No doubt, it may be a very wholesome exercise to pass through all that is here detailed for us with such marvellous vividness and power; and, furthermore, we must declare that we should vastly prefer being honestly in the seventh of Romans to being falsely in the eighth. But all this leaves wholly untouched the question as to the proper application of this profoundly interesting passage of scripture.

We shall now glance, for a moment, at the conflict in Galatians 5:17. We shall quote the passage. "For the flesh lusteth against the Spirit, and the Spirit against the flesh: and these are contrary the one to the other: so that ye cannot do the things that ye would."[1] This passage is often quoted to account for continual *defeat*, whereas it really contains the secret of perpetual *victory*. In verse 16 we read, "This I say, then, walk in the Spirit, and *ye shall not fulfil* the lust of the flesh." This makes it all so clear. The presence of the Holy Ghost secures power. We are assured that God is stronger than "the flesh," and therefore, where He is in conflict the triumph is secured. And be it carefully noted that Galatians 5:17 does not speak of the conflict between the two natures, the old and the new, but between the Holy Ghost and the flesh. This is the reason why it is added, "In order that ye may not do the things that ye would." If the Holy Ghost were not dwelling in us, we should be sure to fulfil the lust of the flesh; but, inasmuch as He is in us to carry on the warfare, we are no longer obliged to do wrong, but blessedly enabled to do right.

Now this precisely marks the point of difference between Romans 7:14, 15 and Galatians 5:17. In the former we have the new nature, but not the power of the indwelling Spirit. In the latter, we have not only the new nature, but also the power of the Holy Ghost. We must ever bear in mind that the new nature in a believer is dependent. It is dependent upon the Spirit for power, and upon the word for guidance. But, clearly, where God the Holy Ghost is, there must be power. He may be grieved and hindered; but Galatians 5:16 distinctly teaches that if we walk in the Spirit, we shall have sure and constant victory over the flesh. Hence, therefore, it would be a very serious mistake indeed to quote Galatians 5:17 as a reason for a low and carnal walk. Its teaching is designed to produce the direct opposite.

And now one word on Ephesians 6:10-17. Here we have the conflict between the Christian and wicked spirits in heavenly places. The Church belongs to heaven, and should ever maintain a heavenly walk and conversation. It should be our constant aim to make good our heavenly standing – to plant the foot firmly upon our heavenly inheritance, and keep it there. This the devil seeks to hinder, in every possible way, and hence the conflict; hence too "the whole armour of God," by which alone we can stand against our powerful spiritual foe.

It is not our purpose to dwell upon the armour, as we have merely called the reader's attention to the above three scriptures in order that he may have the subject of conflict, in all its phases, fully before his mind, in connection with the opening lines of the Book of Numbers. Nothing can be more interesting; nor can we possibly over estimate the importance of being clear as to the real nature and ground of Christian conflict. If we go forth to war without knowing what the war is about, and in a state of uncertainty as to whether our "pedigree" is all right, we shall not make much headway against the enemy.

The order of the camp of Israel

But, as has been already remarked, there was another thing quite as necessary for the man of war as the clear declaration of his pedigree, and that was the distinct recognition of his standard. The two things were essential for the walk and warfare of the wilderness. Moreover, they were inseparable. If a man did not know his pedigree, he could not recognise his standard, and thus all would have been plunged in hopeless confusion. In place of keeping rank, and making steady progress, they would have been in each other's way, and treading one upon another. Each had to know his post and keep it – to know his standard and abide by it. Thus they moved on together; thus progress was made, work done, and warfare carried on. The Benjaminite had his post, and the Ephraimite had his, and neither was to interfere with, or cross the path of, the other. Thus with all the tribes, throughout the camp of the Israel of God. Each had his pedigree, and each had his post; and neither the one nor the other was according to their own thoughts; all was of God. He gave the pedigree, and He assigned the standard. Nor was there any need of comparing one with another, or any ground of jealousy one of another; each had his place to fill, and his work to do, and there was work enough and room enough for all. There was the greatest possible variety, and yet the most perfect unity. "Every man of the children of Israel shall pitch by his own standard, with the ensign of their father's house." "And the children of Israel did according to all that the Lord commanded Moses: so they pitched by their standards, and so they set forward, every one after their families, according to the house of their fathers." (Num. 2:2, 34)

Thus, in the camp of old, as well as in the Church now, we learn that "God is not the author of confusion." Nothing could be more exquisitely arranged than the four camps, of three tribes each, forming a perfect square, each side of the square exhibiting its own specific standard. "Every man of the children of Israel shall pitch by his own standard, with the ensign of their father's house: over against the tabernacle of the congregation shall they pitch." The God of the armies of Israel knew how to marshal His hosts. It would be a great mistake to suppose that God's warriors were not ordered according to the most perfect system of military tactics.

We may plume ourselves upon our progress in arts and sciences, and we may fancy that the host of Israel presented a spectacle of rude disorder and wild confusion, compared with what may be seen in modern times. But this would be an empty conceit. We may rest assured that the camp of Israel was ordered and furnished in the most perfect manner, for the simplest and most conclusive of all reasons, namely, that it was ordered and furnished by the hand of God. Grant us but this, that God has done anything, and we argue, with the most perfect confidence, that it has been perfectly done.

This is a very simple, but a very blessed principle. Of course it would not satisfy an infidel or a sceptic; what would? It is the province and prerogative of a sceptic to doubt everything, to believe nothing. He measures everything by his own standard, and rejects whatever he cannot reconcile with his own notions. He lays down, with marvellous coolness, his own premises, and then proceeds to draw his own conclusions. But if the premises are false, the conclusions must be false likewise. And there is this invariable feature attaching to the premises of all sceptics, rationalists, and infidels, *they always leave out God;* and hence all their conclusions must be fatally false. On the other hand, the humble believer starts with this great first principle, that GOD IS; and not only that He is, but that He has to do with His creatures; that He interests Himself in, and occupies Himself about, the affairs of men.

What consolation for the Christian! But infidelity will not allow this at all. To bring God in is to upset all the reasonings of the sceptic, for they are based upon the thorough exclusion of God.

However, we are not now writing in order to meet infidels, but for the edification of believers, and yet it is sometimes well to call attention to the thorough rottenness of the whole system of infidelity; and surely in no way can this be more clearly or forcibly shewn than by the fact that it rests entirely upon the exclusion of God. Let this fact be seized, and the whole system crumbles into dust at our feet. If we believe that God is, then, assuredly, everything must be viewed in relation to Him. We must look at all from His point of view. Nor is this all. If we believe that God is, then we must see that man cannot judge Him. God must be the judge of right or wrong, of what is and what is not worthy of Himself. So also in reference to God's word. If it be true that God is, and that He has spoken to us, He has given us a revelation, then, assuredly, that revelation is not to be judged by man's reason. It is above and beyond any such tribunal. Only think of measuring God's word by the rules of human arithmetic! And yet this is precisely what has been done in our own day, with this blessed Book of Numbers, with which we are now engaged, and with which we shall proceed, leaving infidelity and its arithmetic aside.

We feel it very needful, in our notes and reflections on this book, as well as on every other book, to remember two things, namely, first, the *book*; and secondly, the *soul*: the book and its contents; the soul and its necessities. There is a danger of becoming so occupied with the former as to forget the latter. And, on the other hand, there is the danger of becoming so wholly engrossed with the latter as to forget the former. Both must be attended to. And we may say that what constitutes an efficient ministry, whether written or oral, is the proper adjustment of these two things. There are some ministers who study the word very diligently, and, it may be, very profoundly. They are well versed in biblical knowledge; they have drunk deeply at the fountain of inspiration. All this is of the utmost importance, and of the very highest value. A ministry without this will be barren indeed. If a man does not study his Bible diligently and prayerfully, he will have little to give to his readers or his hearers; at least little worth their having. Those who minister in the word must dig for themselves, and *"dig deep."*

But then the *soul* must be considered – its condition anticipated, and its necessities met. If this be lost sight of, the ministry will lack point, pungency, and power. It will be inefficient and unfruitful. In short, the two things must be combined and properly adjusted. A man who merely studies the *book* will be unpractical. A man who merely studies the *soul* will be unfurnished. A man who duly studies *both* will be a good minister of Jesus Christ.

A question to the reader

Now, we desire, in our measure, to be this to the reader; and hence as we travel, in his company, through the marvellous book which lies open before us, we would not only seek to point out its moral beauties, and unfold its holy lessons, but we would also feel it to be our bounden duty to put an occasional question to him or her, as to how far those lessons are being learnt, and those beauties appreciated. We trust the reader will not object to this, and hence, ere we close this our first section, we would ask him a question or two thereon.

And first, then, dear friend, Art thou clear and settled as to thy "pedigree?" Is it a settled thing that thou art on the Lord's side? Do not, we beseech thee, leave this grand question unsettled. We have asked it before, and we ask it again. Dost thou know – canst thou declare thy spiritual pedigree? It is the first thing for God's warrior. It is of no use to think of entering the militant host so long as you are unsettled as to this point. We say not that a man cannot be saved without this. Far be the thought. But he cannot take rank as a man of war. He cannot do battle with the world, the flesh, and the devil, so long as he is filled with doubts and fears as to whether he belongs to the true spiritual stock. If there is to be any progress, if there is to be that decision, so essential to a spiritual warrior, we must be able to say, "*We know* that we have passed from death unto life" – "*We know* that we are of God."

This is the proper language of a man of war. Not one of that mighty host that mustered "over against the tabernacle of the congregation" would have understood such a thing as a single doubt, or shadow of a doubt as to *his own very pedigree*. Doubtless, he would have smiled, had any one raised a question on the subject. Each one of the six hundred thousand knew well whence he had sprung, and, therefore, where he was to take his stand. And just so with God's militant host now. Each member thereof will need to possess the most unclouded confidence as to his relationship, else he will not be able to stand in the battle.

And then as to the "standard." What is it? Is it a doctrine? Nay. Is it a theological system? Nay. Is it an ecclesiastical polity? Nay. Is it a system of ordinances, rites, or ceremonies? Nothing of the sort. God's warriors do not fight under any such banner. What is the standard of God's militant host? Let us hear and remember. It is Christ. This is the only standard of God and the only standard of that warrior band which musters in this wilderness world, to wage war with the hosts of evil, and fight the battles of the Lord. Christ is the standard for everything. To have any other would only unfit us for that spiritual conflict to which we are called. What have we, *as Christians,* to do with contending for any system of theology or church organisation? Of what account, in our estimation, are ordinances, ceremonies, or ritualistic observances? Are we going to fight under such banners as these? God forbid! Our theology is the Bible. Our church organisation is the one Body, formed by the presence of the Holy Ghost, and united to the living and exalted Head in the heavens. To contend for anything less than these is entirely below the mark of a true spiritual warrior.

Alas! alas! that so many who profess to belong to the Church of God should so forget their proper standard, and be found fighting under another banner. We may rest assured it superinduces weakness, falsifies the testimony, and hinders progress. If we would stand in the day of battle, we must acknowledge no standard whatsoever but Christ and His word – the living Word, and the written word. Here lies our security in the face of all our spiritual foes. The more closely we adhere to Christ and to Him *alone* the stronger and safer we shall be. To have Him as a perfect covering for our eyes – to keep close to Him – fast by His side, this is our grand moral safeguard. "The children of Israel shall pitch their tents, every man by his own camp, and every man by his own standard throughout their hosts."

Oh! that thus it may be throughout all the host of the Church of God! May all be laid aside for Christ! May He be enough for our hearts. As we trace our "pedigree" up to Him, may His name be inscribed on the "standard" round which we encamp in this wilderness, through which we are passing home to our eternal rest above! Reader, see to it, we beseech thee, that there be not one jot or tittle inscribed on thy banner save Jesus Christ – that name which is above every name, and which shall yet be exalted for ever throughout the wide universe of God.

---

[1] We ought, perhaps, to inform the reader that many able scholars render the last clause of Galatians 5:17 thus, "In order that we may not do the things that we would." We assuredly believe this rendering to be in full keeping with the spirit of the context; though we are, each day, more convinced of the unrivalled excellence of our precious English Bible.

ISRAEL IN THE WILDERNESS, A PICTURE OF THE CHURCH IN THIS WORLD

God in the midst of His people

What a marvellous spectacle was the camp of Israel, in that waste howling wilderness! What a spectacle to angels, to men, and to devils! God's eye ever rested upon it. His presence was there. He dwelt in the midst of His militant people. It was there He found His habitation. He did not, He could not, find His abode amid the splendours of Egypt, of Assyria, or of Babylon. No doubt those nations presented much that was attractive to nature's eye. The arts and sciences were cultivated amongst them. Civilization had reached a far loftier point amongst those ancient nations than we moderns are disposed to admit. Refinement and luxury were probably carried to as great an extent there as amongst those who put forth very lofty pretensions.

But, be it remembered, Jehovah was not known among those nations. His name had never been revealed to them. He did not dwell in their midst. True, there were the ten thousand testimonies to His creative power. And moreover, His superintending providence was over them. He gave them rain and fruitful seasons, filling their hearts with food and gladness. The blessings and benefits of His liberal hand were showered upon them, from day to day, and year to year. His showers fertilized their fields, His sunbeams gladdened their hearts. But they knew Him not, and cared not for Him.

His dwelling was not there. Not one of those nations could say, "Jehovah is my strength and song, and he is become my salvation: he is my God, and I will prepare him an habitation; my father's God, and I will exalt Him." Exodus 15:2.

Jehovah found His abode in the bosom of His redeemed people, and nowhere else. Redemption was the necessary basis of God's habitation amongst men. Apart from redemption the divine presence could only prove the destruction of men; but, redemption being known, that presence secures man's highest privilege and brightest glory.

The all-sufficiency of God faced with the needs of the people in the wilderness

God dwelt in the midst of His people Israel. He came down from heaven, not only to redeem them out of the land of Egypt, but to be their travelling companion through the wilderness. What a thought! The most High God taking up His abode on the sand of the desert, and in the very bosom of His redeemed congregation! Truly there was nothing like that throughout the wide, wide world. There was that host of six hundred thousand men, beside women and children, in a sterile desert, where there was not a blade of grass, not a drop of water – no visible source of subsistence. How were they to be fed? God was there! How were they to be kept in order? God was there! How were they to track their way through a howling wilderness where there was no way? God was there!

In a word, God's presence secured everything. Unbelief might say, "What! are three millions of people to be fed on air? Who has charge of the commissariat? Where are the military stores? Where is the baggage? Who is to attend to the clothing?" Faith alone could answer, and its answer is brief, and conclusive: "God was there!" And that was quite sufficient. All is comprehended in that one sentence. In faith's arithmetic, God is the only significant figure, and, having Him, you may add as many ciphers as you please. If all your springs are in the living God, it ceases to be a question of your need, and resolves itself into a question of His sufficiency.

What were six hundred thousand footmen to the Almighty God? What the varied necessities of their wives and children? In man's estimation, these things might seem overwhelming. England has just sent out ten thousand troops to Abyssinia; but only think of the enormous expense and labour; think of the number of transports required to convey provisions and other necessaries for that small army. But imagine an army sixty times the size, together with the women and children. Conceive this enormous host entering upon a march that was to extend over the space of forty years, through "a great and terrible wilderness," in which there was no corn, no grass, no water-spring. How were they to be sustained? No supplies with them – no arrangements entered into with friendly nations to forward supplies – no transports despatched to meet them at various points along their route – in short, not a single visible source of supply – nothing that nature would consider available.

All this is something worth pondering. But we must ponder it in the divine presence. It is of no possible use for reason to sit down and try to solve this mighty problem by human arithmetic. No, reader; it is only faith that can solve it, and that, moreover, by the word of the living God. Here lies the precious solution. Bring God in, and you want no other factors to work out your answer. Leave Him out, and the more powerful your reason, and the more profound your arithmetic, the more hopeless must be your perplexity.

Thus it is that faith settles the question. God was in the midst of His people. He was there in all the fulness of His grace and mercy – there in His perfect knowledge of His people's wants, and of the difficulties of their path – there in His almighty power and boundless resources, to meet these difficulties and supply these wants. And so fully did He enter into all these things, that He was able, at the close of their long wilderness wanderings, to appeal to their hearts in the following touching accents, "for the Lord thy God hath blessed thee in all the works of thy hand; he knoweth thy walking through this great wilderness: these forty years the Lord thy God hath been with thee; *thou hast lacked nothing."* And again, "Thy raiment waxed not old upon thee, neither did thy foot swell, these forty years." Deut. 2:7; 8:4.

Now, in all these things, the camp of Israel was a type – a vivid, striking type. A type of what? A type of the Church of God passing through this world. The testimony of scripture is so distinct on this point, as to leave no room and no demand for the exercise of imagination. "All these things happened unto them for ensamples; and they are written for our admonition, upon whom the ends of the world are come." 1 Cor. 10:11.

Hence, therefore, we may draw near and gaze, with intense interest, upon that marvellous spectacle, and seek to gather up the precious lessons which it is so eminently fitted to teach. And, oh, what lessons! Who can duly estimate them? Look at that mysterious camp in the desert, composed, as we have said, of warriors, workers, and worshippers! What separation from all the nations of the world! What utter helplessness! What exposure! What absolute dependence upon God! They had nothing – could do nothing – could know nothing. They had not a morsel of food, nor a drop of water, but as they received it day by day from the immediate hand of God. When they retired to rest at night, there was not a single atom of provision for the morrow. There was no storehouse, no larder, no visible source of supply, nothing that nature could take any account of.

But God was there, and that, in the judgment of faith, was quite enough. *They were shut up to God.* This is the one grand reality. Faith owns nothing real, nothing solid, nothing true, but the one true, living, eternal God. Nature might cast a longing look at the granaries of Egypt, and see something tangible, something substantial there. Faith looks up to heaven and finds *all* its springs there.

Thus it was with the camp in the desert; and thus it is with the Church in the world. There was not a single exigency, not a single contingency, not a single need of any sort whatsoever, for which the Divine Presence was not an all-sufficient answer. The nations of the uncircumcised might look on and marvel. They might, in the bewilderment of blind unbelief, raise many a question as to how such a host could ever be fed, clothed, and kept in order. Most certainly they had no eyes to *see* how it could be done. They knew not Jehovah, the Lord God of the Hebrews; and therefore to tell them that He was going to undertake for that vast assembly would indeed seem like idle tales.

The assembly separated from this world

And so it is now, in reference to the assembly of God, in this world, which may truly be termed a moral wilderness. Looked at from God's point of view, that assembly is not of the world; it is in complete separation. It is as thoroughly apart from the world, as the camp of Israel was apart from Egypt. The waters of the Red Sea rolled between that camp and Egypt; and the deeper and darker waters of the death of Christ roll between the Church of God and this present evil world. It is impossible to conceive separation more complete. "They," says our Lord Christ, "are not of the world, even as I am not of the world." John 17.

Then, as to entire dependence; what can be more dependent than the Church of God in this world? She has nothing in or of herself. She is set down in the midst of a moral desert, a dreary waste, a vast howling wilderness, in the which there is literally nothing on which she can live. There is not one drop of water, not a single morsel of suited food for the Church of God, throughout the entire compass of this world.

So also as to the matter of exposure to all sorts of hostile influences. Nothing can exceed it. There is not so much as one friendly influence. All is against her. She is in the midst of this world like an exotic – a plant belonging to a foreign clime, and set down in a sphere where both the soil and the atmosphere are uncongenial.

Such is the Church of God in the world – a separated –

dependent – defenceless thing, wholly cast upon the living God. It is calculated to give great vividness, force, and clearness to our thoughts about the Church, to view it as the antitype of the camp in the desert; and that it is in no wise fanciful or far-fetched to view it thus, 1 Corinthians 10:11 does most clearly shew. We are fully warranted in saying that what the camp of Israel was literally, that the Church is morally and spiritually. And, further, that what the wilderness was literally to Israel, that the world is, morally and spiritually, to the Church of God. The wilderness was the sphere of Israel's toil and danger, not of their supplies or their enjoyment; and the world is the sphere of the Church's toil and danger, not of its supplies or its enjoyment.

It is well to seize this fact, in all its moral power. The assembly of God in the world, like "the congregation in the wilderness," is wholly cast upon the living God. We speak, be it remembered, from the divine standpoint – of what the Church is in God's sight. Looked at from man's point of view – looked at as she is, in her own actual practical state, it is, alas! another thing. We are now only occupied with the normal, the true, the divine idea of God's assembly is this world.

And let it not be forgotten, for one moment, that, as truly as there was a camp in the desert, of old – a congregation in the wilderness – so truly is there the Church of God, the body of Christ, in the world now. Doubtless, the nations of the world knew little, and cared less, about that congregation of old; but that did not weaken or touch the great living fact. So now, the men of the world know little and care less about the assembly of God – the body of Christ; but that, in no wise, touches the grand living truth that there *is* such a thing actually existing in this world, and *has been* ever since the Holy Ghost descended on the day of Pentecost. True, the congregation, of old, had its trials, its conflicts, its sorrows, its temptations, its strifes, its controversies – its internal commotions – its numberless and nameless difficulties, calling for the varied resources that were in God – the precious ministrations of prophet, priest, and king which God had provided; for, as we know, Moses was there as "king in Jeshurun," and as the prophet raised up of God; and Aaron was there to exercise all the priestly functions.

But, in spite of all these things that we have named – in spite of the weakness, the failure, the sin, the rebellion, the strife – still there was the striking fact, to be taken cognizance of by men, by devils, and by angels, namely, a vast congregation, amounting to something like three millions of people (according to the usual mode of computation) journeying through a wilderness, wholly dependent upon an unseen arm, guided and cared for by the eternal God, whose eye was never for one moment withdrawn from that mysterious typical host; yea, He dwelt in their midst, and never left them, in all their unbelief, their forgetfulness, their ingratitude, and rebellion. God was there to sustain and guide, to guard and keep them day and night. He fed them with bread from heaven, day by day; and He brought them forth water out of the flinty rock.

This, assuredly, was a stupendous fact – a profound mystery. God had a congregation in the wilderness – apart from the nations around, shut up to Himself. It may be the nations of the world knew nothing, cared nothing, thought nothing, about this assembly. It is certain the desert yielded nothing in the way of sustenance or refreshment. There were serpents and scorpions – there were snares and dangers – drought, barrenness, and desolation. But there was that wonderful assembly maintained in a manner that baffled and confounded human reason.

And, reader, remember this was a type. A type of what? A type of something that has been in existence for over eighteen centuries; is in existence still; and shall be in existence until the moment that our Lord Christ rises from His present position, and descends into the air. In one word, a type of the Church of God in the world. How important to recognise this fact! How sadly it has been lost sight of! How little understood even now! And yet every Christian is solemnly responsible to recognise, and practically to confess it. There is no escaping it. Is it true that there is something in this world, at this very moment, answering to the camp in the desert? Yes, verily; there is, in very truth, the Church in the wilderness. There is an assembly passing through this world, just as the literal Israel passed through the literal desert and, moreover, the world is, morally and spiritually, to that Church what the desert was, literally and practically, to Israel of old. Israel found no springs in the desert; and the Church of God should find no springs in the world. If she does, she proves false to her Lord. Israel was not of the desert, but passing through it; and the Church of God is not of the world, but passing through it.

If this be thoroughly entered into by the reader, it will show him the place of complete separation which belongs to the Church of God as a whole, and to each individual member thereof. The Church, *in God's view of her,* is as thoroughly marked off from this present world, as the camp of Israel was marked off from the surrounding desert. There is as little in common between the Church and the world, as there was between Israel and the sand of the desert. The most brilliant attractions and bewitching fascinations of the world are to the Church of God what the serpents and scorpions, and the ten thousand other dangers of the wilderness, were to Israel.

In the midst of a Christianity in ruin

Such is the divine idea of the Church; and it is with this idea that we are now occupied. Alas! alas! how different it is with that which calls itself the Church! But we want the reader to dwell, for the present, on the true thing. We want him to place himself, by faith, at God's standpoint, and view the Church from thence. It is only by so doing that he can have anything like a true idea of what the Church is, or of his own personal responsibility with respect to it. God *has* a Church in the world. There *is* a body now on the earth, indwelt by God the Spirit, and united to Christ the Head. This Church – this body – is composed of all those who truly believe on the Son of God, and who are united by the grand fact of the presence of the Holy Ghost.

And, be it observed, this is not a matter of opinion – a certain thing which we may take up or lay down at pleasure. It is a divine fact. It is a grand truth, whether we will hear or whether we will forbear. The Church is an existing thing, and we, if believers, are members thereof. We cannot avoid this. We cannot ignore it. We are actually in the relationship – baptised into it by the Holy Ghost. It is as real and as positive a thing as the birth of a child into a family. The birth has taken place, the relationship is formed, and we have only to recognise it, and walk in the sense of it, from day to day. The very moment in the which a soul is born again – born from above, and sealed by the Holy Ghost – he is incorporated into the body of Christ. He can no longer view himself as a solitary individual – an independent person – an isolated atom; he is a member of a body, just as the hand or the foot is a member of the human body. He is a member of *the* Church of God, and cannot, properly or truly, be a member of anything else. How could my arm be a member of any other body? And, on the same principle, we may ask, how could a member of the body of Christ be a member of any other body?

What a glorious truth is this respecting the Church of God – the antitype of the camp in the desert, "the congregation in the wilderness!" What a fact to be governed by! There *is* such a thing as the Church of God, amid all the ruin and the wreck, the strife and the discord, the confusion and division, the sects and parties. This surely is a most precious truth. But not only is it most precious, it is also most practical and formative. We are as bound to recognize, by faith, this Church in the world, as the Israelite was bound to recognise, by sight, the camp in the desert. There *was* one camp, one congregation, and the true Israelite belonged thereto; there *is* one Church – one body, and the true Christian belongs to it.

But how is this body organised? By the Holy Ghost, as it is written, "By one Spirit are we all baptised into one body" (1 Cor. 12:13.). How is it maintained? By its living Head, through the Spirit, and by the word, as it is written, "No man ever yet hated his own flesh; but nourisheth and cherisheth it, even as the Lord the church" (Eph. 5:29). Is not this enough? Is not the Lord Christ sufficient? Doth not the Holy Ghost suffice? Do we want anything more than the varied virtues that are lodged in the name of Jesus? Are not the gifts of the Eternal Spirit quite sufficient for the growth and maintenance of the Church of God? Doth not the fact of the Divine presence in the Church secure *all* that the Church can possibly need? Is it not sufficient for "exigence of every hour?" Faith says, and says it with emphasis and decision – "Yes!" Unbelief – human reason, says, "No! we want a great many things as well." What is our brief reply! Simply this, "If God be not sufficient, we know not whither to turn. If the name of Jesus doth not suffice, we know not what to do. If the Holy Ghost cannot meet all our need, in communion, in ministry, and in worship, we know not what to say."

What is of God endures

It may, however, be said that "Things are not as they were in apostolic times. The professing Church has failed; pentecostal gifts have ceased; the palmy days of the Church's first love have passed away; and therefore we must adopt the best means in our power for the organisation and maintenance of our churches." To all this we reply, "God has not failed. Christ the Head of the Church has not failed. The Holy Spirit has not failed. Not one jot or tittle of God's word has failed." This is the true ground of faith. "Jesus Christ is the same yesterday, to-day, and for ever." He has said, "Lo, I am with you." How long? During the days of first love? during apostolic times? so long as the Church shall continue faithful? No; "I am with you *always,* even unto the end of the age" (Matt. 28). So also, at an earlier moment when, for the first time in the whole canon of scripture, the Church, properly so called, is named, we have those memorable words, "On this rock [the Son of the living God] I will build my church, and the gates of hell shall not prevail against it." Matthew 16.

Now, the question is, "Is that Church on the earth at this moment?" Most assuredly. It is as true that there is a Church now on this earth, as that there was a camp in the desert of old. Yes; and as truly as God was in that camp to meet every exigence, so truly is He, now, in the Church to order and guide in everything, as we read, "Ye are builded together for an habitation of God through the Spirit" (Eph. 2). This is quite sufficient. All we want is to lay hold, by a simple faith, of this grand reality. The name of Jesus is as sufficient for all the exigencies of the Church of God as it is for the soul's salvation. The one is as true as the other. "Where two or three are gathered together in [or, unto] my name, there am I in the midst" (Matt. 18). Has this ceased to be true? And if not, is not Christ's presence quite enough for His Church? Do we need to set about planning or working for ourselves in church matters? No more than in the matter of the soul's salvation. What do we say to the sinner? Trust Christ. What do we say to the saint? Trust Christ. What do we say to an assembly of saints, few or many? Trust Christ. Is there anything that He cannot manage? "Is there a thing too hard for Him?" Has His treasury of gift and grace become exhausted? Is He not able to supply ministerial gifts? Can He not furnish evangelists, pastors, and teachers? Can He not perfectly meet all the manifold necessities of His Church in the wilderness? If not, where are we? What shall we do? Whither shall we turn? What had the congregation of old to do? To look to Jehovah. For everything? Yes, for everything; for food, for water, for clothing, for guidance, for protection, for all. All their springs were in Him. Must we turn to some one else? Never. Our Lord Christ is amply sufficient, in spite of all our failure and ruin, our sin and unfaithfulness. He has sent down the Holy Ghost, the blessed Paraclete, to dwell with and in His people – to form them into one body, and unite them to their living Head in heaven. He is the power of unity, of communion, of ministry, and of worship. He has not left us, and He never will. Only let us trust Him; let us use Him; let us give Him room to act.

Let us carefully guard against everything that might tend to quench, to hinder, or to grieve Him. Let us acknowledge Him, in His own proper place in the assembly, and yield ourselves, in all things, to His guidance and authority.

Here, we are persuaded, lies the true secret of power and blessing. Do we deny the ruin? How could we? Alas! alas! it stands forth as a fact too palpable and glaring to admit of denial. Do we seek to deny our share in the ruin – our folly and sin? Would to God we felt it more deeply! But shall we add to our sin by denying our Lord's grace and power to meet us in our folly and ruin? Shall we forsake Him, the fountain of living waters, and hew out for ourselves broken cisterns that can hold no water? Shall we turn from the Rock of Ages and lean upon the broken reeds of our own devising? God forbid! Rather let the language of our hearts be, as we think of the name of Jesus,

> "Salvation in that name is found,
> Cure for my grief and care;
> A healing balm for every wound,
> *All, all I want is there."*

But let not the reader suppose that we want to lend the smallest countenance to ecclesiastical pretension. We perfectly abhor any such thing. We look upon it as utterly contemptible. We believe we cannot possibly take too low a place. A low place and a lowly spirit are what alone become us in view of our common sin and shame. All we seek to maintain is this, the all-sufficiency of the name of Jesus for all the exigencies of the Church of God, at all times, and under all circumstances. There was all power in that name in apostolic times; and why not now? Has any change passed over that glorious name? No, blessed be God! Well then it is sufficient for us, at this moment, and all we want is to confide in it fully, and to show that we so confide by discarding thoroughly every other ground of confidence, and coming out, with bold decision, to that peerless and precious name. He has, blessed be His name, come down to the smallest congregation – the smallest plurality, inasmuch as He has said, "Where two or three are gathered together in my name, there am I." Does this still hold good? Has it lost its power? Does it no longer apply? Where has it been repealed?

Oh! Christian reader, we call upon you, by every argument which ought to weigh with your heart, to give your cordial assent and consent to this one eternal truth, namely, *the all-sufficiency of the name of the Lord Jesus Christ for the assembly of God, in every possible condition in which it can be found, throughout its entire history.*[2] We call upon you not merely to hold this as a true theory, but, to confess it practically and then, assuredly, you will taste the deep blessedness of the presence of Jesus in the outside place – a blessedness which must be tasted in order to be known; but, when once really tasted, it can never be forgotten or surrendered for anything beside.

But we had no intention of pursuing the foregoing line of thought so far, or of penning such a lengthened introduction to the section of our book which lies open before us, and to which we shall now invite the reader's particular attention.

Warriors, workers and worshippers

On looking attentively at "the congregation in the wilderness" (Acts 7:38), we find it composed of three distinct elements, namely, *warriors, workers,* and *worshippers.* There was a *nation* of warriors, a tribe of *workers,* a *family* of worshippers or priests. We have glanced at the first of these and seen each one according to his "pedigree," taking up his position by his "standard," according to the direct appointment of Jehovah; and we shall now dwell for a few moments on the second, and see each one at his work and service, according to the same appointment. We have considered the warriors; let us meditate on the workers.

The families of the Levites and their service

The Levites were distinctly marked off from all the other tribes, and called to a very specific place and service. Thus we read of them, "But the Levites after the tribe of their fathers were not numbered among them. For the Lord had spoken unto Moses, saying, Only thou shalt not number the tribe of Levi, neither take the sum of them among the children of Israel. But thou shalt appoint the Levites over the tabernacle of testimony, and over all the vessels thereof, and over all things that belong to it: they shall bear the tabernacle, and all the vessels thereof; and they shall minister unto it, and shall encamp round about the tabernacle. And when the tabernacle setteth forward, the Levites shall take it down; and when the tabernacle is to be pitched, the Levites shall set it up: and the stranger that cometh nigh shall be put to death. And the children of Israel shall pitch their tents, every man by his own camp, and every man by his own standard, throughout their hosts. But the Levites shall pitch round about the tabernacle of testimony, that there be no wrath upon the congregation of the children of Israel: and the Levites shall keep the charge of the tabernacle of testimony" (chap. 1:47-53). And again we read, "But the Levites were not numbered among the children of Israel, as the Lord commanded Moses." Chap. 2:33.

But why the Levites? Why was this tribe specially marked off from all the others, and set apart for so holy and elevated a service? Was there any special sanctity or goodness about them to account for their being so distinguished? Not by nature, certainly, nor yet by practice, as we may see by the following words "Simeon and Levi are brethren; instruments of cruelty are in their habitations. O, my soul, come not thou into their secret; unto their assembly, mine honour, be not thou united: for *in their anger they slew a man,* and in their self-will they digged down a wall. Cursed be their anger, for it was fierce; and their wrath, for it was cruel: I will divide them in Jacob, and scatter them in Israel." Genesis 49.

Such was Levi by nature and by practice – self-willed,

fierce, and cruel. How remarkable that such an one should be singled out and brought into a place of such high and holy privilege! Surely we may say it was grace from first to last. It is the way of grace to take up the very worst cases. It stoops to the lowest depths and gathers up its brightest trophies from thence. "This is a faithful saying, and worthy of all acceptation, that Christ Jesus came into the world to save sinners, of whom I am chief" (2 Tim. 1:16). "Unto me, who am less than the least of all saints, is this grace given, that I should preach among the Gentiles the unsearchable riches of Christ." Ephesians 3.

But how striking the language, "O, my soul, come not thou into their secret; unto their assembly, mine honour, be not thou united." God is of purer eyes than to behold evil, and cannot look on iniquity. God could not come into Levi's secret, or be united unto his assembly. That was impossible. God could have nought to do with self-will, fierceness, and cruelty. But yet He could bring Levi into His secret, and unite him to His assembly. He could take him out of his habitation, wherein were instruments of cruelty, and bring him into the tabernacle to be occupied with the holy instruments and vessels that were there. This was grace – free, sovereign grace; and herein must be sought the basis of all Levi's blessed and elevated service. So far as he was personally concerned there was an immeasurable distance between him and a holy God – a chasm which no human art or power could bridge. A holy God could have nothing to do with self-will, fierceness, and cruelty; but a God of grace could have to do with Levi. He could visit such an one in sovereign mercy, and raise him up from the depths of his moral degradation, and bring him into a place of nearness to Himself.

And oh! what a marvellous contrast between Levi's position by nature, and his position by grace! between the instruments of cruelty and the vessels of the sanctuary! between Levi in Genesis 34 and Levi in Numbers 3 and 4.

The purification of the Levites

But let us look at the mode of God's dealing with Levi – the ground on which he was brought into such a place of blessing. In doing this, it will be needful for us to refer chapter 8 of our book, and there we are let into the secret of the whole matter. We shall see that there was, and could be, no allowance of anything that belonged to Levi, no sanction of any of his ways; and yet there was the most perfect display of grace – grace reigning through righteousness. We speak of the type and its significance. We do so in view of that statement already referred to: "Now all these things happened unto them for types." It is not a question of how far the Levites saw through these things. This is not at all the point. We are not to ask, What did the Levites see in God's dealings with them? But, What do we learn?

"And the Lord spake unto Moses, saying, Take the Levites from among the children of Israel, and cleanse them. And thus shalt thou do unto them, to cleanse them: sprinkle water of purifying upon them, and let them shave all their flesh, and let them wash their clothes, and so make themselves clean." Num. 8:5-7.

Here we have, in type, the only divine principle of cleansing. It is the application of death to nature and all its habits. It is the word of God brought to bear upon the heart and conscience, in a living way. Nothing can be more expressive than the double action presented in the above passage. Moses was to sprinkle water of purifying upon them; and then they were to shave off all their hair, and wash their garments. There is great beauty and precision here. Moses, as representing the claims of God, cleanses the Levites according to those claims; and they, being cleansed, are able to bring the sharp razor to bear upon all that was the mere growth of nature, and to wash their garments, which expresses, in typic form, the cleansing their habits according to the word of God. This was God's way of meeting all that appertained to Levi's natural state – the self-will, the fierceness, and the cruelty. The pure water and the sharp razor were called into action – the washing and shaving had to go on, ere Levi was fit to approach the vessels of the sanctuary.

Thus it is in every case. There is, there can be, no allowance of nature among God's workers. There never was a more fatal mistake than to attempt to enlist nature in the service of God. It matters not how you may endeavour to improve or regulate it. It is not improvement, but death that will avail. It is of the very last possible importance for the reader to lay hold, with clearness and force, of this great practical truth. Man has been weighed in the balance and found wanting. The plummet has been applied to him, and he has been found crooked. It is of no possible use seeking to reform. Nothing will do save the *water* and the *razor*. God has closed up man's history. He has brought it to an end in the death of Christ. The first grand fact that the Holy Ghost presses upon the human conscience is, that God has delivered His solemn verdict upon human nature, and that each one must accept that verdict against himself personally. It is not a matter of opinion, or a matter of feeling. A person may say, "I do not see, or I do not feel, that I am so bad as you seem to make out." We reply, That does not affect the question in the least. God has declared His judgment about us, and it is man's first duty to fall in with, and bow to that. Of what use would it have been for Levi to say that he did not agree with what God's word had said about him? Would that – could that, have altered the question as to him? In no wise. The divine record remained the same whether Levi felt it or not; but clearly, it was the first step in wisdom's pathway to bow down under the weight of that record.

All this is expressed, in type, in the "water" and the "razor" – the "washing" and the "shaving." Nothing could be more significant or impressive. These acts set forth the solemn truth of the sentence of death upon nature, and the execution of judgment upon all that nature produces.

And what, let us ask, is the meaning of the initiatory act of Christianity – the act of baptism? Does it not set forth the blessed fact that "our old man" – our fallen nature – is completely set aside, and that we are introduced into an entirely new position? Truly so. And how do we use the razor? By rigid self-judgment, day by day; by the stern disallowance of all that is of nature's growth. This is the true path for all God's workers in the wilderness. When we look at Levi's conduct at Shechem, in Genesis 34, and the record concerning him in Genesis 49, we may ask, How can such an one ever be allowed to carry the vessels of the sanctuary? The answer is, Grace shines in Levi's call; and holiness shines in Levi's cleansing. He was called to the work, according to the riches of divine grace; but he was fitted for the work according to the claims of divine holiness.

Thus it must be with all God's workers. We are most thoroughly convinced that we are fit for God's work just so far as nature is brought under the power of the cross, and the sharp razor of self-judgment. Self-will can never be made available in the service of God; nay, it must be set aside, if we would know what true service is. There is, alas! a large amount of what which passes for service which, if judged in the light of the divine presence, would be seen to be but the fruit of a restless will. This is most solemn, and demands our most earnest attention. We cannot exercise too severe a censorship over ourselves, in this very thing. The heart is so deceitful that we may be led to imagine that we are doing the Lord's work, when, in reality, we are only pleasing ourselves. But, if we would tread the path of true service, we must seek to be, more and more, apart from nature. The self-willed Levi must pass through the typic process of washing and shaving, ere he can be employed in that elevated service assigned him by the direct appointment of the God of Israel.

"Who is on the Lord's side?"

But, ere proceeding to examine particularly the work and service of the Levites, we must look for a moment at a scene in Exodus 32, in which they act a very prominent and a very remarkable part. We allude, as the reader will at once perceive, to the golden calf. During the absence of Moses, the people so completely lost sight of God and His claims as to set up a molten calf and bow down thereto. This terrible act called for summary judgment. "And when Moses saw that the people were naked; (for Aaron had made them naked to their shame among their enemies:) then Moses stood in the gate of the camp, and said, Who is on the Lord's side? let him come unto me. And all the sons of Levi gathered themselves together unto him. And he said unto them, Thus saith the Lord God of Israel, Put every man his sword by his side, and go in and out from gate to gate throughout the camp, and slay every man his brother, and every man his companion, and every man his neighbour. And the children of Levi did according to the word of Moses: and there fell of the people that day about three thousand men. For Moses had said, Consecrate yourselves to-day to the Lord, even every man upon his son, and upon his brother; that he may bestow upon you a blessing this day." Exodus 32:25-29.

This was a testing moment. It could not be otherwise, when this great question was pressed home upon the heart and conscience, *"Who is on the Lord's side?"* Nothing could be more searching. The question was not, "Who is willing to work?" No; it was a far deeper and more searching question. It was not who will go here or there – do this or that? There might be a vast amount of doing and going, and, all the while, it might be but the impulse of an unbroken will which, acting upon religious nature, gave an appearance of devotedness and piety eminently calculated to deceive oneself and others.

But to be "on the Lord's side" implies the surrender of one's own will – yea, the surrender of oneself, and this is essential to the true servant – the real workman. Saul of Tarsus was on this ground when he exclaimed, "Lord, what wilt *thou* have *me* to do?" What words, from the self-willed, fierce, and cruel persecutor of the Church of God!

"Who is on the Lord's side?" Reader, art thou? Search and

see. Examine thyself closely. Remember, the question is not at all "What art thou doing?" No; it is far deeper. If thou art on the Lord's side, thou art ready for anything and everything. Thou art ready to stand still, or ready to go forward; ready to go to the right or to the left; ready to be active, and ready to be quiet; ready to stand on thy feet, and ready to lie on thy back. The grand point is this, namely, the surrender of thyself to the claims of another, and that other the Lord Christ.

This is an immense point. Indeed we know of nothing more important, at the present moment, than this searching question, "Who is on the Lord's side?" We live in days of immense self-will. Man exults in his liberty. And this comes out, very prominently, in religious matters. Just as it was in the camp of Israel, in the days of the thirty-second of Exodus – the days of the golden calf. Moses was out of sight, and the human will was at work; the graving tool was called into operation. And what was the result? The molten calf; and when Moses returned, he found the people in idolatry and nakedness. Then came forth the solemn and testing question, "Who is on the Lord's side?" This brought things to an issue, or rather it put people to the test. Nor is it otherwise now. Man's will is rampant, and that too in matters of religion. Man boasts of his rights, of the freedom of his will, the freedom of his judgment. There is the denial of the Lordship of Christ; and therefore it behoves us to look well to it, and see that we really are taking sides with the Lord against ourselves; that we are in the attitude of simple subjection to His authority. Then we shall not be occupied with the amount or character of our service; it will be our one object to do the will of our Lord.

Now, to act thus under the Lord may often give an appearance of narrowness to our sphere of action; but with this we have nothing whatever to do. If a master tells his servant to stand in the hall, and not to stir until he rings the bell, what is the servant's duty? Clearly to stand still; nor should he be moved from this position or this attitude, even though his fellow-servants should find fault with his apparent inactivity and good-for-nothingness; he may rest assured his Master will approve and vindicate. This is enough for any true-hearted servant, whose one desire will ever be not so much to do a great deal, as to do the will of his Lord.

In a word, then, the question for the camp of Israel, in the day of the golden calf, and the question for the Church, in this day of human will, is this, "Who is on the Lord's side?" Momentous question! It is not, Who is on the side of religiousness, philanthropy, or moral reform? There may be a large amount of any or all of these things, and yet the will be thoroughly unbroken. Let us not forget this; nay, rather we should say, let us continually bear it in mind. We may be very zealous in promoting all the various schemes of philanthropy, religiousness, and moral reform, and, all the while, be ministering to self, and feeding self-will. This is a most solemn and weighty consideration; and it behoves us to give earnest heed to it. We are passing through a moment in the which man's will is being pampered with unparalleled diligence. We believe, most assuredly, that the true remedy for this evil will be found wrapped up in this one weighty question, "Who is on the Lord's side" There is immense practical power in this question. To be really on *the Lord's side* is to be ready for anything to which He may see fit to call us, no matter what. If the soul is brought to say, in real truth, "*Lord*, what wilt thou have me to do?" "Speak, *Lord*, for *thy servant heareth*," then we are ready for everything. Hence, in the case of the Levites, they were called to "slay every man his brother, and every man his companion, and every man his neighbour." This was terrible work for flesh and blood. But the moment demanded it. God's claims had been openly and grossly dishonoured. Human invention had been at work, with the graving tool, and a calf had been set up. The glory of God had been changed into the similitude of an ox that eateth grass; and therefore all who were on the Lord's side were called to gird on the sword. Nature might say, "No; let us be tender, and gentle, and gracious. We shall accomplish more by kindness than by severity. It can do no good to wound people. There is far more power in love than in harshness. Let us love one another." Thus might nature throw out its suggestions – thus it might reason and argue. But the command was distinct and decisive: "Put every man his sword by his side." The sword was the only thing when the golden calf was there. To talk of love at such a moment, would be to fling overboard the just claims of the God of Israel. It belongs to the true spirit of obedience to render the very service which suits the occasion. A servant has no business to reason, he is simply to do as he is bid. To raise a question, or put forth a demur, is to abandon our place as a servant. It might seem most dreadful work to have to slay a brother, a companion, or a neighbour; but the word of the Lord was imperative. It left no room for evasion; and the Levites, through grace, yielded a full and ready obedience. "The children of Levi did according to the word of Moses."

This is the only true path for those who will be God's workers, and Christ's servants in this world where self-will is dominant. It is immensely important to have the truth of the Lordship of Christ deeply engraved upon the heart. It is the only regulator of the course and conduct. It settles a thousand questions. If the heart be really subject to the authority of Christ, it is in readiness for anything and everything to which He calls us, be it to stand still or to go forward, to do little or much, to be active or passive. To a really obedient heart, the question is not at all, "What am I doing? or where am I going?" It is simply, "Am I doing the will of my Lord?"

The covenant with Levi

Such was the ground occupied by Levi. And mark the divine comment on this, as given in Malachi. "And ye shall know that I have sent this commandment unto you, that my covenant might be with Levi, saith the Lord of hosts. My covenant was with him of life and peace; and I gave them to him for the fear wherewith he feared me, and was afraid before my name. The law of truth was in his mouth, and iniquity was not found in his lips: he walked with me in peace and equity, and did turn many away from iniquity" (Mal. 2:4-6). Mark also the blessing pronounced by the lips of Moses, "And of Levi he said, Let thy Thummim and thy Urim be with thy holy one, whom thou didst prove at Massah, and with whom thou didst strive at the waters of Meribah; who said unto his father and to his mother, I have not seen him; neither did he acknowledge his brethren, nor knew his own children; for they have observed thy word and kept thy covenant. They shall teach Jacob thy judgments, and Israel thy law; they shall put incense before thee, and whole burnt sacrifice upon thine altar. Bless, Lord, his substance, and accept the work of his hands: smite through the loins of them that rise against him, and of them that hate him, that they rise not again." Deuteronomy 33:8-11.

It might have appeared unwarrantably harsh and severe in Levi not to have seen his parents or known or acknowledged his brethren. But God's claims are paramount; and our Lord Christ hath declared these solemn words, "If any man come to me, and hate not his father, and mother, and wife, and children, and brethren, and sisters, yea, and his own life also, he cannot be my disciple." Luke 14:26.

These are plain words; and they let us into the secret of what it is which lies at the bottom of all true service. Let no one imagine that we are to be without natural affection. Far be the thought. To be so would be to connect us, morally, with the apostasy of the last days (see 2 Tim. 3:3). But when the claims of natural affection are allowed to stand in the way of our whole-hearted service to Christ, and when the so-called love of our brethren receives a higher place than faithfulness to Christ, then are we unfit for His service and unworthy of the name of His servants. Let it be carefully noted that what formed the *moral* ground of Levi's title to be employed in the Lord's service was the fact that he did not *see* his parents, *acknowledge* his brethren, or *know* his children. In a word, he was enabled to set the claims of nature completely aside, and to give the claims of Jehovah the paramount place in his heart. This, we repeat, is the only true basis of the servant's character.

This is a most weighty consideration, and one which demands the most serious attention of the Christian reader. There may be a vast amount of what looks like service – a great deal of activity, of coming and going, of doing and saying – and, all the while, there may not be a single atom of true Levite service, yea, it may, in God's estimation, be only the restless activity of the will. "What," it may be said, "can the will show itself in the service of God – in matters of religion?" Alas, alas, it can and does. And very often the apparent energy and fruitfulness in work and service is just in proportion to the energy of the will. This is peculiarly solemn. It calls for the most rigid self-judgment, in the light of the divine presence. True service doth not consist in great activity, but in profound subjection to the will of our Lord, and where this exists there will be the readiness to sink the claims of parents, brethren, and children, in order to carry out the will of Him whom we own as Lord. True, we should love our parents, our brethren, and our children. It is not that we should love these less, but we should love Christ more. He and His claims must ever have the paramount place in the heart, if we would be true workers for God, true servants of Christ, true Levites in the wilderness. It was this that marked the actings of Levi, on the occasion to which we are referring. God's claims were in question, and hence the claims of nature were not to be entertained for a moment. Parents, brethren, and children, how dear soever these might be, were not to stand in the way when the glory of the God of Israel had been changed into the similitude of an ox that eateth grass.

Here lies the whole question, in all its weight and magnitude. The ties of natural relationship, with all the claims, duties, and responsibilities arising out of such ties, will ever get their proper place, their due respect, from those whose hearts, and minds, and consciences have been brought under the adjusting power of the truth of God. Nought save what is really due to God and His Christ should ever be suffered to infringe those rights which are founded upon natural relationship. This is a most necessary and wholesome consideration, and one which we would particularly press upon the young Christian reader. We have ever to be on our guard against a spirit of self-will and self-pleasing which is never so dangerous as when it clothes itself in the garb of religious service, and work so called. It behoves us to be *very sure indeed* that we are directly and simply governed by the claims of God when we disregard the claims of natural relationship. In Levi's case, the matter was as clear as a sunbeam, and hence the *"sword"* of judgment, not the kiss of affection, befitted the critical moment. So, also, in our history, there are moments in which it would be open disloyalty to our Lord Christ to hearken, for one instant, to the voice of natural relationship.

The above remarks may help the reader to understand the actings of the Levites in Exodus 32, and the words of our Lord in Luke 14:26. May God's Spirit enable us to realize and exhibit the adjusting power of truth!

The consecration of the Levites

We shall now dwell, for a few moments, on the consecration of the Levites, in Numbers 8, in order that we may have the whole subject before our minds. Truly it is a theme full of instruction for all who desire to be workers for God.

After the ceremonial acts of "washing" and "shaving" already referred to, we read, "Then let them (i.e., the Levites) take a young bullock with his meat offering, even fine flour mingled with oil, and another young bullock shalt thou take for a sin offering. And thou shalt bring the Levites before the tabernacle of the congregation: and thou shalt gather the whole assembly or the children of Israel together. And thou shalt bring the Levites before the Lord: and the children of Israel shall put their hands upon the Levites. And Aaron shall offer the Levites before the Lord for an offering of the children of Israel, that they may execute the service of the Lord. And the Levites shall lay their hands upon the heads of the bullocks; and thou shalt offer the one for a sin offering, and the other for a burnt offering, unto the Lord, to make an atonement for the Levites."

Here we have presented to us, in type, the two grand aspects of the death of Christ. The sin offering furnishes the one; the burnt offering furnishes the other. Into the details of those offerings we do not enter here, having sought to do so in the opening chapters of our "Notes on Leviticus." We would merely observe here, that, in the sin offering, we see Christ bearing sin in His own body on the tree, and enduring the wrath of God against sin. In the burnt offering, we see Christ glorifying God even in the very matter of making atonement for sin. Atonement is made in both; but in the former, it is atonement according to the depth of the sinner's need; in the latter, it is atonement according to the measure of Christ's devotedness to God. In that, we see the hatefulness of sin; in this, the preciousness of Christ. It is, we need hardly say, the same atoning death of Christ, but presented in two distinct aspects.[3]

Now, the Levites laid their hands on both the sin offering and the burnt offering; and this act of the imposition of hands expressed the simple fact of identification. But how different the result in each case! When Levi laid his hands on the head of the sin offering, it involved the transfer of all his sins, of all his guilt, of all his fierceness, cruelty, and self-will to the victim. And on the other hand, when he laid his hands on the head of the burnt offering, it involved the transfer of all the acceptableness of the sacrifice, of all its perfectness, to Levi. Of course, we speak of what the type set forth. We do not undertake to state anything as to Levi's intelligent entrance into these things; we merely seek to unfold the meaning of the ceremonial figure; and, most assuredly, no figure could be more expressive than the imposition of hands, whether we view it in the case of the sin offering, or in the case of the burnt offering. The doctrine of all this is embodied in that most weighty passage at the close of 2 Corinthians 5, "He hath made him [Christ] to be sin for us, who knew no sin, that we might become the righteousness of God in him." "And thou shalt set the Levites before Aaron, and before his sons, and offer them for an offering unto the Lord. Thus shalt thou separate the Levites from among the children of Israel; and the Levites shall be mine, and after that shall the Levites go in to do the service of the tabernacle of the congregation; and thou shalt cleanse them, and offer them for an offering. For they are wholly given unto me from among the children of Israel; instead of such as open every womb, even instead of the firstborn of all the children of Israel, have I taken them unto me. For all the firstborn of the children of Israel are mine, both man and beast: on the day that I smote every firstborn in the land of Egypt I sanctified them for myself. And I have taken the Levites for all the firstborn of the children of Israel. And I have given the Levites as a gift to Aaron and to his sons from among the children of Israel, to do the service of the children of Israel in the tabernacle of the congregation, and to make an atonement for the children of Israel: that there be no plague among the children of Israel, when the children of Israel come nigh unto the sanctuary. And Moses, and Aaron, and all the congregation of the children of Israel, did to the Levites according unto all that the Lord commanded Moses concerning the Levites, so did the children of Israel unto them." Numbers 8:13-20.

How forcibly are we reminded, by the foregoing lines, of the words of our Lord in John 17, "I have manifested thy name unto the men which thou gavest me out of the world: thine they were, and thou gavest them me, and they have kept thy word . . . I pray for them: I pray not for the world, but for them which thou hast given me; for they are thine. And all mine are thine, and thine are mine; and I am glorified in them." Verses 6-10.

The Levites were a separated people – God's special possession. They took the place of all the firstborn in Israel – of those who were saved from the sword of the destroyer by the blood of the lamb. They were, typically, a dead and risen people, set apart to God, and by Him presented as a gift to

Aaron the high priest, to do the service of the tabernacle.

What a place for the self-willed, fierce, and cruel Levi! What a triumph of grace! What an illustration of the efficacy of the blood of atonement and the water of purification! They were, by nature and by practice, far off from God; but the "blood" of atonement, and the "water" of cleansing, and the "razor" of self-judgment had done their blessed work, and hence the Levites were in a condition to be presented as a gift to Aaron and to his sons, to be associated with them in the hallowed services of the tabernacle of the congregation.

In all this the Levites were a striking type of God's people now. These latter have been lifted from the depths of their degradation and ruin as sinners. They are washed in the precious blood of Christ, purified by the application of the word, and called to the exercise of habitual and rigid self-judgment. Thus are they fitted for that holy service to the which they are called. God has given them to His Son in order that they may be His workers in this world. "Thine they were and thou gavest them me." Wondrous thought! To think that such as we could be thus spoken of! To think of our being God's property and God's gift to His Son! Well may we say it surpasses all human thought. It is not merely that we are saved from hell; that is true. It is not merely that we are pardoned, justified, and accepted; all this is true; but we are called to the high and holy work of bearing through this world the Name, the testimony, the glory of our Lord Jesus Christ. This is our work as true Levites. As men of war, we are called to fight; as priests, we are privileged to worship; but as Levites, we are responsible to serve, and our service is to carry through this dreary desert scene the antitype of the tabernacle, and that tabernacle was the figure of Christ. This is our distinct line of service. To this we are called – to this we are set apart.

The reader will, we doubt not, notice, with interest, the fact that it is in this book of Numbers, and here alone, that we are furnished with all the precious and deeply instructive details respecting the Levites. In this we have a fresh illustration of the character of our book. It is from a wilderness standpoint that we get a full and proper view of God's workers as well as of God's warriors.

The service of the Levites

And, now, let us examine for a few moments, the service of the Levites, as detailed in Numbers 3 and 4. "And the Lord spake unto Moses, saying, Bring the tribe of Levi near, and present them before Aaron the priest, that they may minister unto him. And they shall keep his charge, and the charge of the whole congregation before the tabernacle of the congregation, to do the service of the tabernacle. And they shall keep all the instruments of the tabernacle of the congregation, and the charge of the children of Israel, to do the service of the tabernacle. And thou shalt give the Levites unto Aaron and to his sons: they are wholly given unto him out of the children of Israel." Num. 3:5-9.

The Levites represented the whole congregation of Israel, and acted on their behalf. This appears from the fact that the children of Israel laid their hands on the heads of the Levites, just as the Levites laid their hands on the heads of the sacrifices (see chap. 8:10). The act of imposition expressed identification, so that, according to this, the Levites furnish a distinct view of the people of God in the wilderness. They present them to us as a company of earnest workers, and that too, be it noted, not as mere desultory labourers, running to and fro, and doing each one what seemed right in his own eyes. Nothing of the sort. If the men of war had their pedigree to show and their standard to adhere to, so had the Levites their centre to gather round and their work to do. All was as clear, distinct, and defined as God could make it; and, moreover, all was under the immediate authority and direction of the high priest.

It is most needful for all who would be true Levites, proper workmen, intelligent servants, to weigh, with all seriousness, this point. Levite service was to be regulated by the appointment of the priest. There was no more room for the exercise of self-will in the service of the Levites, than there was the position of the men of war. All was divinely settled; and this was a signal mercy to all whose hearts were in a right condition. To one whose will was unbroken it might seem a hardship and a most irksome task to be obliged to occupy the same position, or to be engaged in precisely the same line of work. Such an one might sigh for something fresh – some variety in his work. But, on the contrary, where the will was subdued, and the heart adjusted, each one would say, "My path is perfectly plain; I have only to obey." This is ever the business of the true servant. It was pre-eminently so with Him who was the only perfect servant that ever trod the earth. He could say, "I came down from heaven, not to do mine own will, but the will of Him that sent me." And again, "My meat is to do the will of him that sent me, and to finish his work."

But there is another fact which claims our attention, in reference to the Levites; and that is, their service had exclusively to do with the tabernacle and its belongings. They had nothing else to do. For a Levite to think of putting his hand to anything beside would have been to deny his calling, to abandon his divinely appointed work, and to fly in the face of God's commandments.

Just so is it with Christians now. Their exclusive business – their one grand work – their absorbing service, is Christ and His belongings. They have nothing else to do. For a Christian to think of putting his hand to anything beside is to deny his calling, to abandon his divinely-appointed work, and fly in the face of the divine commandments. A true Levite of old could say, "To me to live is the tabernacle;" and a true Christian, now, can say, "To me to live is Christ." The grand question, in every matter which may present itself before the Christian, is this, "Can I connect Christ with it?" If not, I have nothing whatsoever to do with it.

This is the true way to look at things. It is not a question as to the right or wrong of this or that. No; it is simply a question as to how far it concerns the name and glory of Christ. This simplifies everything amazingly. It answers a thousand questions, solves a thousand difficulties, and makes the path of the true and earnest Christian as clear as a sunbeam.

To each his work

A Levite had no difficulty as to his work. It was all settled for him with divine precision. The burden that each had to carry, and the work that each had to do, was laid down with a clearness which left no room for the questionings of the heart. Each man could know his own work and do it; and let us add the work was done by each one discharging his own specific functions. It was not by running hither and thither, and doing this or that; but by each man sedulously adhering to his own particular calling, that the service of the tabernacle was duly discharged.

It is well to bear this in mind. We, as Christians, are very apt to jostle one another; indeed we are sure to do so if we do not each one pursue his own divinely-appointed line of work. We say *"divinely* appointed," and would press the word. We have no right to choose our own work. If the Lord has made one man an evangelist, another a teacher, another a pastor, and another an exhorter, how is the work to go on? Surely it is not by the evangelist trying to teach, and the teacher to exhort, or one who is not fitted for either trying to do both. No; it is by each one exercising his own divinely-imparted gift. No doubt it may please the Lord to endow one individual with a variety of gifts; but this does not, in the smallest degree, touch the principle on which we are dwelling, which is simply this, every one of us is responsible to know his own special line and pursue it. If this be lost sight of we shall get into hopeless confusion. God has His quarrymen, His stone-squarers, and His masons. The work progresses by each man attending diligently to his own work. If all were quarry-men, where were the stone-squarers? if all were stone-squarers, where were the masons? The greatest possible damage is done to the cause of Christ, and to God's work in the world, by one man aiming at another's line of things, or seeking to imitate another's gift. It is a grievous mistake, against which we would solemnly warn the reader. Nothing can be more senseless. God never repeats Himself. There are not two faces alike, not two leaves in the forest alike, not two blades of grass alike. Why then should any one aim at another's line of work, or affect to possess another's gift? Let each one be satisfied to be just what His Master has made him. This is the secret of real peace and progress.

Three classes of Levite

All this finds a very vivid illustration in the inspired record concerning the service of the three distinct classes of the Levites, which we shall now proceed to quote at length for the reader. There is nothing, after all, to be compared with the veritable language of holy scripture.

"And the Lord spake unto Moses in the wilderness of Sinai, saying, number the children of Levi after the house of their fathers, by their families: every male from a month old and upward shalt thou number them. And Moses numbered them *according to the word of the Lord, as He was commanded.* And these were the sons of Levi by their names, Gershon, and Kohath, and Merari. And these are the names of the sons of Gershon by their families; Libni, and Shimei. And the sons of Kohath by their families; Amram, and Izehar, Hebron, and Uzziel. And the sons of Merari by their families; Mahli, and Mushi. These are the families of the Levites according to the house of their fathers. Of Gershon was the family of the Libnites, and the family of the Shimites: these are the families of the Gershonites. Those that were numbered of them, according to the number of all the males, from a month old and upward, even those that were numbered of them were seven thousand and five hundred. The families of the Gershonites shall pitch behind the tabernacle westward. And the chief of the house of the father of the Gershonites shall be Eliasaph the son of Lael. And the charge of the sons of Gershon in the tabernacle of the congregation shall be the tabernacle, and the tent, the covering thereof, and the hanging for the door of the tabernacle of the congregation, and the hangings of the court, and the curtain for the door of the court, which is by the tabernacle, and by the altar round about, and the cords of it for all the service thereof" (chap. 3:14-26). And again, we read, "And the Lord spake unto Moses, saying, Take also the sum of the sons of Gershon, throughout the houses of their fathers, by their families; from thirty years old and upward until fifty years old shalt thou number them; all that enter in to perform the service, to do the work in the tabernacle of the congregation. This is the service of the families of the Gershonites, to serve, and for burdens: and they shall bear the curtains of the tabernacle, and the tabernacle of the congregation, his covering, and the covering of the badgers' skins that is above upon it, and the hanging for the door of the tabernacle of the congregation, and the hangings of the court, and the hanging for the door of the gate of the court, which is by the tabernacle and by the altar round about, and their cords, and all the instruments of their service, and all that is made for them: so shall they serve. At the appointment of Aaron and his sons shall be all the service of the sons of the Gershonites, in all their burdens, and in all their service: and ye shall appoint unto them in charge all their burdens. This is the service of the families of the sons of Gershon in the tabernacle of the congregation: and their charge shall be under the hand of Ithamar the son of Aaron the priest." Numbers 4:21-28.

Thus much as to Gershon and his work. He, with his brother Merari, had to carry "the tabernacle" whereas Kohath was called to bear "the sanctuary," as we read in Numbers 10. "And the tabernacle was taken down; and the sons of Gershon, and the sons of Merari set forward, bearing *the tabernacle* . . . And the Kohathites set forward, bearing the *sanctuary*: and the other (i.e., the Gershonites and the Merarites) did set up the tabernacle against they came" (Ver. 17, 21). There was a strong moral link connecting Gershon and Merari in their service, although their work was perfectly distinct, as we shall see from the following passage.

"As for the sons of Merari, thou shalt number them after their families, by the house of their fathers; from thirty years old and upward, even unto fifty years old, shalt thou number them, every one that entereth into the service, to do the work of the tabernacle of the congregation. And this is the charge of their burden, according to all their service in the tabernacle of the congregation; the boards of the tabernacle, and the bars thereof, and the pillars thereof, and sockets thereof, and the pillars of the court round about, and their sockets, and their pins, and their cords, with all their instruments, and with all their service: and by name ye shall reckon the instruments of the charge of their burden. This is the service of the families of the sons of Merari, according to all their service in the tabernacle of the congregation, under the hand of Ithamar, the son of Aaron the priest." Chapter 4:29-33.

All this was clear and distinct. Gershon had nothing to do with the boards and pins; and Merari had nothing to do with the curtains or the coverings. And yet they were very intimately connected, as they were mutually dependent. "The boards and sockets" would not do without "the curtains;" and the curtains would not do without the boards and sockets. And as to "the *pins,*" though apparently so insignificant, who could estimate their importance in keeping things together, and maintaining the visible unity of the whole? Thus all worked together to one common end, and that end was gained by each attending to his own special line. If a Gershonite had taken it into his head to abandon "the curtains" and address himself to "the pins," he would have left his own work undone and interfered with the work of the Merarite. This would never do. It would have thrown everything into hopeless confusion; whereas by adhering to the divine rule, all was maintained in the most exquisite order.

Subjection to the God-given order

It must have been perfectly beautiful to mark God's workers in the wilderness. Each one was at his post, and each moved in his divinely appointed sphere. Hence, the moment the cloud was lifted up, and the order issued to strike, every man knew what he had to do, and he addressed himself to that and to nothing else. No man had any right to think for himself. Jehovah thought for all. The Levites had declared themselves "on the Lord's side;" they had yielded themselves to His authority; and this fact lay at the very base of all their wilderness work and service. Looked at in this light it would be deemed a matter of total indifference whether a man had to carry a pin, a curtain, or a golden candlestick. The grand question for each and for all was simply, "Is this my work? Is this what the Lord has given me to do?"

This settled everything. Had it been left to human thinking or human choosing, one man might like this; another might like that; and a third might like something else. How then could the tabernacle ever be borne along through the wilderness, or set up in its place? Impossible! There could be but one supreme authority, namely Jehovah Himself. He arranged for all, and all had to submit to Him. There was no room at all for the exercise of the human will. This was a signal mercy. It prevented a world of strife and confusion. There must be subjection – there must be a broken will – there must be a cordial yielding to divine authority, otherwise it will turn out to be like the book of Judges, "Every man doing that which is right in his own eyes." A Merarite might say, or think if he did not say it, "What! am I to spend the very best portion of my life upon earth – the days of my prime and vigour – in looking after a few pins? Was this the end for which I was born? Am I to have nothing higher before me as an object in life? Is this to be my occupation from the age of thirty to fifty?"

To such questions there was a twofold reply. In the first place, it was enough for the Merarite to know that Jehovah had assigned him his work. This was sufficient to impart dignity to what nature might esteem the smallest and meanest matter. It does not matter what we are doing, provided always we are doing our divinely appointed work. A man may pursue what his fellows would deem a most brilliant career; he may spend his energies, his time, his talents, his fortune, in pursuits which the men of this world esteem grand and glorious, and, all the while, his life may prove to be but a splendid bubble. But, on the other hand, the man that simply does the will of God, whatever that may be – the man who executes his Lord's commands, whatever such commands may enjoin – that is the man whose path is illuminated by the beams of divine approbation, and whose work shall be remembered when the most splendid schemes of the children of this world have sunk in eternal oblivion.

But, besides the moral worth attaching always to the act of doing what we are told to do, there was also a special dignity belonging to the work of a Merarite, even though that work was merely attending to a few "pins" or "sockets." Everything connected with the tabernacle was of the very deepest interest and highest value. There was not, in the whole world, anything to be compared with that boarded tent with all its mystic belongings. It was a holy dignity and privilege to be allowed to touch the smallest pin that formed a part of that wonderful tabernacle in the wilderness. It was more glorious, by far, to be a Merarite looking after the pins of the tabernacle, than to wield the sceptre of Egypt or Assyria. True, that Merarite, according to the import of his name, might seem a poor "sorrowful," labouring man; but oh! his labour stood connected with the dwelling-place of the Most High God, the possessor of heaven and earth. His hands handled the things which were the patterns of things in the heavens. Every pin, every socket; every curtain, and every covering was a shadow of good things to come – a foreshadowing of Christ.

We do not mean to assert that the poor labouring Merarite or Gershonite understood these things. This is not, by any means, the point. *We* can understand them. It is our privilege to bring all these things – the tabernacle and its mystic furniture – under the brilliant light of the New Testament, and there read Christ in all.

While, therefore, we predicate nothing as to the measure of intelligence possessed by the Levites, in their respective work; we at the same time, may say, with confidence, that it was a very precious privilege to be allowed to touch and handle, and bear through the wilderness, the earthly shadows of heavenly realities. Moreover, it was a special mercy to have the authority of a "Thus saith the Lord" for everything they put their hand to. Who can estimate such a mercy – such a privilege? Each member of that marvellous tribe of workers had his own particular line of things marked out by God's hand, and superintended by God's priest. It was not each doing what he liked himself, nor one man running in the wake of another, but all bowing to the authority of God, and doing precisely what they were told to do. This was the secret of order throughout the eight thousand five hundred and eighty workers (Num. 4:48). And, we may say, with all possible confidence, it is the only true secret of order still. Why is it that we have so much confusion in the professing church? Why such conflicting thoughts, feelings, and opinions? Why such clashing one with another? Why such crossing of each other's path? Simply from the lack of entire and absolute submission to the word of God. Our *will* is at work. We choose our own ways, instead of allowing God to choose for us. We want that attitude and temper of soul in the which *all* human thoughts, our own amongst them, shall be put down at what they are really worth; and God's thoughts shall rise into full unqualified dominion.

This, we feel persuaded, is the grand desideratum – the crying want of the day in which our lot is cast. Man's will is everywhere gaining the ascendant. It is rising like a mighty tide and bearing away those ancient barriers which have, in some measure, kept it in check. Many an old and time-honoured institution is, at this moment, giving way before the rushing torrent. Many an edifice, whose foundations, as we supposed, were laid deep down in the fond and reverent affections of the people, is giving way beneath the battering ram of popular feeling. "Let us break their bands asunder, and cast away their cords from us."

Such is, pre-eminently, the spirit of the age. What is the

antidote? *Subjection*! Subjection to what? Is it to what is called the authority of the Church? Is it to the voice of tradition? Is it to the commandments and doctrines of men? No; blessed be God, it is not to any of these things, nor to all of them put together. To what then? To the voice of the living God – the voice of holy scripture. This is the grand remedy for self-will, on the one hand, and submission to human authority, on the other. "We must *obey*." This is the answer to self-will. "We must obey *God*." This is the answer to mere bowing down to human authority. We see these two elements all around us. The former, self-will, resolves itself into infidelity. The latter, subjection to man, resolves itself into superstition. These two will bear sway over the whole civilized world. They will carry away all save those who are divinely taught to say, and feel, and act upon, that immortal sentence, "We must obey God rather than man."

The value of everything that is connected to Christ

It was this that enabled the Gershonite, in the wilderness, to look after those rough unattractive looking "badger skins;" and that enabled the Merarite to look after these, apparently, insignificant "pins." Yes, and it is this which will enable the Christian, now, to address himself to that special line of service to which his Lord may see fit to call him. What, though, to human eyes, it seems rough and unattractive, mean and insignificant: it is enough for us that our Lord has assigned us our post, and given us our work; and that our work has direct reference to the Person and glory of Him who is the chiefest among ten thousand, and altogether lovely. We, too, may have to confine ourselves to the antitype of the rough unsightly badger skin, or the insignificant pin. But let us remember that whatever has reference to Christ – His name – His Person – His cause, in the world, is unspeakably precious to God. It may be very small, in man's account; but what of that? We must look at things from God's point of view, we must measure them by His standard, and that is Christ.

God measures everything by Christ. Whatever has even the very smallest reference to Christ is interesting and important in God's account. Whereas the most splendid undertakings, the most gigantic schemes, the most astonishing enterprises of the men of this world, all pass away like the morning cloud and the early dew. Man makes *self* his centre, his object, his standard. He values things according to the measure in which they exalt himself, and further his interests. Even religion itself, so called, is taken up in the same way, and made a pedestal on which to display himself. Everything, in short, is marked up as capital for self, and used as a reflector to throw light upon, and call attention to, that one object. Thus there is a mighty gulf between God's thoughts and man's thoughts; and the shores of that gulf are as far apart as *Christ* and *self*. All that belongs to Christ is of eternal interest and moment. All that belongs to self shall pass away and be forgotten. Hence, therefore, the most fatal mistake into which any man can fall is to make *self* his object. It must issue in everlasting disappointment. But, on the other hand, the very wisest, safest, best thing that any man can do, is to make Christ his one absorbing object. This must, infallibly, issue in everlasting blessedness and glory.

Beloved reader, pause here a moment and commune with thine own heart and conscience. It seems to us, at this point, that we have a sacred responsibility to discharge in reference to thy soul. We are penning these lines in the solitude of our chamber at Bristol, and you may, perchance, read them in the solitude of thy chamber in New Zealand, Australia, or some other distant spot. We would therefore remember that our object is not to write a book, nor yet, merely, to expound scripture. We desire to be used of God in the blessed work of dealing with thy very inmost soul. Permit us, therefore, to put this solemn and pointed question home to thee, *What is thy object?* Is it Christ or self? Be honest with thyself before the Almighty and All-seeing Searcher of hearts. Sit in stern judgment upon thyself, as in the very light of the divine presence. Be not deceived by any gilding or false colouring. God sees below the surface of things, and He would have thee do so likewise. He presents Christ to thee in contrast with all beside. Hast thou accepted Him? Is He thy wisdom, thy righteousness, thy sanctification, and thy redemption? Canst thou say, without hesitation, "My Beloved is mine, and I am his?" Search and see. Is this a thoroughly settled point, deep down in the very depths of thy soul? If so, art thou making Christ thy exclusive object? Art thou measuring everything by Him?

Ah! dear friend, these are searching questions. Be assured we do not put them to thee without feeling their edge and power for ourselves. As God is our witness, we do feel, though in a very small degree, their weight and seriousness. We are deeply and thoroughly convinced that nothing will stand save that which is connected with Christ; and, moreover, that the very smallest matter which refers, however remotely, to Him is of commanding interest in the judgment of heaven. If we may be permitted to awaken a sense of this in any heart, or to deepen the sense where it has been awakened, we shall feel we have not penned this volume in vain.

The service of the Kohathites

We must now, ere closing this lengthened section, glance, for a few moments, at the Kohathites and their work.

"And the Lord spake unto Moses and unto Aaron, saying, Take the sum of the sons of Kohath from among the sons of Levi, after their families, by the house of their fathers, from thirty years old and upward even until fifty years old, all that enter into the host, to do the work in the tabernacle of the congregation. This shall be the service of the sons of Kohath in the tabernacle of the congregation, about the most holy things: and when the camp setteth forward, Aaron shall come, and his sons, and they shall take down the covering vail, and cover *the ark* of testimony with it: and shall put thereon the covering of badgers' skins, and shall spread over it a cloth wholly of blue, and shall put in the staves thereof. And upon the *table* of shewbread they shall spread a cloth of blue, and put thereon the dishes, and the spoons, and the bowls, and covers to cover withal: and the continual bread shall be thereon: and they shall spread upon them a cloth of scarlet, and cover the same with a covering of badgers' skins, and shall put in the staves thereof. And they shall take a cloth of blue, and cover the candlestick of the light, and his lamps, and his tongs, and his snuffdishes, and all the oil vessels thereof, wherewith they minister unto it; and they shall put it and all the vessels thereof within a covering of badgers skins, and shall put it upon a bar. And upon *the golden altar* they shall spread a cloth of blue, and cover it with a covering of badgers' skins, and shall put to the staves thereof: and they shall take all the instruments of ministry, wherewith they minister in the sanctuary, and put them in a cloth of blue, and cover them with a covering of badgers' skins, and shall put them on a bar: and they shall take away the ashes from the altar, and spread a purple cloth thereon: and they shall put upon it all the vessels thereof, wherewith they minister about it, even the censers, the flesh-hooks, and the shovels, and the basons, all the vessels of the altar; and they shall spread upon it a covering of badgers' skins, and put to the staves of it. And when Aaron and his sons have made an end of covering the sanctuary, and all the vessels of the sanctuary, as the camp is to set forward; after that, the sons of Kohath shall come to bear it: but they shall not touch any holy thing, lest they die. These things are the burden of the sons of Kohath in the tabernacle of the congregation." Numbers 4:1-15.

Here we see what precious mysteries were committed to the charge of the Kohathites. The ark, the golden table, the golden candlestick, the golden altar, and the altar of burnt offering – all these were shadows of good things to come – the patterns of things in the heavens – the figures of the true – the types of Christ, in His Person, His work, and His offices, as we have sought to show in our "Notes on Exodus" (chap. 24 – 30). They are here presented in the wilderness, and, if we may be allowed the expression, in their travelling dress. With the exception of the ark of the covenant, all these things presented the one unvarying appearance to the human eye, namely, the rough covering of the badgers' skins. With the ark there was this difference, that above the badgers' skins there was "a cloth wholly of blue," setting forth, doubtless, the entirely heavenly character of the Lord Jesus Christ, in His own divine Person. That which was essentially heavenly in Him lay upon the very surface of His blessed life here below. He was ever the entirely heavenly man – "the Lord from heaven." Underneath this covering of blue were the badgers' skins, which may be viewed as the expression of that which protects from all evil. The ark was the only thing that was covered in this peculiar manner.

With regard to "the table of shewbread," which was a type of our Lord Jesus Christ, in His connection with the twelve tribes of Israel, there was first "a cloth of *blue*," and then a "cloth of *scarlet*;" and over all, the badgers' skins. In other words, there was that which is essentially heavenly; then that which expresses human splendour; and above all, that which protects from evil. It is the purpose of God that Israel's twelve tribes shall be pre-eminent in the earth – that in them the very highest type of human splendour shall be exhibited. Hence the appropriateness of the "scarlet" covering on the table of shewbread. The twelve loaves evidently point to the twelve tribes; and as to the scarlet colour, the reader has only to look through scripture in order to see that it sets forth that which man considers splendid.

The coverings of the golden candlestick and of the golden altar were identical, namely, first the heavenly covering; and then the external badgers' skin. In the candlestick we see our Lord Christ, in connection with the work of the Holy Ghost in light and testimony. The golden altar shows us Christ and the preciousness of His intercession – the fragrance and value of what He is before God. Both these, when passing along the sand of the desert, were wrapped up in that which was heavenly, and protected above by the badgers' skins.

Finally, in reference to the brazen altar, we observe a marked distinction. It was covered with "purple" instead of "blue," or "scarlet." Why was this? Doubtless because the brazen altar prefigured Christ as the one who "*suffered* for sins," and who shall therefore wield the sceptre of royalty. "Purple" is the royal colour. The One who suffered in this world, shall reign. The One who wore the crown of thorns, shall wear the crown of glory. Hence the moral fitness of the "purple" covering on the brazen altar – for on that altar the victim was offered. We know there is nothing in scripture without its own divine meaning, and it is our privilege as well as our duty to seek to know the meaning of all that our God has graciously written for our learning. This, we believe, can only be reached by humble, patient, prayerful waiting upon Him. The One who has penned the Book knows perfectly the scope and object of the book as a whole, and of each division of the Book in particular. This will have the effect of checking the unhallowed flights of the imagination. The Spirit of God alone can open scripture to our souls. "God is His own interpreter" in revelation, as well as in providence, and the more we lean on Him, in true self-emptiness, the deeper insight we shall have both into His word and His ways.

We would therefore say to the Christian reader, Take the first fifteen verses of Numbers 4 and read them in the presence of God. Ask Him to explain to thee the meaning of each clause – the meaning of the ark, and why it alone was covered with "a cloth wholly of blue." And so of all the rest. We have ventured, we trust in humility of mind, to suggest the meaning, but we earnestly desire that thou shouldst get it directly from God, for thyself, and not accept it merely from man. We confess we are terribly afraid of imagination; and we know not that we have ever sat down to write on sacred scripture with a deeper sense of this that none but the Holy Ghost can really explain it.

Thou wilt say, then, "Why sit down to write at all?" Well, it is with the fond hope of being permitted, in some feeble manner, to help the earnest student of scripture to catch sight of the rare and exquisite gems that lie scattered along the inspired page, so that he may pick them up for himself.

Thousands of readers might read, again and again, the fourth of Numbers, and not even perceive the fact that the ark was the only part of the mystic furniture of the tabernacle that did not exhibit the badger skin. And if the simple fact be not laid hold of, how can its import be seen? So also, as to the brazen altar, how many have failed to notice that it alone put on the "purple?"

Now, we may rest assured that both these facts are full of spiritual meaning. The ark was the very highest manifestation of God, and, therefore, we may understand why it should exhibit, at first sight, that which was purely heavenly. The brazen altar was the place where sin was judged – it typified Christ in His work as a sin bearer – it set forth that most distant place to which He travelled for us; and yet that brazen altar was the only thing that was wrapped in *royal* covering. Can anything be more exquisite than the teaching here? What infinite wisdom in all these fine distinctions! The ark conducts us to the very highest point in heaven. The brazen altar conducts us to the lowest point on earth. They stood at extreme points in the tabernacle. In the former, we see the One who magnified the law; in the latter, we see the One who was made sin. In the one, that which was heavenly was seen at the first sight; and it was only when you looked deeper, you saw the badger skin; and deeper still, that mysterious veil, the type of Christ's flesh. But, in the other, the first thing you saw was the badger skin, and deeper down we see the royal covering. Christ in each, though in a different aspect. In the ark, we have Christ maintaining the glory of God. In the brazen altar, we have Christ meeting the sinner's need. Blessed combination for us!

But, further, has the reader noticed that in the entire of this marvellous passage to which we have been calling his particular attention, there is no mention of a certain piece of furniture which we know, from Exodus 30 and other scriptures, occupied a, very important place in the tabernacle? We allude to the brazen laver. Why is this omitted in Numbers 4? It is more than probable that some of our keen-eyed rationalists would find here what they would pronounce an error – a defect – a discrepancy. But is it so? No, thank God! The devout Christian student knows full well that such things are wholly incompatible with the volume of God. He knows and confesses this, even though he may not be able to account for the absence of this or the presence of that particular thing in any given passage. But just in so far as we are enabled, through the mercy of God, to see the spiritual reason of things, do we always find that where the rationalist, sees, or affects to see flaws, the pious student sees brilliant gems.

Thus it is, we doubt not, in reference to the omission of the brazen laver from the catalogue in Numbers 4. It is only one of the ten thousand illustrations of the beauty and perfectness of the inspired volume.

But, the reader may enquire, "Why is the laver omitted?" The reason may be found in the double fact of what that laver was made from, and what it was made for. This double fact we have noticed in Exodus. The laver was made of the looking-glasses of the women who assembled at the door of the tabernacle of the congregation (Ex. 38:8). This was its material. And, as to its object, it was provided as a means of purification for man. Now, in all those things which formed the special burden and charge of the Kohathites, we see only the varied manifestations of God in Christ, from the ark in the holiest of all, to the brazen altar in the court of the tabernacle; and, inasmuch as the laver was not a manifestation of God, but a purification for man, it is therefore not found in the custody and charge of the Kohathites.

But we must now leave the reader to meditate alone on this most profound section of our book (chap. 3, 4). It is really inexhaustible. We might go on expatiating upon it until we had filled volumes instead of pages, and, after all, we should feel as though we had barely penetrated the surface of a mine whose depth never can be sounded – whose treasures never can be exhausted. What human pen can bring out the marvellous instruction contained in the inspired account of the tribe of Levi? Who can attempt to unfold that sovereign grace which shines in the fact that the self-willed Levi should be the very first to respond to that soul-stirring call, "Who is on the Lord's side?" Who can speak aright of that rich, abounding, distinguishing mercy illustrated in the fact that those whose hands had been embued in blood should be permitted to handle the vessels of the sanctuary; and that those into whose assembly God's Spirit could not enter should be brought into the very bosom of the congregation of God, there to be occupied with that which was so precious to Him?

And then those three divisions of workers, Merarites, Gershonites, and Kohathites! What instruction is here! What a type of the various members of the Church of God, in their various service! What depth of mysterious wisdom in all this! Is it speaking too strongly – is it too much to say that nothing, at this moment, so deeply impresses us as the sense of the utter feebleness and poverty of all that we have advanced on one of the very richest sections of the inspired volume! Still we have conducted the reader to a mine of infinite depth and richness, and we must leave him to penetrate thereinto by the gracious aid of Him to whom the mine belongs and who alone is able to evolve its wealth. All that man can write or say on any portion of God's word can, at best, be but suggestive; to speak of it as exhaustive would be to cast a slight upon the sacred canon. May we tread the holy place with unshod feet, and be as those who inquire in the temple, and whose studies are perfumed by the spirit of worship.[4]

---

[2] In using the expression, "The all-sufficiency of the name of the Lord Jesus Christ," we understand by it all that is secured to His people in that name – life; righteousness; acceptance; the presence of the Holy Ghost with all His varied gifts: a divine centre or gathering point. In a word, we believe that everything that the Church can possibly need, for time or eternity, is comprehended in that one glorious name, The Lord Jesus Christ.

[3] For further instruction on the doctrine of the sin offering and the burnt offering, the reader is referred to "Notes on Leviticus," chapters 1 and 4. This little volume can be had of the publisher.

[4] For further suggestions on the subjects touched upon in the foregoing section, the reader is referred to "Notes on Exodus" (chap. 24 – 30). Also to a small pamphlet entitled, "the History of the Tribe of Levi Considered."

Chapter 5

UNCLEANNESS OUTSIDE THE CAMP

"And the Lord spake unto Moses, saying, Command the children of Israel, that they put out of the camp every leper, and every one that hath an issue, and whosoever is defiled by the dead: both male and female shall ye put out, without the camp shall ye put them; that they defile not their camps, *in the midst whereof I dwell.* And the children of Israel did so, and put them out without the camp: as the Lord spake unto Moses, so did the children of Israel." Numbers 5:1-4.

A picture of discipline in the assembly

Here we have unfolded to us, in few words, the great foundation principle on which the discipline of the assembly is founded – a principle, we may say, of the very last importance, though, alas! so little understood or attended to. It was the presence of God in the midst of His people Israel that demanded holiness on their part. "That they defile not their camps in the midst of which I dwell." The place where the Holy One dwells must be holy. This is a plain and a necessary truth.

We have already remarked that *redemption* was the *basis* of God's dwelling in the midst of His people. But we must remember that *discipline* was essential to His continuance amongst them. He could not dwell where evil was deliberately and avowedly sanctioned. Blessed be His name, He can and does bear with weakness; but He is of purer eyes than to behold evil, and cannot look on iniquity. Evil cannot dwell with Him, nor can He have fellowship with it. It would involve a denial of His very nature; and He cannot deny Himself.

It may, however, be said, in reply, "Does not God the Holy Ghost dwell in the individual believer, and yet there is much evil in him?" True, the Holy Ghost dwells in the believer, on the ground of accomplished redemption. He is there, not as the sanction of what is of nature, but as the seal of what is of Christ: and His presence and fellowship are enjoyed just in proportion as the evil in us is habitually judged. Will any one assert that we can realise and delight in the Spirit's indwelling while allowing our indwelling pravity, and indulging the desires of the flesh and of the mind? Far away be the impious thought! No; we must judge ourselves, and put away everything inconsistent with the holiness of the One who dwells in us. Our "old man" is not recognised at all. It has no existence before God. It has been condemned, utterly, in the cross of Christ. We feel its workings, alas! and have to mourn over them, and judge ourselves on account of them; but God sees us in Christ – in the Spirit – in the new creation. And, moreover, the Holy Ghost dwells in the body of the believer, on the ground of the blood of Christ; and His indwelling demands the judgment of evil in every shape and form.

So also, in reference to the assembly. No doubt, there is evil there – evil in each individual member, and therefore evil in the body corporate. But it must be judged; and, if judged, it is not allowed to act, it is rendered null. But to say that an assembly is not to judge evil is nothing more or less than corporate antinomianism. What should we say to a professing Christian who maintained that he was not solemnly responsible to judge evil, in himself and in his ways? We should, with great decision, pronounce him an antinomian. And if it be wrong for a single individual to take such ground, must it not be proportionally wrong for an assembly? We cannot see how this can be called in question.

What would have been the result, had Israel refused to obey the peremptory "command" given at the opening of the chapter before us? Supposing they had said, "We are not responsible to judge evil; and we do not feel that it becomes poor, failing, erring mortals such as we to judge anybody. These people with the leprosy, and the issue, and so forth, are as much Israelites as we are, and have as good a right to all the blessings and privileges of the camp as we have; we do not therefore feel it would be right for us to put them out."

The example of Achan

Now what, we ask, would have been God's rejoinder to such a reply? If the reader will just turn for an instant to Joshua 7 he will find as solemn an answer as could well be given. Let him draw near and carefully inspect that "great heap of stones" in the valley of Achor. Let him read the inscription thereon. What is it? "God is greatly to be feared in the assembly of his saints, and to be had in reverence of all them that are round about him." "*Our* God is a consuming fire." What is the meaning of all this? Let us hear it and consider it! Lust had conceived in the heart of one member of the congregation, and brought forth sin. What then? Did this involve the whole congregation? Yes, verily, this is the solemn truth, "*Israel* (not merely Achan) hath sinned, and *they* have also transgressed my covenant which I commanded them: for *they* have even taken of the accursed thing, and have also stolen, and dissembled also, and *they* have put it even among their own stuff. Therefore the children of Israel could not stand before their enemies, but turned their backs before their enemies, because *they* were accursed: *neither will I be with you any more, except ye destroy the accursed thing from among you.*" Joshua 7:11, 12.

This is peculiarly solemn and searching. It, most assuredly, utters a loud voice in our ears, and conveys a holy lesson to our hearts. There were, so far as the narrative informs us, many hundreds of thousands throughout the camp of Israel as ignorant, as Joshua himself seems to have been, of the fact of Achan's sin and yet the word was, "*Israel* hath sinned – transgressed – taken the accursed thing – stolen and dissembled." How was this? The assembly was one. God's presence in the midst of the congregation constituted it one, so one, that the sin of each was the sin of all. "A little leaven leaveneth the whole lump." Human reason may demur to this, as it is sure to demur to everything that lies beyond its narrow range. But God says it, and this is enough for the believing mind. It doth not become us to ask, "Why? how? or wherefore?" The testimony of God settles everything, and we have only to believe and obey. It is enough for us to know that the fact of God's presence demands holiness, purity, and the judgment of evil. Let us remember this. It is not upon the principle so justly repudiated by every lowly mind, "Stand by thyself, I am holier than thou." No, no; it is entirely on the ground of what God is. "Be ye holy, for I am holy." God could not give the sanction of His holy presence to unjudged wickedness. What! Give a victory at Ai with an Achan in the camp? Impossible! A victory, under such circumstances, would have been a dishonour to God, and the very worst thing that could have happened to Israel. It could not be. Israel must be chastised. They must be humbled and broken. They must be brought down to the valley of Achor – the place of trouble, for there alone can "a door of hope" be opened when evil has come in.

To judge or not to judge?

Let not the reader misunderstand this great practical principle. It has, we fear, been greatly misunderstood by many of God's people. Many there are who seem to think that it can never be right for those who are saved by grace, and who are themselves signal monuments of mercy, to exercise discipline in any form, or on any ground whatsoever. To such persons, Matthew 7:1 seems to condemn utterly the thought of our undertaking to judge. Are we not, say they, expressly told by our Lord, not to judge? Are not these His own veritable words, "Judge not, that ye be not judged?" No doubt. But what do these words mean? Do they mean that we are not to judge the doctrine and manner of life of such as present themselves for Christian fellowship? Do they lend any support to the idea that, no matter what a man holds, or what he teaches, or what he does, we are to receive him all the same? Can this be the force and meaning of our Lord's words? Who could, for one moment, cede anything so monstrous as this? Does not our Lord, in this very same chapter, tell us to "beware of false prophets?" But how can we beware of any one, if we are not to judge? If judgment is not to be exercised in any case, why tell us to beware?

Christian reader, the truth is as simple as possible. God's assembly is responsible to judge the doctrine and morals of all who claim entrance at the door. We are not to judge motives, but we are to judge ways. We are directly taught by the inspired apostle, in 1 Corinthians 5, that we are bound to judge all who take the ground of being inside the assembly. "For what have I to do to judge them also that are without? Do not ye judge them that are within? But them that are without God judgeth. *Therefore* put away from among yourselves that wicked person." Verses 12, 13.

This is most distinct. We are not to judge those "without" but we are to judge those "within." That is, those who take the ground of being Christians – of being members of God's assembly – all such come within the range of judgment. The very moment a man enters the assembly, he takes his place in that sphere where discipline is exercised upon everything contrary to the holiness of the One who dwells there.

The unity of the body of Christ

And let not the reader suppose, for a moment, that the unity of the *body* is touched when the discipline of the *house* is maintained. This would be a very serious mistake indeed; and yet alas! it is a very common one. We frequently hear it said of those who rightly seek to maintain the discipline of the house of God, that they are rending the body of Christ. There could hardly be a greater mistake. The fact is, the former is our bounden duty; the latter, an utter impossibility.

The discipline of God's house must be carried out; but the unity of Christ's body can never be dissolved.

Again, we sometimes hear persons speak of cutting off the limbs of the body of Christ. This also is a mistake. Not a single limb of the body of Christ can ever be disturbed. Each member has been incorporated into its place by the Holy Ghost, in pursuance of the eternal purpose of God, and on the ground of the accomplished atonement of Christ; nor can any power of men or devils ever sever a single limb from the body. All are indissolubly joined together in a perfect unity, and maintained therein by divine power. The unity of the Church of God may be compared to a chain stretching across a river; you see it at either side, but it dips in the middle, and if you were to judge by the sight of your eyes, you might suppose that the chain had given way at the centre. So is it with the Church of God; it was seen to be one at the beginning; it will be seen to be one by and by; and it is, in God's sight, one now, though the unity be not visible to mortal eyes.

It is of the very last moment that the Christian reader should be thoroughly clear on this great Church question. The enemy has sought, by every means in his power, to cast dust into the eyes of God's dear people, in order that they might not see the truth in this matter. We have, on the one side, the boasted unity of Roman Catholicism; and, on the other hand, the deplorable divisions of Protestantism. Rome points, with an air of triumph, to the numerous sects of Protestants; and Protestants likewise point to the numerous errors, corruptions, and abuses of Romanism. Thus the earnest seeker after truth hardly knows where to turn or what to think; while, on the other hand, the careless, the indifferent, the self-indulgent, and the world-loving are only too ready to draw a plea, from all that they see around them, for flinging aside all serious thought and concern about divine things; and even if, like Pilate, they sometimes flippantly ask the question, "What is truth?" they, like him, turn on their heel without waiting for an answer.

Now, we are firmly persuaded that the true secret of the

whole matter – the grand solution of the difficulty – the real relief for the hearts of God's beloved saints, will be found in the truth of the indivisible unity of the church of God, the body of Christ, on the earth. This truth is not merely to be held as a doctrine, but to be confessed, maintained, and carried out, at all cost to ourselves. It is a great formative truth for the soul, and contains in it the only answer to Rome's boasted unity on the one hand, and to Protestant divisions on the other. It will enable us to testify to Protestantism that we have found unity, and to Roman Catholicism that we have found the unity of the Spirit.

It may, however, be argued, in reply, that it is the veriest Utopianism to seek to carry out such an idea, in the present condition of things. Everything is in such ruin and confusion that we are just like a number of children who have lost their way in a wood, and are trying to make the best of their way home, some in large parties, some in groups of two or three, and some all alone.

Now this may seem very plausible; and we do not doubt, in the least, but that it would carry immense weight with a large number of the Lord's people, at the present moment. But, in the judgment of faith, such a mode of putting the matter possesses no weight whatever. And for this simple reason, that the one all-important question for faith is this, namely, "Is the unity of the Church a human theory or a divine reality?" A divine reality, most surely, as it is written, "There is one body, and one Spirit" (Eph 4:4). If we deny that there is "one body," we may, with equal force, deny that there is "one Lord, one faith, one baptism, one God and Father of all," inasmuch as all lie side by side, on the page of inspiration, and if we disturb one, we disturb all.

Nor are we confined to one solitary passage of scripture on this subject; though had we but one, it were amply sufficient. But we have more that one. Hearken to the following: "The cup of blessing which we bless, is it not the communion of the blood of Christ? The bread which we break, is it not the communion of the body of Christ? For we, being many, are one bread, and one body; for we are all partakers of that one bread" (1 Cor. 10:16, 17). Read also 1 Corinthians 12:12-27, where this whole subject is unfolded and applied.

In a word, then, the word of God doth, most clearly and fully, establish the truth of the indissoluble unity of the body of Christ; and, moreover, it establishes, as clearly and as fully, the truth of the discipline of God's house. But, be it observed, the proper carrying out of the latter will never interfere with the former. The two things are perfectly compatible. Are we to suppose that when the apostle commanded the church of Corinth to put away from amongst them "that wicked person," the unity of the body was touched? Surely not. And yet was not that man a member of the body of Christ? Truly so, for we find him restored in the second epistle. The discipline of the house of God had done its work with a member of the body of Christ, and the erring one was brought back. Such was the object of the Church's act.

The holiness of the house of God

All this may help to clear the mind of the reader as to the deeply interesting subject of reception at the Lord's table and exclusion from it. There seems to be a considerable amount of confusion in the minds of many Christians as to these things. Some there are who seem to think that provided a person be a Christian, he should, on no account, be refused a place at the Lord's table. The case in 1 Corinthians 5 is quite sufficient to settle this question. Evidently that man was not put away on the ground of his not being a Christian. He was, as we know, spite of his failure and sin, a child of God; and yet was the assembly at Corinth commanded to put him away; and had they not done so, they would have brought down the judgment of God upon the whole assembly. God's presence is in the assembly, and therefore evil must be judged.

Thus, whether we look at the fifth chapter of Numbers or at the fifth chapter of 1 Corinthians, we learn the same solemn truth, namely, that "Holiness becometh God's house for ever."

And further we learn that it is with God's own people that discipline must be maintained, and not with those outside. For what do we read in the opening lines of Numbers 5? Were the children of Israel commanded to put out of the camp every one that was not an Israelite, every one that was not circumcised, every one who could not trace his pedigree, in an unbroken line, up to Abraham? Were these the ground of exclusion from the camp? Not at all. Who then were to be put out? "Every leper" – that is, every one in whom sin is *allowed* to work. "Every one that hath an issue" – that is, every one from whom a defiling influence is emanating: and, "whosoever is defiled by the dead." These were the persons that were to be separated from the camp in the wilderness, and their antitypes are to be separated from the assembly now.

And why, we may ask, was this separation demanded? Was it to uphold the reputation or respectability of the people? Nothing of the sort. What then? "That they defile not their camps in the midst whereof *I dwell*." And so is it now. We do not judge and put away bad doctrine, in order to maintain *our* orthodoxy; neither do we judge and put away moral evil, in order to maintain *our* reputation and respectability. The only ground of judgment and putting away is this, "Holiness becometh thine house, O Lord, for ever." God dwells in the midst of His people. "Where two or three are gathered together in my name, there am I." "Know ye not that ye are the temple of God, and that the Spirit of God dwelleth in you?" (1 Cor. 3:16). And again, "Now therefore, ye are no more strangers and foreigners, but fellow citizens with the saints, and of the household of God; and *are* built upon the foundation of the apostles and prophets, Jesus Christ himself being the chief corner stone; in whom all the building, fitly framed together, groweth unto *an holy temple* in the Lord; in whom ye also *are* builded together for an habitation of God through the Spirit." Ephesians 2:19-22.

But it may be that the reader feels disposed to put some such question as the following, "How is it possible to find a pure, a perfect church? Is there not – will there not – must there not be some evil in every assembly, in spite of the most intense pastoral vigilance and corporate faithfulness? How then can this high standard of purity be maintained?" No doubt there is evil in the assembly, inasmuch as there is indwelling sin in each member of the assembly. But it must not be allowed; it must not be sanctioned; it must be judged and kept under. It is not the presence of judged evil that defiles, but the allowance and sanction of evil. It is with the Church, in its corporate character, as with the members in their individual character. "If we would judge ourselves, we should not be judged" (1 Cor. 11:31). Hence, therefore, no amount of evil should lead a man to separate from the Church of God; but if an assembly denies its solemn responsibility to judge evil, both in doctrine and morals, it is no longer on the ground of the Church of God at all, and it becomes your bounden duty to separate from it. So long as an assembly is on the ground of the Church of God, however feeble it be, and few in number, to separate from it is schism. But if an assembly be not on God's ground – and most certainly it is not, if it denies its duty to judge evil – then it is schism to continue in association with it.

But will not this tend to multiply and perpetuate divisions? Most assuredly not. It may tend to break up mere human associations; but this is not schism, but the very reverse, inasmuch as all such associations, however large, powerful, and apparently useful, are positively antagonistic to the unity of the body of Christ, the Church of God.

It cannot fail to strike the thoughtful reader that the Spirit of God is awakening attention, on all hands, to the great question of the Church. Men are beginning to see that there is very much more in this subject than the mere notion of an individual mind, or the dogma of a party. The question, "What is the Church?" is forcing itself upon many hearts and demanding an answer. And what a mercy to have an answer to give! an answer as clear, as distinct, and as authoritative as the voice of God, the voice of holy scripture, can give. Is it not an unspeakable privilege, when assailed on all sides, by the claims of churches, "High Church," "Low Church," "Broad Church," "State Church," "Free Church," to be able to fall back upon the one true Church of the living God, the body of Christ? We most assuredly esteem it as such; and we are firmly persuaded that here alone is the divine solution of the difficulties of thousands of the people of God.

But where is this Church to be found? Is it not a hopeless undertaking to set out to look for it amid the ruin and confusion which surround us? No, blessed be God! for, albeit we may not see *all* the members of the Church gathered together, yet it is our privilege and holy duty to know and occupy *the ground* of the Church of God, and no other. And how is this ground to be discerned? We believe that the first step towards discerning the true ground of the Church of God is, to stand apart from everything that is contrary thereto. We need not expect to discover what is true while our minds are beclouded by what is false. The divine order is, "Cease to do evil; learn to do well." God does not give us light for two steps at a time. Hence, the moment we discover that we are on wrong ground, it is our duty to abandon it, and wait on God for further light, which He will, most surely, give.

Confession and reparation

But we must proceed with our chapter.

"The Lord spake unto Moses, saying, Speak unto the children of Israel; when a man or woman shall commit any sin that men commit, to do a trespass against the Lord, and that person be guilty; then they shall confess their sin which they have done; and he shall recompense his trespass with the principal thereof, and add unto it the fifth part thereof, and give it unto him against whom he hath trespassed. But if the man have no kinsman to recompense the trespass unto, let the trespass be recompensed unto the Lord, even to the priest; beside the ram of the atonement, whereby an atonement shall be made for him."

Restitution

The doctrine of the trespass offering has been considered in our "Notes on Leviticus," chapter 5; and to that we must refer our reader, as we do not mean to occupy his time or our own in going into any points which have been already considered. We shall merely notice here the very important questions of confession and restitution. Not only is it true that both God and man are gainers by the Great Trespass Offering presented on the cross at Calvary; but we also learn, from the foregoing quotation, that God looked for confession and restitution, when any trespass had been committed. The sincerity of the former would be evidenced by the latter. It was not sufficient for a Jew, who had trespassed against his brother, to go and say, "I am sorry," He had to restore the thing wherein he had trespassed and add a fifth thereto. Now, although we are not under the law, yet may we gather much instruction from its institutions; although we are not under the schoolmaster, we may learn some good lessons from him. If, then, we have trespassed against any one, it is not enough that we confess our sin to God and to our brother, we must make restitution; we are called upon to give practical proof of the fact that we have judged ourselves on account of that thing in which we have trespassed.

The tender conscience

We question if this is felt as it ought to be. We fear there is a light, flippant, easy-going style in reference to sin and failure, which must be very grievous indeed to the Spirit of God. We rest content with the mere lip confession, without the deep, heartfelt sense of the evil of sin in God's sight. The thing itself is not judged in its moral roots, and, as a consequence of this trifling with sin, the heart becomes hard, and the conscience loses its tenderness. *This is very serious.* We know of few things more precious than a tender conscience. We do not mean a *scrupulous* conscience, which is governed by its own crotchets; or a *morbid* conscience, which is governed by its own fears. Both these are most troublesome guests for any one to entertain. But we mean a *tender* conscience, which is governed, in all things, by the word of God, and which refers, at all times, to His authority. This sound description of conscience we consider an inestimable treasure. It regulates everything, takes cognisance of the very smallest matter connected with our daily walk and habits – our mode of dress – our houses – our furniture – our table – our entire deportment, spirit, and style – our mode of conducting our business, or, if it be our lot to serve others, the mode in which we discharge the service, whatever it be. In short, everything falls under the healthful moral influence of a tender conscience. "Herein," says the blessed apostle, "do I exercise myself, to have *always* a conscience void of offence toward God and men." Acts 24:16.

This is what we may well covet. There is something morally beautiful and attractive in this exercise of the greatest and most gifted servant of Christ. He, with all his splendid gifts, with all his marvellous powers, with all his profound insight into the ways and counsels of God, with all he had to speak of and glory in, with all the wonderful revelations made to him in the third heavens; in a word, he, the most honoured of apostles and privileged of saints, gave holy diligence to keep always a conscience void of offence both toward God and man; and if, in an unguarded moment, he uttered a hasty word, as he did to Ananias the high priest, he was ready, the very next moment, to confess and make restitution, so that the hasty utterance, "God shall smite thee, thou whited wall" was withdrawn, and God's word given instead – "Thou shalt not speak evil of the ruler of thy people."

Now we do not believe that Paul could have retired to rest, that night, with a conscience void of offence, if he had not withdrawn his words. There must be confession, when we do or say what is wrong; and if there be not the confession, our communion will assuredly be interrupted. Communion, with unconfessed sin upon the conscience, is a moral impossibility.

We may talk of it; but it is all the merest delusion. We must keep a clean conscience if we would walk with God. There is nothing more to be dreaded than moral insensibility, a slovenly conscience, an obtuse moral sense that can allow all sorts of things to pass unjudged; that can commit sin, pass on, and coolly say, "What evil have I done?"

Reader, let us, with holy vigilance, watch against all this. Let us seek to cultivate a tender conscience. It will demand from us what it demanded from Paul, namely, "exercise." But it is blessed exercise, and it will yield most precious fruits. Do not suppose that there is anything that savours of the legal in this exercise; nay, it is most thoroughly Christian; indeed we look upon those noble words of Paul as the very embodiment, in a condensed form, of the whole of a Christian's practice. "To have *always* a conscience void of offence toward God and men" comprehends everything.

But alas! how little do we habitually ponder the claims of God, or the claims of our fellow-man! How little is our conscience up to the mark! Claims of all sorts are neglected, yet we feel it not. There is no brokenness and contrition before the Lord. We commit trespass in a thousand things, yet there is no confession or restitution. Things are allowed to pass that ought to be judged, confessed, and put away. There is sin in our holy things; there is lightness and indifference of spirit in the assembly and at the Lord's table; we rob God, in various ways; we think our own thoughts, speak our own words, do our own pleasure; and what is all this but robbing God, seeing that we are not our own but bought with a price?

Now, we cannot but think that all this must sadly hinder our spiritual growth. It grieves the Spirit of God and hinders His gracious ministry of Christ to our souls whereby alone we grow up into Him. We know, from various parts of God's word, how much He prizes a tender spirit, a contrite heart. "To this man will I look, even to him that is of a contrite spirit and trembles at my word." With such an one God can dwell; but with hardness and insensibility, coldness and indifference, He can have no fellowship. Oh! then let us exercise ourselves to have always a pure and uncondemning conscience, both as to God and as to our fellow-man.

Infidelity and jealousy

The third and last section of our chapter, which we need not quote at length, teaches us a deeply solemn lesson, whether we view it from a dispensational or a moral point of view. It contains the record of the great ordinance designed for the trial of jealousy. Its place here is remarkable. In the first section, we have the corporate judgment of evil: in the second, we have individual self-judgment, confession, and restitution: and in the third, we learn that God cannot endure even the mere suspicion of evil.

Now, we fully believe that this very impressive ordinance has a dispensational bearing upon the relationship between Jehovah and Israel. The prophets dwell largely upon Israel's conduct as a wife, and upon Jehovah's jealousy, on that score. We do not attempt to quote the passages, but the reader will find them throughout the pages of Jeremiah and Ezekiel. Israel could not abide the searching trial of the bitter water. Her unfaithfulness has been made manifest. She has broken her vows. She has gone aside from her Husband, the Holy One of Israel, whose burning jealousy has been poured forth upon the faithless nation. He is a jealous God, and cannot bear the thought that the heart that He claims as His own should be given to another.

Thus we see that this ordinance for the trial of jealousy bears very distinctly upon it the impress of the divine character. In it He most fully enters into the thoughts and feelings of an injured husband, or of one who even suspected an injury. The bare suspicion is perfectly intolerable, and where it takes possession of the heart, the matter must be sifted to the very bottom. The suspected one must undergo a process of such a searching nature that only the faithful one can endure. If there was a trace of guilt, the bitter water would search down into the very depths of the soul, and bring it all out. There was no escape for the guilty one; and, we may say, that the very fact of there being no possible escape for the guilty, only made the vindication of the innocent more triumphant. The self-same process that declared the guilt of the guilty, made manifest the innocence of the faithful. To one who is thoroughly conscious of integrity, the more searching the investigation the more welcome it is. If there were a possibility of a guilty one escaping, through any defect in the mode of trial, it would only make against the innocent. But the process was divine, and therefore perfect; and hence, when the suspected wife had gone through it in safety, her fidelity was perfectly manifested, and full confidence restored.

What a mercy, then, to have had such a perfect mode of settling all suspected cases! Suspicion is the death blow to all loving intimacy, and God would not have it in the midst of His congregation. He would not only have His people collectively to judge evil, and individually to judge themselves; but where there was even the suspicion of evil, and no evidence forthcoming, He Himself devised a method of trial which perfectly brought the truth to light. The guilty one had to drink death, and found it to be judgment.[5] The faithful one drank death, and found it victory.

---

[5] The *"dust"* lifted from the floor of the tabernacle may be viewed as the figure of death. "Thou hast brought me into the dust of death." The *"water"* prefigures the word, which, being brought to bear upon the conscience, by the power of the Holy Ghost, makes everything manifest. If there has been any unfaithfulness to Christ, the true Husband of His people, it must be thoroughly judged. This holds good with regard to the nation of Israel, to the Church of God, and to the individual believer. If the heart be not true to Christ, it will not be able to stand the searching power of the word. But if there be truth in the inward parts, the more one is searched and tried, the better. How blessed it is when we can truly say, "Search me, O God, and know my heart: try me, and know my thoughts; and see if there be any wicked way in me, and lead me in the way everlasting." Psalm 139:23, 24.

Chapter 6

THE NAZARITE

The institution of the Nazarite

"And the Lord spake unto Moses, saying, Speak unto the children of Israel, and say unto them, When either man or woman shall separate themselves to vow a vow of a Nazarite, to separate themselves unto the Lord: he shall separate himself from wine and strong drink, and shall drink no vinegar of wine, or vinegar of strong drink, neither shall he drink any liquor of grapes, nor eat moist grapes, or dried. All the days of his separation shall he eat nothing that is made of the vine tree, from the kernels even to the husk. All the days of the vow of his separation there shall no razor come upon his head: until the days be fulfilled, in the which he separateth himself unto the Lord, he shall be holy, and shall let the locks of the hair of his head grow. All the days that he separateth himself unto the Lord he shall come at no dead body. He shall not make himself unclean for his father, or for his mother, for his brother, or for his sister, when they die: because the consecration of his God is upon his head. All the days of his separation he is holy unto the Lord." Verse 1-8.

The ordinance of Nazariteship is full of interest and practical instruction. In it we see the case of one setting himself apart, in a very special manner, from things which, though not absolutely sinful in themselves, were, nevertheless, calculated to interfere with that intense consecration of heart which is set forth in true Nazariteship.

In the first place, the Nazarite was not to drink wine. The fruit of the vine, in every shape and form, was to him a forbidden thing. Now, wine, as we know, is the apt symbol of earthly joy – the expression of that social enjoyment which the human heart is so fully capable of entering into. From this the Nazarite in the wilderness was sedulously to keep himself. With him it was a literal thing. He was not to excite nature by the use of strong drink. All the days of his separation he was called to exercise the strictest abstinence from wine.

Such was the type, and it is written for our learning – written too, in this marvellous book of Numbers, so rich in its wilderness lessons. This is only what we might expect. The impressive institution of the Nazarite finds its appropriate place in the book of Numbers. It is in perfect keeping with the character of the book, which, as has been already remarked, contains all that specially belongs to life in the wilderness.

Let us then inquire into the nature of the lesson taught us in the Nazarite's abstinence from everything pertaining to the vine, from the kernel even to the husk.

The perfect Nazarite

There has been but one true and perfect Nazarite in this world – but one who maintained, from first to last, the most complete separation from all mere earthly joy. From the moment He entered upon His public work, He kept Himself apart from all that was of this world. His heart was fixed upon God and His work, with a devotion that nothing could shake. No claims of earth or nature were ever allowed, for a single moment, to come in between His heart and that work which He came to do. "Wist ye not that I must be about my Father's business?" And again, "Woman, what have I to do with thee?" With such words did the true Nazarite seek to adjust the claims of nature. He had one thing to do, and to that He separated Himself perfectly. His eye was single and His heart undivided. This is apparent from first to last. He could say to His disciples, "I have meat to eat that ye know not of;" and when they, not knowing the deep significance of His words, said, "Hath any man brought Him anything to eat?" He replied, "My meat is to do the will of him that sent me, and to finish his work (John 4). So also, at the close of His course here below, we hear Him giving utterance to such words as these, as He took into His hand the paschal cup: "Take this, and divide it among yourselves: for I say unto you, I will not drink of the fruit of the vine, until the kingdom of God shall come." Luke 22:17, 18.

Thus we see how the perfect Nazarite carried himself throughout. He could have no joy in the earth, no joy in the nation of Israel. The time had not come for that, and therefore He detached Himself from all that which mere human affection might find in association with His own, in order to devote Himself to the one grand object which was ever before His mind. The time will come when He, as the Messiah, will rejoice in His people and in the earth; but, until that blissful moment arrives, He is apart as the true Nazarite, and His people are linked with Him. "They are not of the world, even as I am not of the world. Sanctify them through thy truth: thy word is truth. As thou hast sent me into the world, even so have I also sent them into the world. And for their sakes I sanctify myself, that they also might be sanctified through the truth." John 17:16-19.

Separation from the joys of this world

Christian reader, let us deeply ponder this first grand feature of the Nazarite character. It is important we should faithfully examine ourselves in the light of it. It is a very grave question indeed how far we, as Christians, are really entering into the meaning and power of this intense separation from all the excitement of nature, and from all merely earthly joy. It may perhaps be said, "What harm is there in having a little amusement or recreation? Surely we are not called to be monks. Has not God given as richly all things to enjoy? And while we are in the world, is it not right we should enjoy it?"

To all this we reply, It is not a question of the harm of this, that, or the other. There was no harm, as a general rule, in wine, nothing abstractedly wrong in the vine tree. But the point is this, if any one aimed a being a Nazarite, if he aspired to this holy separation unto the Lord, then was he to abstain *wholly* from the use of wine and strong drink. Others might drink wine; but the Nazarite was not to touch it.

Now, the question for us is this, Do we aim at being Nazarites? Do we sigh after thorough separation and devotion of ourselves, in body, soul, and spirit, unto God? If so, we must be apart from all these things in which mere nature finds its enjoyment. It is upon this one hinge that the whole question turns. The question, most assuredly, is not "Are we to be monks?" but "Do we want to be Nazarites?" Is it, our heart's desire to be apart, with our Lord Christ, from all mere earthly joy – to be separated unto God from those things which, though not absolutely sinful in themselves, do, nevertheless, tend to hinder that entire consecration of heart which is the true secret of all spiritual Nazariteship? Is not the Christian reader aware that there are, in very deed, many such things? Is he not conscious that there are numberless things which exert a distracting and weakening influence upon his spirit, and yet were they to be tried by the standard of ordinary morality, they might be allowed to pass as harmless?

But we must remember that God's Nazarites do not measure things by any such standard. Theirs is not an ordinary morality at all. They look at things from a divine and heavenly standpoint, and hence they cannot suffer anything to pass as harmless which tends, in any wise, to interfere with that high tone of consecration to God after which their souls are fervently breathing.

May we have grace to weigh these things, and to watch against every defiling influence. Each one must be aware of what it is which, in his case, would prove to be wine and strong drink. It may seem to be a trifle; but we may rest assured that nothing is a trifle which breaks the current of our soul's communion with God, and robs us of that holy intimacy which it is our privilege ever to enjoy.

Renouncement of our personal dignity

But there was another thing which marked the Nazarite. He was not to shave his head. "All the days of the vow of his separation there shall no razor come upon his head: until the days be fulfilled in the which he separateth himself unto the Lord, he shall be holy, and shall let the locks of the hair of his head grow."

In 1 Corinthians 11:14, we learn that it argues a lack of dignity for a man to have long hair. "Doth not even nature itself teach you, that if a man have long hair, it is a shame unto him?" From this we learn that if we really desire to live a life of separation to God, we must be prepared to surrender our dignity in nature. This our Lord Jesus Christ did perfectly. He made Himself of no reputation. He surrendered His rights in everything. He could say, "I am a worm and no man." He emptied Himself thoroughly, and took the very lowest place. He neglected Himself, while He cared for others. In a word, His Nazariteship was perfect in this as in all beside.

Now here is just the very thing which we so little like to do. We naturally stand up for our dignity and seek to maintain our rights. It is deemed manly so to do. But the perfect Man never did so; and if we aim at being Nazarites we shall not do so either. We must surrender the dignities of nature, and forego the joys of earth, if we would tread a path of thorough separation to God in this world. By and by both will be in place; but not now.

Here again, be it remarked, the question it is not as to the right or wrong of the case. As a general rule, it was right for a man to shave his locks; but it was not right, nay it was altogether wrong, for a Nazarite to do so. This made all the difference. It was quite right for an ordinary man to shave and drink wine; but the Nazarite was not an ordinary man; he was one set apart from all that was ordinary to tread a path peculiar to himself; and to use a razor or taste wine would involve the entire surrender of that peculiar path. Hence, if any inquire, "Is it not right to enjoy the pleasures of earth, and maintain the dignities of nature?" We reply, "Quite right, if we are to walk as men but wholly wrong, yea, absolutely fatal, if we want to walk as Nazarites."

This simplifies the matter amazingly. It answers a thousand questions and solves a thousand difficulties. It is of little use to split hairs about the harm of this or that particular thing. The question is, What is our real purpose and object? Do we merely want to get on as men, or do we long to live as true Nazarites? According to the language of 1 Corinthians 3:3, to "walk as men" and to be "carnal" are synonymous. Does such language really govern us? Do we drink into the spirit and breathe the atmosphere of such a scripture? Or are we ruled by the spirit and principles of a Godless, Christless world? It is useless to spend our time arguing points which would never be raised at all if our souls were in the right temper and attitude. No doubt, it is perfectly right, perfectly natural, perfectly consistent, for the men of this world to enjoy all that it has to offer them, and to maintain their rights and their dignities to the very utmost of their power. It were childish to question this. But, on the other hand, what is right, and natural, and consistent for the men of this world, is wrong, unnatural, and inconsistent for God's Nazarites. Thus the matter stands, if we are to be governed by the simple truth of God. We learn from Numbers 6, that if a Nazarite drank wine or shaved his locks, he defiled the head of his consecration. Has this no voice, no lesson for us? Assuredly it has. It teaches as that if our souls desire to pursue a path of whole-hearted consecration to God, we must abstain from the joys of earth, and surrender the dignities and the rights of nature. It must be thus, seeing that God and the world, flesh and spirit, do not and cannot coalesce. The time will come when it will be otherwise; but, just now, all who *will* live to God, and walk in the Spirit, must live apart from the world, and mortify the flesh. May God, of His great mercy, enable us so to do!

No contact with a dead body

One other feature of the Nazarite remains to be noticed. He was not to touch a dead body. "All the days that he separateth himself unto the Lord, he shall come at no dead body. He shall not make himself unclean for his father, or for his mother, for his brother, or for his sister, when they die; because the consecration of his God is upon his head."

Thus we see that whether it was drinking wine, shaving his locks, or touching a dead body, the effect was the same; any one of the three involved the defilement of the head of the Nazarite's consecration. Wherefore it is plain that it was as defiling to the Nazarite to drink wine or to shave his head, as it was to touch a dead body. It is well to see this. We are prone to make distinctions which will not stand for a moment in the light of the divine presence. When once the consecration of God rested upon the head of any one, that great and important fact became the standard and touchstone of all morality. It placed the individual on entirely new and peculiar ground, and rendered it imperative upon him to look at everything from a new and peculiar point of view. He was no longer to ask what became him as a man; but what became him as a Nazarite. Hence, if his dearest friend lay dead by his side he was not to touch him. He was called to keep himself apart from the defiling influence of death, and all because "the consecration of God" was upon his head.

Communion with God

Now, in this entire subject of Nazariteship, it is needful for the reader to understand, very distinctly, that it is not, by any means, a question of the soul's salvation, of eternal life, or of the believer's perfect security in Christ. If this be not clearly seen it may lead the mind into perplexity and darkness. There are two grand links in Christianity which, though very intimately connected, are perfectly distinct, namely, the link of eternal life, and the link of personal communion. The former can never be snapped by anything; the latter can be snapped in a moment, by the weight of a feather. It is to the second of these that the doctrine of Nazariteship pertains.

We behold, in the person of the Nazarite, a type of one who sets out in some special path of devotedness or consecration to Christ. The power of continuance in this path consists in secret communion with God; so that if the communion be interrupted, the power is gone. This renders the subject peculiarly solemn. There is the greatest possible danger of attempting to pursue the path in the absence of that which constitutes the source of his power. This is most disastrous, and demands the utmost vigilance. We have briefly glanced at the various things which tend to interrupt the Nazarite's communion; but it would be wholly impossible, by any words of ours, to set forth the moral effect of any attempt to keep up the appearance or Nazariteship when the inward reality is gone. It is dangerous in the extreme. It is infinitely better to confess our failure, and take our true place, than to keep up a false appearance. God will have reality; and we may rest assured that, sooner or later, our weakness and folly will be made manifest to all. It is very deplorable and very humbling when "the Nazarites that were purer than snow," become "blacker than a coal;" but it is far worse when those who have become thus black, keep up the pretence of being white.

The example of Samson

Let us look at the solemn case of Samson, as set before us in the sixteenth chapter of Judges. He, in an evil hour, betrayed his secret and lost his power – lost it though he knew it not. But the enemy soon knew it. It was soon made manifest to all that the Nazarite had defiled the head of his consecration. "And it came to pass, when Delilah pressed him daily with her words, and urged him, so that his soul was vexed unto death; that he told her all his heart, and said unto her, There hath not come a razor upon mine head; for I have been a Nazarite unto God from my mother's womb: if I be shaven, then my strength will go from me, and I shall become weak, and be like any other man." Verses 16, 17.

Here alas! was the betrayal of the deep and holy secret of all his power. Up to this, his path had been one of strength and victory, simply because it had been one of holy Nazariteship. But the lap of Delilah proved too much for the heart of Samson, and what a thousand Philistines could not do was done by the ensnaring influence of a single woman. Samson fell from the lofty elevation of the Nazarite down to the level of an ordinary man.

"And when Delilah saw that he had told her all his heart, she sent and called for the lords of the Philistines, saying, Come up this once, for he hath showed me all his heart. Then the lords of the Philistines came up unto her, and brought money in their hand. And she made him sleep upon her knees; [alas! alas! a fatal sleep to God's Nazarite!] and she called for a man, and she caused him to shave off the seven locks of his head; and she began to afflict him, and his strength went from him. And she said, The Philistines be upon thee, Samson. And he awoke out of his sleep, and said, I will go out as at other times before, and shake myself. And he wist not that the Lord was departed from him. But the Philistines took him, and put out his eyes, and brought him down to Gaza, and bound him with fetters of brass; and he did grind in the prison house." Judges 16:18-21.

Oh! reader, what a picture! How solemn! How admonitory! What a melancholy spectacle was Samson, going out to shake himself, "*as* at other times!" Alas! the "*as*" was out of place. He might shake himself, but it was no longer "as at other times," for the power was gone; the Lord was departed from him; and the once powerful Nazarite became a blind prisoner; and instead of triumphing over the Philistines, he had to grind in their prison house. So much for yielding to mere nature. Samson never regained his liberty. He was permitted, through the mercy of God, to gain one more victory over the uncircumcised; but that victory cost him his life. God's Nazarites must keep themselves pure or lose their power. In their case, power and purity are inseparable. They cannot get on without inward holiness; and hence the urgent need of being ever on the watch against the various things which tend to draw away the heart, distract the mind, and lower the tone of spirituality. Let us ever keep before our souls those words of our chapter, "all the days of his separation he is holy unto the Lord." Holiness is the grand and indispensable characteristic of all the days of Naziriteship; so that when once holiness is forfeited, Naziriteship is at an end.

Divine resources

What then, it may be asked, is to be done? The scripture before us supplies the answer. "And if any man die very suddenly by him, and he hath defiled the head of his consecration; then he shall shave his head in the day of his cleansing, on the seventh day shall he shave it. And on the eighth day he shall bring two turtles, or two young pigeons, to the priest, to the door of the tabernacle of the congregation; and the priest shall offer the one for a sin offering, and the other for a burnt offering, and make an atonement for him, for that he sinned by the dead, and shall hallow his head that same day. And he shall consecrate unto the Lord the days of his separation, and shall bring a lamb of the first year for a trespass offering; but the days that were before shall be lost, because his separation was defiled." Numbers 6:9-12.

Here we find atonement, in its two grand aspects, as the only ground on which the Nazarite could be restored to communion. He had contracted defilement, and that defilement could only be removed by the blood of the sacrifice. We might deem it a very trifling matter to touch a dead body, and particularly under such circumstances. It might be said, "How could he help touching it when the man had suddenly dropped dead by his side?" To all this the reply is at once simple and solemn. God's Nazarites must maintain personal purity; and, moreover, the standard by which their purity is to be regulated is not human but divine. The mere touch of death was sufficient to break the link of communion; and had the Nazarite presumed to go on as though nothing had happened, he would have been flying in the face of God's commandments, and bringing down heavy judgment upon himself.

But, blessed be God, grace had made provision. There was the burnt offering – the type of the death of Christ to Godward. There was the sin offering – the type of that same death to usward. And there was the trespass offering – the type of the death of Christ, not only in its application to the root or principle of sin in the nature, but also to the actual sin committed. In a word, it needed the full virtue of the death of Christ to remove the defilement caused by the simple touch of a dead body. This is peculiarly solemnizing. Sin is a dreadful thing in God's sight – most dreadful. A single sinful thought, a sinful look, a sinful word is enough to bring a dark, heavy cloud over the soul, which will hide from our view the light of God's countenance, and plunge us into deep distress and misery.

Let us, then, beware how we trifle with sin. Let us remember that ere one stain of the guilt of sin – even the very smallest – could be removed, the blessed Lord Jesus Christ had to pass through all the unutterable horrors of Calvary. That intensely bitter cry, "My God, my God, why hast thou forsaken me?" is the only thing that can give us any proper idea of what sin is; and into the profound depths of that cry no mortal or angel can ever enter. But though we can never fathom the mysterious depths of the sufferings of Christ, we should at least seek to meditate more habitually upon His cross and passion, and, in this way, reach a much deeper view of the awfulness of sin, in the sight of God. If, indeed, sin was so dreadful, so abhorrent to a holy God, that He was constrained to turn away the light of His countenance from that blessed One who had dwelt in His bosom from all eternity; if He had to forsake Him because He was bearing sin in His own body on the tree, then what must sin be?

Oh! reader, let us seriously consider these things. May they ever have a place deep down in these hearts of ours that are so easily betrayed into sin! How lightly, at times, do we think of that which cost the Lord Jesus everything, not only life, but that which is better and dearer than life, even the light of God's countenance! May we have a far deeper sense of the hatefulness of sin! May we, most sedulously, watch against the bare movement of the eye in a wrong direction, for we may rest assured that the heart will follow the eye, and the feet will follow the heart, and thus we get away from the Lord, lose the sense of His presence and His love, and become miserable, or, if not miserable, what is far worse, dead, cold, and callous – "hardened through the deceitfulness of sin."

May God, in His infinite mercy, keep as from falling! May we have grace to watch, more jealously, against everything, no matter what, that might defile the head of our consecration! It is a serious thing to get out of communion; and a most perilous thing to attempt to go on in the Lord's service with a defiled conscience. True it is that grace pardons and restores, but we never regain what we have lost. This latter is set forth, with solemn emphasis, in the passage of scripture before us: "He shall consecrate unto the Lord the days of his separation, and shall bring a lamb of the first year for a trespass offering; *but the days that were before shall be lost* (or shall fall, as the margin reads it), because his separation was defiled."

Removal and return

This is a point, in our subject, full of instruction and admonition for our souls. When the Nazarite became defiled, by any means, even by the touch of a dead body, he had to begin over again. It was not merely the days of his defilement that were lost, or let fall, but actually all the days of his previous Nazariteship. All went for nothing, and this simply by reason of touching a dead body.

What does this teach us? It teaches this, at least, that when we diverge, the breadth of a hair, from the narrow path of communion, and get away from the Lord, we must return to the very point from which we set out, and begin *de novo.* We have many examples of this in scripture; and it would be our wisdom to consider them, and also to weigh the great practical truth which they illustrate.

Take the case of Abraham, in his descent into Egypt, as recorded in Genesis 12. This was, very evidently, a divergence from his proper path. And what was the consequence? The days were lost or let fall, and he had to get back to the point whence he had swerved, and begin over again. Thus, in Genesis 12:8, we read, "And he removed from thence unto a mountain on the east of Bethel, and pitched his tent, having Bethel on the west, and Hai on the east; and there he builded an altar unto the Lord, and called upon the name of the Lord." Then, after his return out of the land of Egypt, we read, "He went on his journeys from the south even to Bethel, unto the place where his tent had been *at the beginning,* between Bethel and Hai; unto the place of the altar which he had made there *at the first:* and there Abram called on the name of the Lord" (Gen. 13:3, 4). All the time spent in Egypt went for nothing. There was no altar there, no worship, no communion; and Abraham had to get back to the self-same point from which he had diverged, and begin on the new.

Thus it is in every case; and this will account for the miserably slow progress which some of us make in our practical career. We fail, turn aside, get away from the Lord, are plunged in spiritual darkness; and then His voice of love reaches us in restoring power, and brings us back to the point from which we had wandered; our souls are restored, but we have lost time and suffered incalculably. This is most serious, and it should lead us to walk with holy vigilance and circumspection, so that we may not have to double back upon our path, and lose what can never be regained. True it is that our wanderings, and our stumblings, and our failings give us an insight into our own hearts, teach us to distrust ourselves, and illustrate the boundless and unchangeable grace of our God. All this is quite true; but still there is a very much higher way of learning both ourselves and God, than by wandering, stumbling, or failing. *Self,* in all the terrible depths of that word, should be judged in the holy light of the divine presence; and there, too, our souls should grow in the knowledge of God as He unfolds Himself, by the Holy Ghost, in the face of Jesus Christ, and in the precious pages of holy scripture. This surely is the more excellent way of learning both ourselves and God; and this, too, is the power of all true Nazarite separation. The soul that habitually lives in the sanctuary of God, or, in other words, that walks in unbroken communion with God, is the one who will have a just sense of what nature is, in all its phases, though it be not learnt by sad experience. And not only so; but he will have a deeper and juster sense of what God is, in Himself, and to all who put their trust in Him. It is poor work to be learning self by experience. We may depend upon it, the true way to learn it is in communion; and when we learn it thus, we shall not be characterised by perpetually dwelling upon our personal vileness, but rather we shall be occupied with that which is outside and above self altogether, even the excellency of the knowledge of Christ Jesus our Lord.

The end of the Nazarite's time of consecration

We shall, in closing this section, quote, at length, for the reader, the statement of "The law of the Nazarite, when the days of his separation are fulfilled: he shall be brought unto the door of the tabernacle of the congregation; and he shall offer his offering unto the Lord, one he lamb of the first year without blemish for a burnt offering, and one ewe lamb of the first year without blemish for a sin offering, and one ram without blemish for peace offerings; and a basket of unleavened bread, cakes of fine flour mingled with oil, and wafers of unleavened bread anointed with oil, and their meat offering, and their drink offerings. And the priest shall bring them before the Lord, and shall offer his sin offering and his burnt offering. And he shall offer the ram for a sacrifice of peace offerings unto the Lord, with the basket of unleavened bread: the priest shall offer also his meat offering, and his drink offering. And the Nazarite shall shave the head of his separation at the door of the tabernacle of the congregation, and shall take the hair of the head of his separation, and put it in the fire which is under the sacrifice of the peace offerings. And the priest shall take the sodden shoulder of the ram, and one unleavened cake out of the basket, and one unleavened wafer, and shall put them upon the hands of the Nazarite, after the hair of his separation is shaven; and the priest shall wave them for a wave offering before the Lord: this is holy for the priest, with the wave breast and the heave shoulder: and *after that the Nazarite may drink wine.* This is the law of the Nazarite who hath vowed, and of his offering unto the Lord for his separation, beside that that his hand shall get: according to the vow which he vowed, so he must do after the law of his separation." Numbers 6:13-21.

This marvellous "law" leads us onward to something future, when the full result of Christ's perfect work shall appear; and when He, as the Messiah of Israel, shall, at the close of his Nazarite separation, taste true joy in His beloved people, and in this earth. The time will then have come for the Nazarite to drink wine. From all this He set Himself apart, for the accomplishment of that great work, so fully set forth, in all its aspects and in all its bearings, in the foregoing "law." He is apart from the nation, and apart from this world, in the power of true Nazariteship, as He said to His disciples on that memorable night, "I will not drink henceforth (*ap' arti*) of this fruit of the vine, until *that day* when I drink it new with you in my Father's kingdom." Matthew 26:29.

But there is a bright day coming, when Jehovah-Messiah shall rejoice in Jerusalem, and joy in His people. The prophets, from Isaiah to Malachi, are full of the most glowing and soul-stirring allusions to that bright and blissful day. To quote the passages would literally fill a volume. But if the reader will turn to the closing section of Isaiah's prophecy, he will find a sample of that to which we refer; and he will find many similar passages throughout the various books of the prophets.

There is no Church in the Old Testament

We must not attempt to quote; but we would warn the reader against the danger of being led astray by the uninspired headings attached to those magnificent passages which refer to Israel's future, such, for example, as "The blessings of the gospel" – "The enlargement of the Church." These expressions are calculated to mislead many pious readers who are apt to take for granted that the headings are as much inspired as the text; or, if not inspired, that they, at least, contain a correct statement of what the text sets forth. The fact is, there is not a syllable about the Church from beginning to end of the prophets. That the Church can find most precious instruction, light, comfort, and edification from this grand division of the inspired volume, is blessedly true; but she will do this just in proportion as she is enabled, by the Spirit's teaching, to discern the real scope and object of this portion of the book of God. To suppose, for a moment, that we can only derive comfort and profit from that which exclusively or primarily refers to ourselves, would be to take a very narrow, if not an egotistical, view of things. Can we not learn from the Book of Leviticus? And yet who would assert that that section refers to the Church?

No, reader; you may rest assured that a calm, unprejudiced, prayerful study of "The law and the prophets" will convince you that the great theme of both the one and the other is God's government of the world in immediate connection with Israel. True it is, that throughout "Moses and all the prophets" there are things concerning (the Lord) Himself. This is plain from Luke 24:27. But it is "Himself" in His government of this world, and of Israel in particular. If this fact be not distinctly seized, we shall study the Old Testament with little intelligence or profit.

It may seem to some of our readers, a strong statement to assert that there is nothing about the Church, properly so called, throughout the prophets, or indeed in the Old Testament; but a statement or two from the inspired pen of St. Paul will settle the whole question for any one who is really willing to submit to the authority of holy scripture. Thus in Romans 16 we read, "Now to him that is of power to stablish you according to my gospel, and the preaching of Jesus Christ, according to the revelation of the mystery, *which was kept secret since the world began, but now is made manifest,* and by the scriptures of the prophets [evidently of the New Testament], according to the commandment of the everlasting God, made known to all nations for the obedience of faith." Verses 25, 26.

So also in Ephesians 3 we read, "For this cause I Paul, the prisoner of Jesus Christ for you Gentiles, if ye have heard of the dispensation of the grace of God, which is given me to you-ward; how that by revelation he made known unto me the mystery; (as I wrote afore in few words, whereby, when ye read, ye may understand my knowledge in the mystery of Christ;) *which in other ages was not made known unto the sons of men, as it is now revealed unto his holy apostles and prophets by the Spirit*[6] that the Gentiles should be fellow heirs, and of the same body, and partakers of his promise in Christ by the gospel . . . And to make all men see what is the fellowship of the mystery, which *from the beginning of the world hath been* HID IN GOD, who created all things by Jesus Christ: to the intent that now unto the principalities and powers in heavenly places might be known by the church the manifold wisdom of God." Verses 1-10.

But we must not pursue this deeply interesting subject of the Church; we have merely referred to the foregoing plain passages of scripture, in order to settle the reader's mind as to the fact that the doctrine of the Church, as taught by Paul, finds no place in the page of the Old Testament; and therefore, when he reads the prophets and meets the words "Israel," "Jerusalem," "Zion," he is not to apply such terms to the Church of God, inasmuch as they belong to the literal people of Israel, the seed of Abraham, the land of Canaan, and the city of Jerusalem.[7] God means what He says; and, therefore, we must not countenance anything that borders upon, or looks like, a loose and irreverent mode of handling the word of God. When the Spirit speaks of Jerusalem, He means Jerusalem; if He meant the Church, He would say so. We should not attempt to treat a respectable human document as we treat the inspired volume. We take it for granted that a man not only knows what he means to say, but says what he means; and if this be so, in regard to a poor fallible mortal, how much more so, in regard to the only wise and living God, who cannot lie?

But we must draw this section to a close, and leave the reader to meditate alone upon the ordinance of the Nazarite, so pregnant with sacred teaching for the heart. We wish him to ponder, in a special way, the fact that the Holy Ghost has given us the full statement of the law of Nazariteship in the Book of Numbers – the wilderness book. And not only so, but let him carefully consider the institution itself. Let him see that he understands why the Nazarite was not to drink wine; why he was not to shave his locks; and why he was not to touch a dead body. Let him meditate upon these three things, and seek to gather up the instruction contained therein. Let him ask himself, "Do I really long to be a Nazarite – to walk along the narrow path of separation unto God and, if so, am I prepared to surrender all those things which tend to defile, to distract, and to hinder God's Nazarites?" And, finally, let him remember that there is a time coming when "the Nazarite may drink wine;" or, in other words, when there will be no need to watch against the varied forms of evil within or around; all will be pure; the affections may flow out without check; the garments may flow around us without a girdle; there will be no evil to be separated from, and therefore there will be no need of separation. In a word, there will be "a new heavens and a new earth wherein *dwelleth* righteousness." May God, in His infinite mercy, keep us until that blessed time, in true consecration of heart unto Himself!

The final benediction on the people of Israel

The reader will observe that we here reach the close of a very distinct section of our book. The camp is duly arranged; every warrior is set in his proper place (chap. 1, 2); every workman is set to his proper work (chap. 3, 4); the congregation is purified from defilement (chap. 5). Provision is made for the highest character of separation to God (chap. 6). All this is very marked. The order is strikingly beautiful. We have before us not only a cleansed and well ordered camp, but also a character of consecration to God beyond which it is impossible to go, inasmuch as it is that which is only seen, in its integrity, in the life of our blessed Lord Jesus Christ Himself. Having then reached this lofty point, nothing remains but for Jehovah to pronounce His blessing upon the whole congregation, and accordingly we get that blessing at the close of chapter 6; and surely we may say, a right royal blessing it is. Let us read and consider.

"And the Lord spake unto Moses, saying, Speak unto Aaron and unto his sons, saying, On this wise ye shall bless the children of Israel, saying unto them, The Lord bless thee and keep thee; the Lord make his face shine upon thee, and be gracious unto thee. The Lord lift up his countenance upon thee, and give thee peace. And they shall put my name upon the children of Israel; and I will bless them."

This copious blessing flows through the channel of priesthood. Aaron and his sons are commissioned to pronounce this wonderful benediction. God's assembly is to be blessed and kept of Him, continually; it is ever to bask in the sunlight of His gracious countenance; its peace is to flow as a river; Jehovah's name is to be called upon it; He is ever there to bless.

What a provision! Oh! that Israel had entered into it, and lived in the power of it! But they did not. They quickly turned aside, as we shall see. They exchanged the light of God's countenance for the darkness of Mount Sinai. They abandoned the ground of grace and placed themselves under law. In place of being satisfied with their portion in the God of their Fathers, they lusted after other things (compare Psalms 105 and 106). In place of the order, the purity, and the separation to God with which our book opens, we have disorder, defilement, and giving themselves to idolatry.

But, blessed be God, there is a moment approaching in the which the magnificent benediction of Numbers 6 shall have its full application; when Israel's twelve tribes shall be ranged round that imperishable standard, "Jehovah-shammah" (Ezek. 48:35); when they shall be purified from all their defilements, and consecrated unto God in the power of true Nazariteship. These things are set forth in the fullest and clearest manner, throughout the pages of the prophets. All these inspired witnesses, without so much as one dissentient voice, bear testimony to the glorious future in store for the literal Israel; they all point forward to that time when the heavy clouds which have gathered and still hang upon the nation's horizon shall be chased away before the bright beams of "the Sun of righteousness;" when Israel shall enjoy a cloudless day of bliss and glory, beneath the vines and fig-trees of that very land which God gave as an everlasting possession unto Abraham, Isaac, and Jacob.

If we deny the foregoing, we may as well cut out a large portion of the Old Testament, and not a small part of the New, for in both the one and the other the Holy Ghost doth most clearly and unequivocally bear testimony to this precious fact, namely, mercy, salvation, and blessing to the seed of Jacob. We hesitate not to declare our conviction that no one can possibly understand the Prophets who does not see this. There is a bright future in store for God's beloved, though now rejected people. Let us beware how we deal with this fact. It is a very grave matter to attempt to interfere, in any wise, with the true and proper application of the word of God. If He has pledged Himself to bless the nation of Israel, let us have a care how we seek to force the stream of blessing to flow in a different channel. It is a serious thing to tamper with the declared purpose of God. He has declared it to be His purpose to give the land of Canaan an everlasting possession to the seed of Jacob; and if this be called in question, we do not see how we can hold fast the integrity of any one portion of the word of God. If we show ourselves to trifle with a large division of the inspired canon – and most assuredly it is trifling with it when we seek to divert it from its true object – then what security have we in reference to the application of scripture at all? If God does not mean what He says when He speaks of Israel and the land of Canaan, how do we know that He means what He says when He speaks of the Church and her heavenly portion in Christ? If the Jew be robbed of his glorious future, what security has the Christian as to his?

Reader, let us remember that "*All* (not merely some of) the promises of God are yea and amen in Christ Jesus," and while we rejoice in the application of this precious statement to ourselves, let as not seek to deny its application to others. We most fully believe that the children of Israel shall yet enjoy the full tide of blessing presented in the closing paragraph of Numbers 6; and until then the Church of God is called to partake of blessings peculiar to herself. She is privileged to know the presence of God with her and in her midst continually – to dwell in the light of His countenance – to drink of the river of peace – to be blessed and kept, from day to day, by Him who never slumbers nor sleeps. But let us never forget – yea, let us deeply and constantly remember – that the practical sense and experimental enjoyment of these immense blessings and privileges will be in exact proportion to the measure in which the Church seeks to maintain the order, the purity, and the Nazarite separation to which she is called as the dwelling-place of God – the body of Christ – the habitation of the Holy Ghost.

May these things sink down into our hearts, and exert their sanctifying influence upon our whole life and character!

---

[6] The "prophets" in the above quotations, are those of the New Testament, as is evident from the form of expression. Had the apostle meant Old Testament prophets, he would have said, "His holy prophets and apostles." But the very

point he is insisting upon is, that the mystery had never been revealed until his time – that it had not been made known to the sons of men in other ages – that it was hid in God; not hid in the scriptures, but in the infinite mind of God.

⁷ The statement in the text refers, of course, to the Old Testament prophecies. There are passages in the Epistles to the Romans and Galatians in which all believers are viewed as the seed of Abraham (see Rom. 4:9-17; Gal. 3:7, 9, 21; Gal. 6:16); but this is, obviously, a different thing altogether. We have no revelation of "the Church," properly so called, in the Old Testament scriptures.

Chapter 7

THE OFFERINGS OF ISRAEL'S PRINCES

This is the very longest section in the entire Book of Numbers. It contains a detailed statement of the names of the twelve princes of the congregation, and of their respective offerings on the occasion of the setting up of the tabernacle.

The wagons

"It came to pass on the day that Moses had fully set up the tabernacle, and had anointed it, and sanctified it, and all the instruments thereof, both the altar and all the vessels thereof, and had anointed them, and sanctified them, that the princes of Israel, heads of the house of their fathers, who were the princes of the tribes, and were over them that were numbered, offered. And they brought their offering before the Lord, six covered wagons, and twelve oxen; a wagon for two of the princes, and for each one an ox; and they brought them before the tabernacle. And the Lord spake unto Moses, saying, Take it of them, that they may be to do the service of the tabernacle of the congregation; and thou shalt give them unto the Levites, to every man according to his service. And Moses took the wagons and the oxen, and gave them unto the Levites. Two wagons and four oxen he gave unto the sons of Gershon, according to their service. And four wagons and eight oxen he gave unto the sons of Merari, according unto their service, under the hand of Ithamar, the son of Aaron the priest. But unto the sons of Kohath he gave none; because the service of the sanctuary belonging unto them was that they should bear upon their shoulders." Verses 1-9.

We noticed, when meditating on Numbers 3 and 4, that the sons of Kohath were privileged to carry all that was most precious of the instruments and furniture of the sanctuary. Hence they did not receive any of the princes' offering. It was their high and holy service to bear upon their shoulders, and not to make use of wagons or oxen. The more closely we examine those things which were committed to the custody and charge of the Kohathites, the more we shall see that they set forth, in type, the deeper and fuller manifestations of God in Christ. The Gershonites and Merarites, on the contrary, had to do with those things which were more external. Their work was rougher and more exposed, and therefore they were furnished with the needed help which the liberality of the princes placed at their disposal. The Kohathite did not want the aid of a wagon or an ox in his elevated service. His own shoulder was to bear the precious mystic burden.

The offerings for the dedication of the altar

"And the princes offered for dedicating of the altar in the day that it was anointed, even the princes offered their offering before the altar. And the Lord said unto Moses, They shall offer their offering, *each prince on his day,* for the dedicating of the altar."

An unspiritual reader, in running his eye over this unusually long chapter, might feel disposed to ask why so much space is occupied, in an inspired document, with what might be given in the compass of a dozen lines. If a man were giving an account of the transaction of those twelve days, he would, in all probability, have very briefly summed up all in one statement, and told us that the twelve princes offered each such and such things.

But that would not have suited the divine mind at all. God's thoughts are not as our thoughts, nor His ways as our ways. Nothing could satisfy Him but the fullest and most detailed account of each man's name, of the tribe which he represented, and of the offering which he made to the sanctuary of God. Hence this long chapter of eighty-nine verses. Each name shines out in its own distinctness. Each offering is minutely described and duly estimated. The names and the offerings are not huddled promiscuously together. This would not be like our God; and He can only act like Himself, in whatever He does, and speak like Himself, whatever He says. Man may pass hastily or carelessly over gifts and offerings; but God never can, never does, and never will. He delights to record every little act of service, every little loving gift. He never forgets the smallest thing; and not only does He not forget it Himself, but He takes special pains that untold millions shall read the record. How little did those twelve princes imagine that their names and their offerings were to be handed down, from age to age, to be read by countless generations! Yet so it was, for God would have it so. He will enter upon what might seem to us tedious detail, yea, if you please, what man might deem tautology, rather than omit a single name of any of His servants, or a single item of their work.

Thus, in the chapter before us, "each prince" gets his own appointed day for the presenting of his offering, and his own allotted space on the eternal page of inspiration, in the which the most complete record of his gifts is inscribed by God the Holy Ghost.

This is divine. And may we not say that this seventh chapter of Numbers is one of those specimen pages from the book of eternity, on which the finger of God has engraved the names of His servants, and the record of their work? We believe it is; and if the reader will turn to the twenty-third of second Samuel, and the sixteenth of Romans, he will find two similar pages. In the former, we have the names and the deeds of David's worthies; in the latter, the names and the deeds of Paul's friends at Rome. In both we have an illustration of what, we feel persuaded, is true of all the saints of God, and the servants of Christ, from first to last. Each one has his own special place on the roll, and each one his place in the Master's heart; and all will come out by and by.

Amongst David's mighty men, we have "the first three" – "the three" and "the thirty." Not one of "the thirty" ever attained a place among "the three;" nor did one of "the three" ever reach to "the first three."

Nor this only. Every act is faithfully set down; and the substance and style most accurately put before us. We have the name of the man, *what* he did, and *how* he did it. All is recorded, with sedulous care and minuteness, by the unerring and impartial pen of the Holy Ghost.

So also, when we turn to that remarkable sample page furnished in Romans 16 we have all about Phebe, what she was and what she did, and what a solid basis she had on which to rest her claim upon the sympathy and succour of the assembly at Rome. Then we have Priscilla and Aquila – the wife put first – and how they had laid down their own necks for the life of the blessed apostle, and earned his thanks and that of all the churches of the Gentiles. Next we have "the *well*-beloved Epaenetus;" and "Mary who bestowed," not merely labour, but "*much* labour" on the apostle. It would not have expressed the mind of the Spirit, or the heart of Christ, merely to say that Epaenetus was "beloved," or that Mary had bestowed "labour." No; the little adjuncts "well" and "much" were necessary in order to set forth the exact *status* of each.

But we must not enlarge, and we shall merely call the reader's attention to verse 12. Why does not the inspired penman place "Tryphena, Tryphosa," and "the beloved Persis" under one head? Why does he not assign them one and the same position? The reason is perfectly beautiful; because he could only say of the two former that they had "laboured in the Lord," whereas it was due to the latter to add that she had "laboured *much* in the Lord." Can anything be more discriminating? It is "the three" – "the first three" – and "the thirty" over again. There is no promiscuous jumbling of names and services together; no haste; no inaccuracy. We are told what each one was, and what he did. Each one gets his own place, and receives his own meed of praise.

And this, be it observed, is a specimen page from the book

of eternity. How solemn! And yet, how encouraging! There is not a single act of service which we render to our Lord that will not be set down in His book; and not only the *substance* of the act, but the *style* of it also, for God appreciates style as well as we do. He loves a cheerful giver, and a cheerful worker, because that is precisely what He is Himself. It was grateful to His heart to see the tide of liberality flowing around His sanctuary from the representatives of the twelve tribes. It was grateful to his heart to mark the actings of David's worthies, in the day of his rejection. It was grateful to His heart to trace the devoted path of the Priscillas, the Aquilas, and the Phebes of a later date. And, we may add, it is grateful to His heart, in this day of so much lukewarmness and vapid profession, to behold, here and there, a true-hearted lover of Christ, and a devoted worker in His vineyard.

May God's Spirit stir up our hearts to more thorough devotedness! May the love of Christ constrain us, more and more, to live, not unto ourselves, but unto Him who loved us and washed us from our scarlet sins in His most precious blood, and made us all we are, or ever hope to be.

Chapter 8

THE LIGHT OF THE CANDLESTICK

"And the Lord spake unto Moses, saying, Speak unto Aaron, and say unto him, When thou lightest the lamps, the seven lamps shall give light over against the candlestick. And Aaron did so; he lighted the lamps thereof over against the candlestick, as the Lord commanded Moses. And this work of the candlestick was of beaten gold, unto the shaft thereof, unto the flowers thereof, was beaten work: according unto the pattern which the Lord had showed Moses, so he made the candlestick." Verses 1-4.

On reading the foregoing paragraph, two things claim the reader's attention, namely, first, the position which the type of the golden candlestick occupies; and, secondly, the instruction which the type conveys.

The place of this teaching

It is not a little remarkable, that the candlestick is the only part of the furniture of the tabernacle introduced in this place. We have nothing about the golden altar, nothing about the golden table. The candlestick alone is before us, and that not in its covering of blue and of badgers' skins, as in chapter 4, where it, like all the rest, is seen in its travelling dress. It is here seen lighted, not covered. It comes in between the offerings of the princes, and the consecration of the Levites, and sheds forth its mystic light according to the commandment of the Lord. Light cannot be dispensed with in the wilderness, and therefore the golden candlestick must be stripped of its covering, and allowed to shine in testimony for God, which, be it ever remembered, is the grand object of everything, whether it be the offering of our *substance*, as in the case of the princes; or the dedication of our *persons*, as in the case of the Levites. It is only in the light of the sanctuary that the true worth of anything or any one can be seen.

Hence the moral order of the whole of this part of our book is striking and beautiful; indeed it is divinely perfect. Having read, in chapter 7, the lengthened statement of the princes' liberality, *we*, in our wisdom, might suppose that the next thing in order would be the consecration of the Levites, thus presenting, in unbroken connection, "our persons and offerings." But no. The Spirit of God causes the light of the sanctuary to intervene, in order that we may learn, in it, the true object of all liberality and service, in the wilderness.

Is there not lovely moral appropriateness in this? Can any spiritual reader fail to see it? Why have we not the golden altar, with its cloud of incense, here? Why not the pure table, with its twelve loaves? Because neither of these would have the least moral connection with what goes before, or what follows after; but the golden candlestick stands connected with both, inasmuch as it shows us that all liberality and all work must be viewed in the light of the sanctuary, in order to ascertain its real worth. This is a grand wilderness lesson, and it is taught us here as blessedly as type can teach us. In our progress through the Book of Numbers, we have just read the account of the large-hearted liberality of the great heads of the congregation, on the occasion of the dedication of the altar; and we are about to read the record of the consecration of the Levites; but between the one and the other, the inspired penman pauses, in order to let the light of the sanctuary shine on both.

This is divine order. It is, we are bold to say, one of the ten thousand illustrations which lie scattered over the surface of scripture, tending to demonstrate the divine perfectness of the volume, as a whole, and of each book, section, and paragraph therein. And we are glad – intensely glad to point out these precious illustrations to our reader, as we pass along in his company. We consider we are doing him good service herein; and, at the same time, presenting our humble tribute of praise to that precious book which our Father has graciously penned for us. Well indeed we know it does not need our poor testimony, nor that of any mortal pen or mortal tongue. But still it is our joy to render the testimony, in the face of the enemy's manifold but futile attacks upon its inspiration. The true source and character of all such attacks will become more and more manifest, as we become more deeply, livingly, and experimentally acquainted with the infinite depths and divine perfections of the Volume. And hence it is that the internal evidences of holy scripture – its powerful effect upon *ourselves*, no less than its intrinsic moral glories – its ability to judge the very roots of character and conduct, no less than its admirable structure, in all its parts – are the most powerful arguments in defence of its divinity. A book that exposes me to myself – that tells me all that is in my heart – that lays bare the very deepest moral springs of my nature – that judges me thoroughly, and at the same time reveals to me One who meets my every need – such a book carries its own credentials with it. It craves not, and needs not, letters of commendation from men. It stands in no need of his favour, in no dread of his wrath. It has often occurred to us that were we to reason about the Bible as the woman of Sychar reasoned about our Lord, we should reach as sound a conclusion about *it* as she reached about *Him*. "Come," said this simple and happy reasoner, "see a man which told me all things that ever I did: is not this the Christ?" May we not, with equal force of reasoning, say, "Come, see a book which told me all things that ever I did; is not this the word of God?" Yes, truly; and not only so, but we may argue, *a fortiori,* inasmuch as the book of God not only tells us all that ever we did, but all we think, and all we say, and all we are. See Romans 3:10-18; Matthew 15:19.

But is it that we despise external evidences? Far from it. We delight in them. We value every argument and every evidence calculated to strengthen the foundations of the heart's confidence in the divine inspiration of holy scripture; and, most assuredly, we have abundance of such material. The very history of the book itself, with all its striking facts, furnishes a broad tributary stream to swell the tide of evidence. The history of its composition; the history of its preservation; the history of its translation from tongue to tongue; the history of its circulation throughout earth's wide domain – in a word, its entire history, "surpassing fable, and yet true," forms a powerful argument in defence of its divine origin. Take, for example, that one fact of most commanding interest, namely, its having been kept for over a thousand years, in the custody of those who would have gladly consigned it, if they could, to eternal oblivion. Is not this a telling fact? Yes; and there are many such facts in the marvellous history of this peerless, priceless Volume.

But after allowing as wide a margin as may be desired, in the which to insert the value of external evidences, we return, with unshaken decision, to our statement, that the internal evidences – the proofs to be gleaned from the book itself – form as powerful a defence as can be erected with which to stem the tide of sceptical and infidel opposition.

We shall not, however, pursue any further this line of thought into which we have been led, while contemplating the remarkable position assigned to the golden candlestick, in the Book of Numbers. We felt constrained to say thus much in testimony to our most precious Bible, and having said it, we shall return to our chapter, and seek to gather up the instruction contained in its opening paragraph.

A light which reflected on the candlestick itself

"And the Lord spake unto Moses, saying, Speak unto Aaron, and say unto him, when thou lightest the lamps, the seven lamps shall give light over against the candlestick." Those "seven lamps" express the light of the Spirit in testimony. They were connected with the beaten shaft of the candlestick which typifies Christ, who, in His Person and work, is the foundation of the Spirit's work in the Church. All depends upon Christ. Every ray of light in the Church, in the individual believer, or in Israel by and by, all flows from Christ.

Nor is this all we learn from our type. "The seven lamps shall give light over against the candlestick." Were we to clothe this figure in New Testament language, we should quote our Lord's words when He says to us, "Let your light so shine before men, that they may see your good works, and glorify your Father which is in heaven" (Matt. 5:16). Wherever the true light of the Spirit shines it will always yield a clear testimony to Christ. It will call attention not to itself, but to Him; and this is the way to glorify God. "The seven lamps shall give light over against the candlestick."

This is a great practical truth for all Christians. The very finest evidence which can be afforded of true spiritual work is that it tends directly to exalt Christ. If attention be sought for the work or the workman, the light has become dim, and the Minister of the sanctuary must use the snuffers. It was Aaron's province to light the lamps; and he it was who trimmed them likewise. In other words, the light which, as Christians, we are responsible to yield, is not only founded upon Christ, but maintained by Him, from moment to moment, throughout the entire night. Apart from Him we can do nothing. The golden shaft sustained the lamps; the priestly hand supplied the oil and applied the snuffers. It is all *in* Christ, *from* Christ, and *by* Christ.

And more, it is all *to* Christ. Wherever the light of the Spirit – the true light of the sanctuary – has shone, in this wilderness world, the object of that light has been to exalt the name of Jesus. Whatever has been done by the Holy Ghost, whatever has been said, whatever has been written, has had for its aim the glory of that blessed One. And we may say with confidence, that whatever has not that tendency – that aim, is not of the Holy Ghost, be it what it may. There may be an immense amount of work done, a great deal of apparent result reached, a quantity of that which is calculated to attract human attention, and elicit human applause, and yet not one ray of light from the golden candlestick. And why? Because attention is *sought* for the work, or for those engaged in it. *Man* and his doings and sayings are exalted, instead of Christ. The light has not been produced by the oil which the hand of the great High Priest supplies; and, as a consequence, it is false light. It is a light which shines not over against the candlestick, but over against the name or the actings of some poor mortal.

All this is most solemn, and demands our deepest attention. There is always the utmost danger when a man or his work becomes remarkable. He may be sure Satan is gaining his object, when attention is drawn to anything or to any one but the Lord Jesus Himself. A work may be commenced in the greatest possible simplicity, but through lack of holy watchfulness and spirituality on the part of the workman, he himself, or the results of his work, may attract general attention, and he may fall into the snare of the devil. Satan's grand and ceaseless object is to dishonour the Lord Jesus; and if he can do this by what seems to be Christian service, he has achieved all the greater victory for the time. He has no objection to work, as such, provided he can detach that work from the name of Jesus. He will even mingle himself, if he can, with the work; he will present himself amongst the servants of Christ, as he once presented himself amongst the sons of God; but his object is ever one and the same, namely, to dishonour the Lord. He permitted the damsel, in Acts 16 to bear testimony to Christ's servants, and say, "These men are the servants of the most high God, which show unto us the way of salvation." But this was simply with a view to ensnare those servants and mar their work. He was defeated, however, because the light that emanated from Paul and Silas was the genuine light of the sanctuary, and it *shone* only for Christ. They sought not a name for themselves; and, inasmuch as it was to them and not to their Master that the damsel bore witness, they refused the witness, and chose rather to suffer for their Master's sake than to be exalted at His expense.

This is a fine example for all the Lord's workmen. And if we turn, for an instant to Acts 3 we shall find another very striking illustration. There the light of the sanctuary shone out in the healing of the lame man, and when attention was drawn, *unsought*, to the workmen, we find Peter and John, at once, with holy jealousy, retiring behind their glorious Master and giving all the praise to Him. "And, as the lame man which was healed held Peter and John, all the people ran together unto them, in the porch that is called Solomon's, greatly wondering. And when Peter saw it, he answered unto the people, ye men of Israel, why marvel ye at this? or why look ye so earnestly *on us*, as though by *our own* power or holiness we had made this man to walk? The God of Abraham, and of Isaac, and of Jacob, the God of our fathers, hath glorified HIS SON JESUS."

Here we have, in very deed, "the seven lamps giving their light over against the candlestick;" or, in other words, the sevenfold or perfect display of the Spirit's light in distinct testimony to the name of Jesus. "Why," said these faithful vessels of the Spirit's light, "look ye so earnestly on *us*?" No need of the snuffers here! The light was undimmed. It was, no doubt, an occasion which the apostles might have turned to their own account, had they been so disposed. It was a moment in the which they might have surrounded their own names with a halo of glory. They might have raised themselves to a pinnacle of fame, and drawn around them the respect and veneration of wondering, if not worshipping, thousands. But had they done so, they would have robbed their Master; falsified the testimony; grieved the Holy Ghost, and brought down upon themselves the just judgment of Him who will not give His glory to another.

But, no; the seven lamps were shining brightly in Jerusalem, at this interesting moment. The true candlestick was in Solomon's porch just then, and not in the temple. At least the seven lamps were there, and doing their appointed work most blessedly. Those honoured servants sought no glory for themselves; yea, they instantly put forth all their energies in order to avert the wondering gaze of the multitude from themselves, and fix it upon the only worthy One, who, though He had passed into the heavens, was still working by His Spirit on earth.

Many other illustrations might be drawn from the pages of the Acts of the Apostles; but the above will suffice to impress upon our hearts the great practical lesson taught in the golden candlestick, with its seven lamps. We are deeply sensible of our need of the lesson at this very moment. There is always a danger of the work and the workman being more the object than the Master. Let us be on our guard against this. It is a sad evil. It grieves the blessed Spirit, who ever labours to exalt the name of Jesus. It is offensive to the Father, who would ever be sounding in our ears, and deep down in our hearts, those words heard, from an open heaven, on the mount of transfiguration: "This is my beloved Son, in whom I am well pleased, hear ye him." It is in the most direct and positive hostility to the mind of heaven, where every eye is fixed on Jesus, every heart occupied with Jesus, and where the one eternal, universal, unanimous cry shall be, "*Thou art worthy.*"

Let us think of all this – think deeply – think habitually; that so we may shrink from everything bordering upon, or savouring of, the exaltation of man – of self – our doings and sayings and thinkings. May we all more earnestly seek the quiet, shady, unobtrusive path where the spirit of the meek and lowly Jesus will ever lead us to walk and serve. In a word, may we so abide in Christ, so receive from Him, day by day, and moment by moment, the pure oil, that our light may shine, without our thinking of it, to His praise, in whom alone we have ALL, and apart from whom we can do absolutely NOTHING.

The remainder of the eighth chapter of Numbers contains the record of the ceremonial connected with the consecration of the Levites, to which we have already referred in our notes on chapter 3 and 4.

Chapter 9

THE PASSOVER IN THE DESERT

"And the Lord spake unto Moses in the wilderness of Sinai, in the first month of the second year after they were come out of the land of Egypt, saying, Let the children of Israel also keep the Passover at his appointed season. In the fourteenth day of this month, at even, ye shall keep it in his appointed season: according to all the rites of it, and according to all the ceremonies thereof, shall ye keep it. And Moses spake unto the children of Israel, that they should keep the Passover. And they kept the Passover on the fourteenth day of the first month, at even, in the wilderness of Sinai: according to all that the Lord commanded Moses, so did the children of Israel." Verses 1-5.

There are three distinct positions in which we find this great redemption-feast celebrated, namely, in Egypt (Exod. 12); in the wilderness (Numb. 9); in the land of Canaan (Josh. 5). Redemption lies at the foundation of everything connected with the history of God's people. Are they to be delivered from the bondage, the death, and the darkness of Egypt? It is by redemption. Are they to be borne along through all the difficulties and dangers of the desert? It is on the ground of redemption. Are they to walk across the ruins of the frowning walls of Jericho, and plant their feet upon the necks of the kings of Canaan? It is in virtue of redemption.

Thus the blood of the paschal lamb met the Israel of God amid the deep degradation of the land of Egypt, and delivered them out of it. It met them in the dreary desert, and carried them through it. It met them on their entrance into the land of Canaan, and established them in it.

In a word, then, the blood of the lamb met the people in

Egypt; it accompanied them through the desert; and planted them in Canaan. It was the blessed basis of all the divine actings in them, with them, and for them. Was it a question of the judgment of God against Egypt? The blood of the lamb screened them from it. Was it a question of the numberless and nameless wants of the wilderness? The blood of the lamb secured a full provision for them. Was it a question of the dreaded power of the seven nations of Canaan? The blood of the lamb was the sure and certain pledge of complete and glorious victory. The moment we behold Jehovah coming forth to act on behalf of His people, on the ground of the blood of the lamb, all is infallibly secured, from first to last. The whole of that mysterious and marvellous journey, from the brick kilns of Egypt to the vine clad hills and honeyed plains of Palestine, served but to illustrate and set forth the varied virtues of the blood of the lamb.

A problem

However, the chapter which now lies open before us presents the Passover entirely from a wilderness standpoint; and this will account to the reader for the introduction of the following circumstance: "There were certain men which were defiled by the dead body of a man, that they could not keep the Passover on that day: and they came before Moses and before Aaron on that day."

Here was a practical difficulty – something abnormal, as we say – something not anticipated, and therefore the question was submitted to Moses and Aaron. "They came before Moses" – the exponent of the claims of God; "and before Aaron" – the exponent of the provisions of the grace of God. There seems something distinct and emphatic in the way in which both these functionaries are referred to. The two elements of which they are the expression would be deemed essential in the solving of such a difficulty as that which here presented itself.

"And those men said unto him, We are defiled by the dead

body of a man: wherefore are we kept back, that we may not offer an offering of the Lord in his appointed season among the children of Israel?" There was the plain confession as to the defilement; and the question raised was this: Were they to be deprived of the holy privilege of coming before the Lord in His appointed way? Was there no resource, no provision for such a case?

A deeply interesting question surely, but one for which no answer had as yet been provided. We have no such case anticipated in the original institution, in Exodus 12; although we have there a very full statement of all the rites and all the ceremonies of the feast. It was reserved for the wilderness to evolve this new point. It was in the actual walk of the people – in the real practical details of desert life, that the difficulty presented itself for which a solution had to be provided. Hence it is that the record of this entire affair is appropriately given in Numbers, the book of the wilderness.

"And Moses said unto them, Stand still, and I will hear what the Lord will command concerning you." Lovely attitude! Moses had no answer to give; but he knew who had, and he waited on Him. This was the very best and wisest thing for Moses to do. He did not pretend to be able to give an answer. He was not ashamed to say, *"I do not know."* With all his wisdom and knowledge, he did not hesitate to show his ignorance. This is true knowledge – true wisdom. It might be humiliating to one in Moses' position to appear before the congregation or any members of it, in the light of one ignorant on any question. He who had led the people out of Egypt, he who had conducted them through the Red Sea, he who had conversed with Jehovah, and received his commission from the great "I am;" could it be possible that he was unable to meet a difficulty arising out of such a simple case as that which was now before him? Was it indeed true that such an one as Moses was ignorant as to the right course, in reference to men defiled by a dead body?

How few there are who, though not occupying such a lofty position as Moses, would not have attempted a reply of some sort to such a query. But Moses was the meekest man in all the earth. He knew better than to presume to speak when he had nothing to say. Would that we more faithfully followed his example in this matter! It would save us from many a sad exhibition, from many a blunder, from many a false attempt. Moreover it would tend to make us very much more real, more simple, more unaffected. We are ofttimes so silly as to be ashamed to expose our ignorance. We foolishly imagine that our reputation for wisdom and intelligence is touched when we give utterance to that fine sentence, so expressive of true moral greatness, "I don't know." It is a total mistake. We always attach much more weight and importance to the words of a man who never pretends to knowledge which he does not possess. But a man who is always ready to speak, in flippant self-confidence, we are never ready to hear. Oh! to walk, at all times, in the spirit of these lovely words, "Stand still, and I will hear what the Lord will command."

The Passover in the second month

"And the Lord spake unto Moses, saying, Speak unto the children of Israel, saying, If any man of you or of your posterity shall be unclean by reason of a dead body: or be in a journey afar off, yet he shall keep the Passover unto the Lord. The fourteenth day of *the second month,* at even, they shall keep it, and eat it with unleavened bread and bitter herbs."

There are two grand foundation truths set forth in the Passover, namely, redemption, and the unity of God's people. These truths are unchangeable. Nothing can ever do away with them. Failure there may be, and unfaithfulness, in various forms; but those glorious truths of the eternal redemption and perfect unity of God's people remain in all their force and value. Hence that impressive ordinance which so vividly shadowed forth those truths was of perpetual obligation. Circumstances were not to interfere with it. Death or distance was not to interrupt it. "If any man of you or of your posterity shall be unclean by reason of a dead body, or be in a journey afar off, yet shall he keep the Passover unto the Lord." So imperative indeed was it upon every member of the congregation to celebrate this feast, that a special provision is made in Numbers 9 for those who were not up to the mark of keeping it according to the due order. Such persons were to observe it "on the fourteenth day of the *second* month." This was the provision of grace for all cases of unavoidable defilement or distance.

If the reader will turn to 2 Chronicles 30 he will see that Hezekiah, and the congregation in his day, availed themselves of this gracious provision. "And there assembled at Jerusalem much people to keep the feast of unleavened bread in the *second* month, a very great congregation . . . Then they killed the passover on the fourteenth day of the second month." Ver. 13, 15.

Grace in no way lowers the divine standard

The grace of God can meet us in our greatest possible weakness, if only that weakness be felt and confessed.[8] But let not this most precious and comfortable truth lead us to trifle with sin or defilement. Though grace permitted the second month, instead of the first, it did not, on that account, allow any laxity as to the rites and ceremonies of the feast. "The unleavened bread and bitter herbs" were always to have their place; none of the sacrifice was to remain till the morning, nor was a single bone of it to be broken. God cannot allow any lowering of the standard of truth or holiness. Man, through weakness, failure, or the power of circumstances, might be behind the time; but he must not be below the mark. Grace permitted the former; holiness forbids the latter; and if any one had presumed upon the grace to dispense with the holiness, he would have been cut off from the congregation.

Has this no voice for us! Assuredly it has. We must ever remember, as we pass along through the pages of this marvellous Book of Numbers, that the things which happened unto Israel are our types, and that it is, at once, our duty and our privilege to hang over these types and seek to understand the holy lessons which they are designed of God to teach.

What then are we to learn from the regulations with respect to the Passover, in the second month! Why was Israel so specially enjoined not to omit a single rite or ceremony on that particular occasion? Why is it that, in this ninth chapter of Numbers, the directions for the second month are much more minute than those for the first? It is not surely that the ordinance was more important in the one case than in the other, for its importance, in God's judgment, was ever the same. Neither is it that there was a shade of difference in the order, in either case, for that, too, was ever the same. Still the fact must strike the reader who ponders the chapter before us, that where reference is made to the celebration of the Passover in the first month, we simply read the words, "according to all the rites of it, and according to all the ceremonies thereof, shall ye keep it." But, on the other hand, when reference is made to the second month, we have a most minute statement of what those rites and ceremonies were: "They shall eat it with unleavened bread and bitter herbs. They shall leave none of it unto the morning, nor break any bone of it: according to all the ordinances of the passover they shall keep it." Compare verse 3 with 11, 12.

What, we ask, does this plain fact teach us? We believe it teaches us, most distinctly, that we are never to lower the standard, in the things of God, because of failure and weakness on the part of God's people; but rather, on that very account, to take special pains to hold the standard up, in all its divine integrity. No doubt, there should be the deep sense of failure – the deeper the better; but God's truth is not to be surrendered. We can always reckon, with confidence, upon the resources of divine grace, while seeking to maintain, with unwavering decision, the standard of divine truth.

Let us seek to keep this ever in the remembrance of the thoughts of our hearts. We are in danger, on the one hand, of forgetting the fact that failure has come in – yea, gross failure, unfaithfulness, and sin. And, on the other hand, we are in danger of forgetting, in view of that failure, the unfailing faithfulness of God, in spite of everything. The professing Church has failed, and become a perfect ruin; and not only so, but we ourselves have individually failed and helped on the ruin. We should feel all this – feel it deeply – feel it constantly. We should ever bear upon our spirits before our God the deep and heart-subduing consciousness of how sadly and how shamefully we have behaved ourselves in the house of God. It would be adding immensely to our failure were we ever to forget that we have failed. The most profound humility and the deepest brokenness of spirit become us in the remembrance of all this; and these inward feelings and exercises will surely express themselves in a lowly walk and carriage in the midst of the scene in which we move.

"Nevertheless the foundation of God standeth sure, having this seal, The Lord knoweth them that are his. And, Let every one that nameth the name of Christ depart from iniquity" (2 Tim. 2:19). Here is the resource of the faithful, in view of the ruins of Christendom. God never fails, never changes, and we have simply to depart from iniquity, and cling to Him. We are to do what is right, and follow it diligently, and leave results to Him.

We would earnestly beg of the reader to give the foregoing line of thought his entire attention. We want him to pause, for a few moments, and prayerfully consider the whole subject. We are convinced that a due consideration of it, in its two sides, would greatly help us to pick our steps amid the surrounding ruins. The remembrance of the Church's condition, and of our own personal unfaithfulness, would keep us humble; while, at the same time, the apprehension of God's unchanging standard, and of His unswerving faithfulness, would detach us from the evil around, and keep us steady in the path of separation. Both together would effectually preserve us from empty pretension, on the one hand, and from laxity and indifference, on the other. We have ever to keep before our souls the humbling fact that we have failed, and yet to hold fast that grand truth that God is faithful.

These are, pre-eminently, lessons for the wilderness – lessons for this very day – lessons for *us*. They are suggested, very forcibly, by the inspired record of the Passover in the second month – a record peculiar to the Book of Numbers – the great wilderness book. It is in the wilderness that human failure comes so fully out; and in the wilderness the infinite resources of divine grace are displayed. But once more, let us reiterate the statement – and may it be engraved, in characters deep and broad, on our hearts – the richest provisions of divine grace and mercy afford no warrant whatever for lowering the standard of divine truth. If any had pleaded defilement or distance as an excuse for not keeping the Passover, or for keeping it otherwise than as God had enjoined, he would, most assuredly, have been cut off from the congregation. And so with us, if we consent to surrender any truth of God, because failure has come in – if we, in sheer unbelief of heart, give up God's standard, and abandon God's ground – if we draw a plea from the condition of things around us to shake off the authority of God's truth over the conscience, or its formative influence upon our conduct and character – it is very evident that our communion is suspended.[9]

We would gladly pursue this great practical line of truth somewhat further, but we must forbear, and close this part of our subject by quoting for our reader the remainder of this wilderness record concerning the Passover.

Negligence in respect of the Passover

"But the man that is clean, and is not in a journey, and forbeareth to keep the Passover, even the same soul shall be cut off from among his people: because he brought not the offering of the Lord in his appointed season, that man shall bear his sin. And if a stranger shall sojourn among you, and will keep the Passover unto the Lord; according to the ordinance of the Passover, and according to the manner thereof, so shall he do: ye shall have one ordinance, both for the stranger, and for him that was born in the land." Verses 13, 14.

The wilful neglect of the Passover would argue, on the part of the Israelite, a total want of appreciation of the benefits and blessings coming out of his redemption and deliverance from the land of Egypt. The more deeply any one entered into the divine reality of that which had been accomplished on that memorable night, in the which the congregation of Israel found refuge and repose beneath the shelter of the blood, the more earnestly would he long for the return of "the fourteenth day of the first month," that he might have an opportunity of commemorating that glorious occasion; and if there was anything preventing his enjoying the ordinance in "the first month" the more gladly and thankfully would he avail himself of "the second." But the man who could be satisfied to go on from year to year, without keeping the Passover, only proved that his heart was far away from the God of Israel. It were worse than vain for any one to speak of loving the God of his fathers, and of enjoying the blessings of redemption, while the very ordinance which God had appointed to set forth that redemption lay neglected from year to year.

And may we not, to a certain extent, apply all this to ourselves, in reference to the matter of the Lord's supper? Doubtless we may, and that with very much profit. There is this connection between the Passover and the Lord's supper, that the former was the type, the latter the memorial, of the death of Christ. Thus we read in 1 Corinthians 5, "Christ our passover is sacrificed for us." This sentence establishes the connection. The Passover was the memorial of Israel's redemption from the bondage of Egypt; and the Lord's supper is the memorial of the Church's redemption from the heavier and darker bondage of sin and Satan. Hence, as every true and faithful Israelite would surely be found keeping the Passover, in the appointed season, according to all the rites and ceremonies thereof, so will every true and faithful Christian be found celebrating the Lord's supper, in its appointed season, and according to all the principles laid down in the New Testament respecting it. If an Israelite had neglected the Passover, even on one single occasion, he would have been cut off from the congregation. Such neglect was not to be tolerated in the assembly of old. It was instantly visited with the divine displeasure.

And, may we not ask in the face of this solemn fact, Is it nothing now – is it a matter of no moment for Christians to neglect, from week to week, and month to month, the supper of their Lord? Are we to suppose that the One who, in Numbers 9, declared that the neglecter of the Passover should be cut off, takes no account of the neglecter of the Lord's table? We cannot believe it for a moment. For, albeit it is not a question of being cut off from the Church of God, the body of Christ, are we, on that account, to be negligent? Far be the thought. Yea, rather should it have the blessed effect of stirring us up to greater diligence in the celebration of that most precious feast wherein "we do show the Lord's death till he come."

The value of the Lord's Supper

To a pious Israelite there was nothing like the Passover, because it was the memorial of his redemption. And, to a pious Christian, there is nothing like the Lord's supper, because it is the memorial of his redemption and of the death of his Lord. Of all the exercises in which the Christian can engage, there is nothing more precious, nothing more expressive, nothing that brings Christ more touchingly or solemnly before his heart, than the Lord's supper. He may sing about the Lord's death, he may pray about it, he may read about it, he may hear about it; but it is only in the supper that he *"shews"* it forth. "And he took bread, and gave thanks, and brake it, and gave unto them, saying, This is my body, which is given for you: this do in remembrance of me. Likewise also the cup after supper, saying, This cup is the new testament in my blood, which is shed for you." Luke 22:19, 20.

Here we have the feast *instituted*; and, when we turn to the Acts of the Apostles, we read that, "upon the first day of the week, the disciples came together to break bread." Acts 20:7.

Here we have the feast *celebrated*; and, lastly, when we

turn to the Epistles, we read, "The cup of blessing which we bless, is it not the communion of the blood of Christ? The bread which we break, is it not the communion of the body of Christ? For we, being many, are one loaf, and one body; for we are all partakers of that one loaf" (1 Cor. 10:16, 17). And again, "For I have received of the Lord that which also I delivered unto you, That the Lord Jesus, the same night in which he was betrayed, took bread; and when he had given thanks, he brake it, and said, Take, eat; this is my body, which is broken for you: this do in remembrance of me. After the same manner also he took the cup, when he had supped, saying, This cup is the new testament in my blood: this do ye, as oft as ye drink it, in remembrance of me. For as often as ye eat this bread, and drink this cup, ye do shew the Lord's death till he come." 1 Corinthians 11:23-26.

Here we have the feast *expounded.* And may we not say that, in the institution, the celebration, and the exposition, we have a threefold cord, not easily broken, to bind our souls to this most precious feast?

How is it, then, that in the face of all this holy authority, any of God's people should be found neglecting the Lord's table? Or, looking at it in another aspect, how is it that any of Christ's members can be satisfied to go on for weeks, and months, and some all their days, without ever remembering their Lord in the way of His own direct and positive appointment? We are aware that some professing Christians regard this subject in the light of a return to Jewish ordinances, and as a coming down from the high ground of the Church. They look upon the Lord's supper and baptism as inward spiritual mysteries; and they consider that we are departing from true spirituality in insisting upon the literal observance of these ordinances.

To all this we very simply reply that God is wiser than we are. If the Lord Christ instituted the supper; if God the Holy Ghost led the early Church to celebrate it; and if He has also expounded it unto us, who are we that we should set up our ideas in opposition to God? No doubt, the Lord's supper should be an inward spiritual mystery to all who partake of it; but it is also an outward, literal, tangible thing. There is literal bread, and literal wine – literal eating, and literal drinking. If any deny this, they may, with equal force, deny that there are literal people gathered together. We have no right to explain away scripture after such a fashion. It is our happy and holy duty to submit to scripture, to bow down, absolutely and implicitly, to its divine authority.

Nor is it merely a question of subjection to the authority of scripture. It is that, most assuredly, as we have abundantly proved by quotation after quotation from the divine word; and that alone is simply sufficient for every pious mind. But there is more than this. There is such a thing as the response of love in the heart of the Christian, answering to the love of the heart of Christ. Is not this something? Ought we not to seek, in some small degree, to meet the love of such a heart? If our blessed and adorable Lord has, in very deed, appointed the bread and the wine, in the supper, as memorials of His broken body and shed blood; if He has ordained that we should eat of that bread and drink of that cup, in remembrance of Him, ought we not, in the power of responsive affection, to meet the desire of His loving heart? Surely no earnest Christian will question this. It ought ever to be the very joy of our hearts to gather round the table of our loving Lord, and remember Him in the way of His appointment – to show forth His death till He come. It is only marvellous to think that He should seek a place in the remembrance of such hearts as ours; but so it is; and it would be sad indeed if we, on any ground, and for any reason whatsoever, should neglect that very feast with which He has linked His precious name.

This, of course, would not be the place to enter upon anything like an elaborate exposition of the ordinance of the Lord's supper. We have sought to do this elsewhere. What we specially desire here is, to urge upon the Christian reader the immense importance and deep interest of the ordinance as viewed on the double ground of subjection to the authority of scripture, and responsive love to Christ Himself. And, furthermore, we are anxious to impress all who may read these lines with a sense of the seriousness of neglecting to eat the Lord's supper, according to the scriptures. We may depend upon it, it is dangerous ground for any to attempt to set aside this positive institution of our Lord and Master. It argues a wrong condition of soul altogether. It proves that the conscience is not subject to the authority of the word, and that the heart is not in true sympathy with the affections of Christ. Let us therefore see to it that we are honestly endeavouring to discharge our holy responsibilities to the table of the Lord – that we forbear not to keep the feast – that we celebrate it according to the order laid down by God the Holy Ghost.

Thus much as to the Passover in the wilderness, and the impressive lessons which it conveys to our souls.

Attentive to the movements of the cloud

We shall now dwell for a few moments on the closing paragraph of our chapter, which is as truly characteristic as any portion of the book. In it we are called to contemplate a numerous host of men, women, and children, travelling through a trackless wilderness, "where there was no way" – passing over a dreary waste, a vast sandy desert, without compass or human guide.

What a thought! What a spectacle! There were those millions of people moving along without any knowledge of the route by which they were to travel, as wholly dependent upon God for guidance as for food and all beside; a thoroughly helpless pilgrim host. They could form no plans for the morrow. When encamped, they knew not when they were to march; and when on the march, they knew not when or where they were to halt. Theirs was a life of daily and hourly dependence. They had to look up for guidance. Their movements were controlled by the wheels of Jehovah's chariot.

This truly was a wondrous spectacle. Let us read the record of it, and drink into our souls its heavenly teaching.

"And on the day that the tabernacle was reared up, the cloud covered the tabernacle, namely, the tent of the testimony:

and at even there was upon the tabernacle as it were the appearance of fire, until the morning. *So it was alway:* the cloud covered it by day, and the appearance of fire by night. And when the cloud was taken up from the tabernacle, then after that the children of Israel journeyed: and in the place where the cloud abode, there the children of Israel pitched their tents. At the commandment of the Lord the children of Israel journeyed, and at the commandment of the Lord they pitched: as long as the cloud abode upon the tabernacle, they rested in their tents. And when the cloud tarried long upon the tabernacle many days, then the children of Israel kept the charge of the Lord, and journeyed not. And so it was, when the cloud was a few days upon the tabernacle; according to the commandment of the Lord they abode in their tents, and according to the commandment of the Lord they journeyed. And so it was, when the cloud abode from even unto the morning, and that the cloud was taken up in the morning, then they journeyed; whether it was by day or by night that the cloud was taken up, they journeyed. Or whether it were two days, or a month, or a year, that the cloud tarried upon the tabernacle, remaining thereon, the children of Israel abode in their tents, and journeyed not; but when it was taken up, they journeyed. At the commandment of the Lord they rested in the tents, and at the commandment of the Lord they journeyed: they kept the charge of the Lord, at the commandment of the Lord by the hand of Moses." Verses 15-23.

A more lovely picture of absolute dependence upon, and subjection to, divine guidance it were impossible to conceive than that presented in the foregoing paragraph. There was not a footprint or a landmark throughout that "great and terrible wilderness." It was therefore useless to look for any guidance from those who had gone before. They were wholly cast upon God for every step of the way. They were in a position of constant waiting upon Him. This, to an unsubdued mind – an unbroken will – would be intolerable; but to a soul knowing, loving, confiding, and delighting in God, nothing could be more deeply blessed.

Here lies the real gist of the whole matter. Is God known, loved, and trusted? If He be, the heart will delight in the most absolute dependence upon Him. If not, such dependence would be perfectly insufferable.

Slavery and liberty

The unrenewed man loves to think himself independent – loves to fancy himself free – loves to believe that he may do what he likes, go where he likes, say what he likes. Alas! it is the merest delusion. Man is not free. He is the slave of Satan. It is now well nigh six thousand years since he sold himself into the hands of that great spiritual slaveholder who has held him ever since, and who holds him still. Yes, Satan holds the natural man – the unconverted, unrepentant man in terrible bondage. He has him bound hand and foot with chains and fetters which are not seen in their true character because of the gilding wherewith he has so artfully covered them. Satan rules man by means of his lusts, his passions, and his pleasures. He forms lusts in the heart, and then gratifies them with the things that are in the world, and man vainly imagines himself free because he can gratify his desires. But it is a melancholy delusion; and, sooner or later, it will be found to be such. There is no freedom save that with which Christ makes His people free. He it is who says, "Ye shall know the truth, and the truth shall make you free." And again, "If the Son shall make you free, ye shall be free indeed." John 8.

Here is true liberty. It is the liberty which the new nature finds in walking in the Spirit, and doing those things that are pleasing in the sight of God. "The service of the Lord is perfect freedom." But this service, in all its departments, involves the most simple dependence upon the living God. Thus it was with the only true and perfect Servant that ever trod this earth. He was ever dependent. Every movement, every act, every word – all He did, and all He left undone – was the fruit of the most absolute dependence upon, and subjection to, God. He moved when God would have Him move, and stood still when God would have Him stand. He spoke when God would have Him speak, and was silent when God would have Him silent.

Such was Jesus when He lived in this world; and we, as partakers of His nature – His life, and having His Spirit dwelling in us are called to walk in His steps, and live a life of simple dependence upon God, from day to day. Of this life of dependence, in one special phase of it, we have a graphic and beautiful type at the close of our chapter. The Israel of God – the camp in the desert – that pilgrim host followed the movement of the cloud. They had to *look up* for guidance. This is man's proper work. He was made to turn his countenance upward, in contrast with the brute, who is formed to look downward.[10] Israel could form no plans. They could never say, "To-morrow we shall go to such a place." They were entirely dependent upon the movement of the cloud.

Thus it was with Israel, and thus it should be with us. We are passing through a trackless desert – a moral wilderness. There is absolutely no way. We should not know how to walk, or where to go, were it not for that one most precious, most deep, most comprehensive sentence which fell from the lips of our blessed Lord, "*I am the way.*" Here is divine infallible guidance. We are to follow Him. "I am the light of the world: he that followeth me shall not walk in darkness, but shall have the light of life" (John 8). This is living guidance. It is not acting according to the letter of certain rules and regulations; it is following a living Christ; walking as He walked; doing as He did; imitating His example in all things. This is Christian movement – Christian action. It is keeping the eye fixed upon Jesus, and having the features, traits, and lineaments of His character imprinted on our new nature, and reflected back or reproduced in our daily life and ways.

Now this will, assuredly, involve the surrender of our own will, our own plans, our own management altogether. We must follow the cloud; we must wait *ever* – wait *only* upon God. We cannot say, "We shall go here or there, do this or that, to-morrow, or next week." All our movements must be placed under the regulating power of that one commanding sentence – often alas! lightly penned and uttered by us – *"If the Lord will."*

God's will and ours

Oh! that we better understood all this! Would that we knew more perfectly the meaning of divine guidance! How often do we vainly imagine, and confidently assert, that the cloud is moving in that very direction which suits the bent of our inclination. We want to do a certain thing, or make a certain movement, and we seek to persuade ourselves that our will is the will of God. Thus, instead of being divinely guided, we are self-deceived. Our will is unbroken, and hence we cannot be guided aright, for the real secret of being rightly guided – guided of God – is to have our own will thoroughly subdued. "The meek will he guide in judgment; and the meek will he teach *his way*." And again, "I will guide thee with mine eye." But let us ponder the admonition, "Be ye not as the horse, or as the mule, which have no understanding; whose mouth must be held in with bit and bridle, lest they come near unto thee" (Psalm 32). If the countenance be turned upwards to catch the movement of the divine "eye," we shall not need the "bit and bridle." But here is precisely the point in which we so sadly fail. We do not live sufficiently near to God to discern the movement of His eye. The *will* is at work. We want to have our own way, and hence we are left to reap the bitter fruits thereof. Thus it was with Jonah. He was told to go to Nineveh but he wanted to go to Tarshish; and circumstances seemed to favour; providence seemed to point in the direction of his will. But alas! he had to find his place in the belly of the whale, yea, in "the belly of hell" itself, where "the weeds were wrapped about his head." It was there he learnt the bitterness of following his own will. He had to be taught in the depths of the ocean the true meaning of the "bit and bridle," because he would not follow the gentler guidance of the eye.

But our God is so gracious, so tender, so patient! He will teach and He will guide His poor feeble erring children. He spares no pains with us. He occupies Himself continually about us, in order that we may be kept from our own ways, which are full of thorns and briars, and walk in His ways, which are pleasantness and peace.

There is nothing in all this world more deeply blessed than to lead a life of habitual dependence upon God; to hang upon Him, moment by moment, to wait on Him and cling to Him for everything. To have all our springs in Him. It is the true secret of peace, and of holy independence of the creature. The soul that can really say, "*All* my springs are in thee" is lifted above all creature confidences, human hopes, and earthly expectations. It is not that God does not use the creature, in a thousand ways, to minister to us. We do not at all mean this. He does use the creature; but if we *lean* upon the creature instead of leaning upon Him, we shall very speedily get leanness and barrenness into our souls. There is a vast difference between God's using the creature to bless us, and our leaning on the creature to the exclusion of Him. In the one case, we are blessed and He is glorified; in the other, we are disappointed and He is dishonoured.

It is well that the soul should deeply and seriously consider this distinction. We believe it is constantly overlooked. We imagine, oft-times, that we are leaning upon, and looking to, God, when, in reality, if we would only look honestly at the roots of things, and judge ourselves in the immediate presence of God, we should find an appalling amount of the leaven of creature confidence. How often do we speak of living by faith, and of trusting only in God, when, at the same time, if we would only look down into the depths of our hearts, we should find there a large measure of dependence upon circumstances, reference to second causes, and the like.

Christian reader, let us look well to this. Let us see to it that our eye is fixed upon the living God alone, and not upon man whose breath is in his nostrils. Let us wait on Him – wait patiently – wait constantly. If we are at a loss for anything, let our direct and simple reference be to Him. Are we at a loss to know our way, to know whither we should turn, what step we should take? let us remember that He has said, "I am the way;" let us follow Him. He will make all clear, bright, and certain. There can be no darkness, no perplexity, no uncertainty, if we are following Him; for He has said, and we are bound to believe, "He that followeth me shall not walk in darkness." Hence, therefore, if we are in darkness, it is certain that we are not following Him. No darkness can ever settle down upon that blessed path along which God leads those who, with a single eye, seek to follow Jesus.

But some one, whose eye scans these lines, may say, or at least may feel disposed to say, "Well, after all, I am in perplexity as to my path. I really do not know which way to turn or what step to take." If this be the language of the reader, we would simply ask him this one question, "Art thou following Jesus? If so, thou canst not be in perplexity. Art thou following the cloud? If so, thy way is as plain as God can make it." Here lies the root of the whole matter. Perplexity or uncertainty is very often the fruit of the working of the *will*. We are bent upon doing something which God does not want us to do at all – upon going somewhere that God does not want us to go. We pray about it, and get no answer. We pray again and again, and get no answer. How is this? Why the simple fact is that God wants us to be quiet – to stand still – to remain just where we are. Wherefore, instead of racking our brain and harassing our souls about what we ought to do, let us do nothing, but simply wait on God.

This is the secret of peace and calm elevation. If an Israelite, in the desert, had taken it into his head to make some movement, independent of Jehovah; if he took it upon him to move when the cloud was at rest, or to halt while the cloud was moving, we can easily see what the result would have been. And so it will ever be with us. If we move when we ought to rest, or rest when we ought to move, we shall not have the divine presence with us. "At the commandment of the Lord they rested in the tents, and at the commandment of the Lord they journeyed." They were kept in constant waiting upon God, the most blessed position that any one can occupy;

but it must be occupied ere its blessedness can be tasted. It is a reality to be known, not a mere theory to be talked of. May it be ours to prove it all our journey through!

---

[8] The reader will note with interest and profit, the contrast between the acting of Hezekiah, in 2 Chronicles 30, and the acting of Jeroboam, in 1 Kings 12:32. The former availed himself of the provisions of divine grace; the latter followed his own device. The second month was permitted of God; the eighth month was invented by man. Divine provisions meeting man's need, and human inventions opposing God's word, are totally different things.

[9] Let it be noted here once for all, that the cutting off of any one from the congregation of Israel, answers to the suspension of a believer's communion because of unjudged sin.

[10] The Greek word for man (*anthrōpos*) signifies to turn the face upwards.

Chapter 10

HOW GOD GUIDES HIS PEOPLE

The two silver trumpets

"And the Lord spake unto Moses, saying, Make thee two trumpets of silver; of a whole piece shalt thou make them; that thou mayest use them for the calling of the assembly, and for the journeying of the camp. And when they shall blow with them, all the assembly shall assemble themselves to thee at the door of the tabernacle of the congregation. And if they blow but with one trumpet, then the princes, which are heads of the thousands of Israel, shall gather themselves unto thee. When ye blow an alarm, then the camps that lie on the east parts shall go forward. When ye blow an alarm the second time, then the camps that lie on the south side shall take their journey: they shall blow an alarm for their journeys. But when the congregation is to be gathered together, ye shall blow, but ye shall not sound an alarm. And the sons of Aaron, the priest, shall blow with the trumpets; and they shall be to you for an ordinance for ever throughout your generations. And if ye go to war in your land against the enemy that oppresseth you, then ye shall blow an alarm with the trumpets; and ye shall be remembered before the Lord your God, and ye shall be saved from your enemies. Also in the day of your gladness, and in your solemn days, and in the beginnings of your months, ye shall blow with the trumpets over your burnt offerings, and over the sacrifices of your peace offerings; that they may be to you for a memorial before your God. I am the Lord your God." Verses 1-10.

We have quoted the entire of this interesting passage for the reader, in order that he may have before him, in the veritable language of inspiration, the lovely institution of "The silver trumpets." It comes in, with striking fitness, immediately after the instruction respecting the movement of the cloud, and is bound up, in a very marked way, with the entire history of Israel, not only in the past but also in the future. The sound of the trumpet was familiar to every circumcised ear. It was the communication of the mind of God, in a form distinct and simple enough to be understood by every member of the congregation, however distant he might be from the source whence the testimony emanated. God took care that each one in that vast assembly, however far away, should hear the silvery tones of the trumpet of testimony.

Each trumpet was to be made of *one* piece, and they fulfilled a double purpose. In other words, the source of the testimony was one, however the object and practical result might vary. Every movement in the camp was to be the result of the sound of the trumpet. Was the congregation to be gathered in festive joy and worship? It was by a certain sound of the trumpet. Were the tribes to be gathered in hostile array? It was by a blast of the trumpet. In a word, the solemn assembly, and the warlike host; the instruments of music and the weapons of war – all – all was regulated by the silver trumpet. Any movement, whether festive, religious, or hostile, that was not the result of that familiar sound, could be but the fruit of a restless and unsubdued will, which Jehovah could, by no means, sanction. The pilgrim host in the wilderness was as dependent upon the sound of the trumpet as upon the movement of the cloud. The testimony of God, communicated in that particular manner, was to govern every movement throughout the many thousands of Israel.

Moreover, it pertained to the sons of Aaron, the priests, to blow with the trumpets, for the mind of God can only be known and communicated in priestly nearness and communion. It was the high and holy privilege of the priestly family to cluster round the sanctuary of God, there to catch the first movement of the cloud, and communicate the same to the most distant parts of the camp. They were responsible to give a certain sound, and every member of the militant host was equally responsible to yield a ready and an implicit obedience. It would have been at once positive rebellion for any to attempt to move without the word of command, or to refuse to move when once that word was given. All had to wait upon the divine testimony, and walk in the light thereof the very moment it was given. To move without the testimony would be *to move in the dark;* to refuse to move, when the testimony was given, would be *to remain in the dark*.

Dependence and submission

This is most simple and deeply practical. We can have no difficulty in seeing its force and application, in the case of the congregation in the wilderness. But let us remember that all this was a type; and, further, that it is written for our learning. We are solemnly bound, therefore, to look into it; we are imperatively called upon to seek to gather up and treasure up the great practical instruction contained in the singularly beautiful ordinance of the silver trumpet. Nothing could be more seasonable for the present moment. It teaches a lesson to which the Christian reader should give his most profound attention. It sets forth, in the most distinct manner possible, that God's people are to be absolutely dependent upon, and wholly subject to, divine testimony, in all their movements. A child may read this in the type before us. The congregation in the wilderness dared not assemble for any festive or religious object until they heard the sound of the trumpet; nor could the men of war buckle on their armour, till summoned forth by the signal of alarm to meet the uncircumcised foe. They worshipped and they fought, they journeyed and they halted, in simple obedience to the trumpet call. It was not, by any means, a question of their likings or dislikings, their thoughts, their opinions, or their judgment. It was simply and entirely a question of implicit obedience. Their every movement was dependent upon the testimony of God, as given by the priests from the sanctuary. The song of the worshipper and the shout of the warrior were each the simple fruit of the testimony of God.

How beautiful! How striking! How instructive! And, let us add, how deeply practical! Why do we dwell upon it? Because we firmly believe it contains a needed lesson for the day in which our lot is cast. If there is one feature more characteristic than another of the present hour, it is insubjection to divine authority – positive resistance of the truth when it demands unqualified obedience and self-surrender. It is all well enough so long as it is truth setting forth, with divine fullness and clearness, *our* pardon, *our* acceptance, *our* life, *our* righteousness, *our* eternal security in Christ. This will be listened to, and delighted in. But the very moment it becomes a question of the claims and authority of that blessed One who gave His life to save us from the flames of hell, and introduce us to the everlasting joys of heaven, all manner of difficulties are started; all sorts of reasonings and questions are raised; clouds of prejudice gather round the soul, and darken the understanding. The sharp edge of truth is blunted or turned aside, in a thousand ways. There is no *waiting* for the sound of the trumpet; and when it sounds, with a blast as clear as God Himself can give, there is no response to the summons. We move when we ought to be still; and we halt when we ought to be moving.

Reader, what must be the result of this? Either no progress at all, or progress in a wrong direction, which is worse than none. It is utterly impossible that we can advance in the divine life, unless we yield ourselves, without reserve, to the word of the Lord. Saved we may be, through the rich aboundings of divine mercy, and through the atoning virtues of a Saviour's blood; but shall we rest satisfied with being saved by Christ, and not seek, in some feeble measure, to walk with him, and live for Him? Shall we accept of salvation through the work which He has wrought, and not long after deeper intimacy of communion with Himself, and more complete subjection to His authority in all things? How would it have been with Israel in the wilderness, had they refused attention to the sound of the trumpet? We can see it at a glance. If, for example, they had presumed, at any time, to assemble for a festive or religious object, without the divinely appointed summons; what would have been the result? Or, further, had they taken it upon themselves to move forward on their journey, or go forth to war, ere the trumpet had sounded an alarm; how would it have been? Or, finally, had they refused to move, when called by the sound of the trumpet, either to the solemn assembly, the onward march, or to the battle, how would they have fared?

God occupies Himself with the details of our lives

The answer is as plain as a sunbeam. Let us ponder it. It has a lesson for us. Let us apply our hearts to it. The silver trumpet settled and ordered every movement for Israel of old. The testimony of God ought to settle and order everything for the Church now. That silver trumpet was blown by the priests of old. That testimony of God is known in priestly communion now. A Christian has no right to move or act apart from divine testimony. He must wait upon the word of his Lord. Till he gets that, he must stand still. When he has gotten it, he must *go forward.* God can and does communicate His mind to His militant people now, just as distinctly as He did to His people of old. True, it is not now by the sound of a trumpet, or the movement of a cloud; but by His word and Spirit. It is not by anything that strikes the senses that our Father guides us; but by that which acts on the heart, the conscience, and the understanding. It is not by that which is natural, but by that which is spiritual, that He communicates His mind.

But let us be well assured of this, that our God can and does give our hearts full certainty both as to what we should do, and what we should not do; as to where we should go, and where we should not go. It seems strange to be obliged to insist upon this – passing strange that any Christian should doubt, much less deny it. And yet so it is. We are often in doubt and perplexity; and some there are who are ready to deny that there can be any such thing as certainty as to the details of daily life and action. This surely is wrong. Cannot an earthly father communicate his mind to his child as to the most minute particulars of his conduct? Who will deny this? And cannot our Father communicate His mind to us, as to all our ways, from day to day? Unquestionably He can; and let not the Christian reader be robbed of the holy privilege of knowing his Father's mind in reference to every circumstance of his daily life.

Are we to suppose, for a moment, that the Church of God is worse off, in the matter of guidance, than the camp in the desert? Impossible. How is it, then, that one often finds Christians at a loss as to their movements? It must be owing to the lack of a circumcised ear to hear the sound of the silver trumpet, and of a subject will to yield a response to the sound. It may, however, be said that we are not to expect to hear a voice from heaven telling us to do this or that, or to go hither or thither; nor yet to find a literal text of scripture to guide us in the minor matters of our every day history. How, for example, is one to know whether he ought to visit a certain town, and remain there a certain time? We reply, If the ear is circumcised, you will assuredly hear the silver trumpet. Till that sounds, never stir: when it sounds, never tarry. This will make all so clear, so simple, so safe, so certain. It is the grand cure for doubt, hesitancy, and vacillation. It will save us from the necessity of running for advice to this one and that one, as to how we should act, or where we should go. And, furthermore, it will teach us that it is none of our business to attempt to control the actions or movements of others. Let each one have his ear open, and his heart subject, and then, assuredly, he will possess all the certainty that God can give him, as to his every act and movement, from day to day. Our ever gracious God can give clearness and decision as to everything. If he does not give it, no one can. If He does, no one need.

Thus much as to the beautiful institution of the silver trumpet, which we shall not pursue further now, though, as we have noticed above, it is not confined, in its application to Israel in the wilderness, but is bound up with their entire history right onward to the end. Thus we have the feast of trumpets; the trumpet of the jubilee; the blowing of trumpets over their sacrifices, upon which we do not now dwell, as our immediate object is to help the reader to seize the grand idea presented in the opening paragraph of our chapter. May the Holy Spirit impress upon our hearts the needed lesson of "the silver trumpets!"

The camp of Israel ready to move

We have now reached, in our meditations on this precious book, the moment in the which the camp is called to move forward. All is duly ordered, according to that grand regulator – "The commandment of the Lord." Each man according to his pedigree, and each tribe according to the standard thereof, is in the divinely appointed place. The Levites are at their posts, each with his own clearly defined work to do. Full provision is made for the cleansing of the camp from every species of defilement; and not only so, but the lofty standard of personal holiness is unfurled, and the fruits of active benevolence are presented. Then we have the golden candlestick and its seven lamps, giving forth their pure and precious light. We have the pillar of fire and of cloud; and, finally, the double testimony of the silver trumpet. In short, nothing is lacking to the pilgrim host. A vigilant eye, a powerful hand, and a loving heart have provided for every possible contingency, so that the whole congregation in the wilderness, and each member in particular, might be "thoroughly furnished."

This is only what we might expect. If God undertakes to provide for any one, or for any people, the provision, must of necessity, be perfect. It is wholly impossible that God could omit any one thing needful. He knows all things, and can do all things. Nothing can escape His vigilant eye; nothing is beyond His omnipotent hand. Hence, therefore, all those who can truly say, "The Lord is my Shepherd," may add, without hesitancy or reserve, "I shall not want." The soul that is, in truth and reality, leaning on the arm of the living God can never – shall never – want any *good* thing. The poor foolish heart may imagine a thousand wants; but God knows what we really want, and He will provide for ALL.

The ark in front of the people

Thus, then, the camp is ready to move; but, strange to say, there is a departure from the order laid down in the opening of the book. The ark of the covenant, instead of reposing in the bosom of the camp, goes in the very front. In other words, Jehovah, instead of remaining in the centre of the congregation to be waited upon there, actually condescends, in His marvellous, inimitable grace, to do the work of an *avant-courier*, for His people.

But let us see what it is that leads to this touching display of grace. "And Moses said unto Hobab, the son of Raguel the Midianite, Moses' father-in-law, We are journeying unto the place of which the Lord said, I will give it you; come thou with us and we will do thee good; for the Lord hath spoken good concerning Israel. And he said unto him, I will not go; but I will depart to mine own land, and to my kindred. And he said, Leave us not, I pray thee, forasmuch as thou knowest how we are to encamp in the wilderness, and thou mayest be to us instead of eyes."

Now, if we did not know something of our own hearts, and the tendency thereof to lean on the creature rather than upon the living God, we might well marvel at the above. We might feel disposed to enquire, What could Moses possibly want with Hobab's eyes? Was not Jehovah sufficient? Did not He know the wilderness? Would He suffer them to go astray? What of the cloud and the silver trumpet? Were not they better than Hobab's eyes? Why, then, did Moses seek for human aid? Alas! alas! We can but too well understand the reason. We all know, to our sorrow and loss, the tendency of the heart to lean upon something that our eyes can see. We do not like to occupy the ground of absolute dependence upon God for every step of the journey. We find it hard to lean upon an unseen arm. A Hobab that we can see inspires us with more confidence than the living God whom we cannot see. We move on with comfort and satisfaction when we possess the countenance and help of some poor failing mortal; but we hesitate, falter, and quail when called to move on in naked faith in God.

These statements may seem strong; but the question is, are they true? Is there a Christian who reads these lines that will not freely own that it is even so? We are all prone to lean upon an arm of flesh, and that, too, in the face of a thousand and one examples of the folly of so doing. We have proved, times without number, the vanity of all creature confidences, and yet we *will* confide in the creature. On the other hand, we have, again and again, proved the reality of leaning upon the word and upon the arm of the living God. We have found that He has never failed us, never disappointed us, nay, that He has always done exceeding abundantly above all that we ask or think; and yet we are ever ready to distrust Him, ever ready to lean upon any broken reed, and betake ourselves to any broken cistern.

Thus it is with us; but, blessed be God, His grace abounds toward us, as it did toward Israel, on the occasion to which we are now referring. If Moses will look to Hobab for guidance, Jehovah will teach His Servant that He Himself is all-sufficient as a guide. "And they departed from the mount of the Lord three days' journey; and the ark of the covenant of the Lord went before them in the three days' journey, *to search out a resting place for them.*"

What rich, what precious grace! In place of their finding a resting-place for Him, He would find a resting place for them. What a thought! The mighty God, the Creator of the ends of the earth, going through the wilderness to look out for a suitable camping ground for a people who were ready, at every turn in their path, to murmur and rebel against Him!

Such is our God, ever "patient, gracious, powerful, holy"

– ever rising, in the magnificence of His grace above all our unbelief and failure, and proving Himself superior, in His love, to all the barriers which our unfaithfulness would erect. He, most assuredly, proved to Moses and to Israel, that He was far better as a guide than ten thousand Hobabs. We are not told in this place, whether Hobab went or not. He certainly refused the first appeal, and perhaps the second likewise. But we are told that the Lord went with them. "The cloud of the Lord was upon them by day, when they went out of the camp." Blessed shelter in the wilderness! Blessed, unfailing resource, in everything! He went before His people to search them out a resting place, and when He had found a spot suited to their need, He halted with them, and spread His sheltering wing over them, to protect them from every foe. "He found him in a desert land, and in the waste howling wilderness; he led him about, he instructed him, he kept him as the apple of his eye. As an eagle stirreth up her nest, fluttereth over her young, spreadeth abroad her wings, taketh them, beareth them on her wings; so the Lord alone did lead him, and there was no strange god with him" (Deut. 32:10-12). "He spread a cloud for a covering, and fire to give light in the night." Psalm 105:39.

Thus, then, all was provided for, according to the wisdom, power, and goodness of God. Nothing was, or could be, lacking, inasmuch as God Himself was there. "And it came to pass, when the ark set forward, that Moses said, Rise up, Lord, and let thine enemies be scattered, and let them that hate thee flee before thee. And when it rested, he said, Return, O Lord, unto the many thousands of Israel."

Chapter 11

THE MURMURINGS, THE MANNA AND THE QUAILS

Man and his failures

Hitherto we have been occupied, in our study of this book, with God's mode of ordering and providing for His people in the wilderness. We have travelled over the first ten chapters and seen in them the illustration of the wisdom, goodness, and forethought of Jehovah, the God of Israel.

But, now, we reach a point at which dark clouds gather round us. Up to this, God and His actings have been before us; but, now, we are called to contemplate man and his miserable ways. This is ever sad and humiliating. Man is the same everywhere. In Eden, in the restored earth, in the wilderness, in the land of Canaan, in the Church, in the Millennium, man is proved to be a total failure. The very moment he moves, he breaks down. Thus, in the first two chapters of Genesis God is seen acting as Creator; everything is done and ordered in divine perfection, and man is placed in the scene to enjoy the fruit of divine wisdom, goodness, and power. But in chapter 3 all is changed. The moment man acts, it is to disobey and bring in ruin and desolation. So after the deluge, when the earth had passed through that deep and dreadful baptism, and when man again takes his place therein, he exposes himself, and proves that, so far from being able to subdue and govern the earth, he cannot even govern himself (Gen. 9). Hardly had Israel been brought out of Egypt, when they made the golden calf. No sooner had the priesthood been set up, than the sons of Aaron offered strange fire. Directly Saul was made king, he proved wilful and disobedient.

So also when we turn to the pages of the New Testament, we find the same thing. No sooner is the Church set up and adorned with Pentecostal gifts, than we hear the sad accents of murmuring and discontent. In short, man's history, from first to last, here, there, and everywhere, is marked with failure. There is not so much as a single exception from Eden down to the close of the millennial day.

It is well to consider this solemn and weighty fact, and to give it a deep place in the heart. It is eminently calculated to correct all false notions as to man's real character and condition. It is well to bear in mind that the awful sentence which struck terror into the heart of the voluptuous king of Babylon has, in point of fact, been passed upon the entire human race, and to each individual son and daughter of fallen Adam, namely, *"Thou art weighed in the balance and found wanting."* Has the reader fully accepted this sentence against himself? This is a serious inquiry. We feel imperatively called to press it home. Say, reader, art thou one of Wisdom's children? Dost thou justify God and condemn thyself? Hast thou taken thy place as a self-destroyed, guilty, hell-deserving sinner? If so, Christ is for thee. He died to put away sin, and to bear your many sins. Only trust him and all He is and has is thine. He is thy wisdom, thy righteousness, thy sanctification, and thy redemption. All who simply and heartily believe in Jesus have passed clean off the old ground of guilt and condemnation, and are seen by God on the new ground of eternal life and divine righteousness. They are accepted in the risen and victorious Christ. "As he is, so are we in this world." 1 John 4:17.

We would earnestly entreat the reader not to rest until this most momentous question is clearly and thoroughly settled in the light of God's own word and presence. We pray that God the Holy Ghost may deeply exercise the heart and conscience of the unconverted and undecided reader, and lead such to the Saviour's feet.

Will the bread from heaven be enough for us?

We shall now proceed with our chapter.

"And when the people complained, it displeased the Lord; and the Lord heard it; and his anger was kindled; and the fire of the Lord burnt among them, and consumed them that were in the uttermost parts of the camp. And the people cried unto Moses; and when Moses prayed unto the Lord, the fire was quenched. And he called the name of the place Taberah: because the fire of the Lord burnt among them. And the mixed multitude that was among them fell a lusting: and the children of Israel also wept again, and said, Who shall give us flesh to eat? We remember the fish which we did eat in Egypt freely; the cucumbers, and the melons, and the leeks, and the onions, and the garlic. But now our soul is dried away; there is nothing at all, beside this manna, before our eyes."

Here the poor human heart lets itself thoroughly out. Its tastes and its tendencies are made manifest. The people sigh after the land of Egypt, and cast back wistful looks after its fruits and its fleshpots. They do not say anything about the lash of the taskmaster, and the toil of the brick-kilns. There is total silence as to these things. Nothing is remembered now, save those resources by which Egypt had ministered to the lusts of nature.

How often is this the case with us! When once the heart loses its freshness in the divine life – when heavenly things begin to lose their savour – when first love declines – when Christ ceases to be a satisfying and altogether precious portion for the soul – when the word of God and prayer lose their charm and become heavy, dull, and mechanical; then the eye wanders back toward the world, the heart follows the eye, and the feet follow the heart. We forget, at such moments, what the world was to us when we were in it and of it. We forget what toil and slavery, what misery and degradation, we found in the service of sin and of Satan, and think only of the gratification and ease, the freedom from those painful exercises, conflicts, and anxieties which attend upon the wilderness path of God's people.

All this is most sad, and should lead the soul into the most profound self-judgment. It is terrible when those who have set out to follow the Lord begin to grow weary of the way and of God's provision. How dreadful must those words have sounded in the ear of Jehovah, "But now our soul is dried away: there is nothing at all, beside this manna, before our eyes." Ah! Israel, what more didst thou need? Was not that heavenly food enough for thee? Couldst thou not live upon that which the hand of thy God had provided for thee?

Do we count ourselves free to ask such questions? Do we always find *our* heavenly manna sufficient for us? What means the enquiry inquiry raised by professing Christians as to the right or wrong of such and such worldly pursuits and pleasures? Have we not even heard from the lips of persons making the very highest profession such words as these, "How are we to fill up the day? We cannot be always thinking about Christ and heavenly things. We must have some little recreation." Is not this somewhat akin to Israel's language in Numbers 11? Yes truly; and as is the language, so is the acting. We prove, alas! that Christ is not enough for the heart, by the palpable fact of our betaking ourselves to other things. How often, for example, does the Bible lie neglected for hours, while the light and worthless literature of the world is greedily devoured. What mean the well-thumbed newspaper and the almost dust-covered Bible? Do not these things tell a tale? Is not this despising the manna, and sighing after, nay, devouring, the leeks and onions?

We specially call the attention of young Christians to that which is now before us. We are deeply impressed with a sense of their danger of falling into the very sin of Israel as recorded in our chapter. No doubt we are all in danger; but the young amongst us are peculiarly so. Those of us who are advanced in life are not so likely to be drawn away by the frivolous pursuits of the world – by its concerts, its flower shows, its pleasure parties, its vain songs and light literature. But the young *will* have a dash of the world. They long to taste it for themselves. They do not find Christ an all-sufficient portion for the heart. They want recreation.

Alas! alas! what a thought! How sad to hear a Christian say, "I want some recreation. How can I fill up the day? I cannot be always thinking of Jesus." We should like to ask all who speak thus, How will you fill up eternity? Shall not Christ be sufficient to fill up its countless ages? Shall you want recreation there? Will you sigh for light literature, vain songs, and frivolous pursuits there?

It will, perhaps, be said, "We shall be different then." In what respect? We have the divine nature – we have the Holy Ghost – we have Christ for our portion – we belong to heaven – we are brought to God. "But we have an evil nature in us." Well, are we to cater for that? Is it for that we crave recreation? Must we try to help our wretched flesh – our corrupt nature – to fill up the day? Nay, we are called to deny it, to mortify it, to reckon it dead. This is Christian recreation. This is the mode in which the saint is called to fill up his day. How is it possible for us to grow in the divine life if we are only making provision for the flesh? Egypt's food cannot nourish the new nature; and the great question for us is this, which do we really mean to nourish and cherish – the new or the old? It must be obvious that the divine nature cannot possibly feed upon newspapers, vain songs, and light literature; and hence, if we give ourselves, in any measure, to these latter, our souls must wither and droop.

May we have grace to think of these things – to think seriously. May we so walk in the Spirit that Christ may ever be a satisfying portion for our hearts. Had Israel, in the wilderness, walked with God, they never could have said, "Our soul is dried away: there is nothing at all beside this manna before our eyes." That manna would have been quite enough for them. And so with us. If we really walk with God, in this wilderness world, our souls shall be satisfied with the portion which He gives, and that portion is a heavenly Christ. Can He ever fail to satisfy? Does He not satisfy the heart of God? Does He not fill all heaven with His glory? Is He not the theme of angels' song, and the object of their adoring homage and wondering worship? Is He not the one grand subject of everlasting counsels and purposes? Doth not the history of His ways overlap eternity?

What answer have we to give to all these queries? What but a hearty, unreserved, unhesitating, YES? Well, then, is not this blessed One, in the deep mystery of His Person, in the moral glory of His ways, in the brightness and blessedness of His character, is not He enough for our hearts! Do we want anything beside? Must we get the newspaper or some light magazine to fill up the vacuum in our souls? Must we turn from Christ to a flower show or a concert?

Alas! that we should have to write thus. It is most sad but it is most needful; and we here put this question most pointedly to the reader, Dost thou really find Christ insufficient to satisfy thy heart? Hast thou cravings which He does not fully meet? If so, thou art in a very alarming condition of soul, and it behoves thee to look at once, and to look closely, into this solemn matter. Get down on thy face before God, in honest self-judgment. Pour out thy heart to Him. Tell Him all. Own to Him how thou hast fallen and wandered – as surely thou must have done when God's Christ is not enough for thee. Have it all out in secret with thy God, and take no rest until thou art fully and blessedly restored to communion with Himself – to heart fellowship with Him about the Son of His love.

The bad elements in the midst of God's people

But we must return to our chapter, and in so doing we call the reader's attention to an expression full of weighty admonition for us: "And the *mixed multitude* that was among them fell a lusting: and the children of Israel also wept again." There is nothing more damaging to the cause of Christ or to the souls of His people than association with men of *mixed* principles. It is very much more dangerous than having to do with open and avowed enemies. Satan knows this well, and hence his constant effort to lead the Lord's people to link themselves with those who are only half and half; or, on the other hand, to introduce spurious materials – false professors, into the midst of those who are seeking, in any measure, to pursue a path of separation from the world. We have repeated allusions to this special character of evil, in the New Testament. We have it both prophetically in the Gospels, and historically in the Acts and in the Epistles. Thus we have the tares and the leaven in Matthew 13. Then in the Acts we find persons attaching themselves to the assembly who were like the "mixed multitude" of Numbers 11. And, finally, we have apostolic reference to spurious materials introduced by the enemy for the purpose of corrupting the testimony and subverting the souls of God's people. Thus the apostle Paul speaks of "false brethren unawares brought in" (Gal. 2:4). Jude also speaks of "certain men crept in unawares." Verse 4.

From all this we learn the urgent need of vigilance on the part of God's people; and not only of vigilance, but also of absolute dependence upon the Lord, who alone can preserve them from the entrance in of false materials, and keep them free from all contact with men of mixed principles and doubtful character. "The mixed multitude" is sure to "fall a lusting," and the people of God are in imminent danger of being drawn away from their proper simplicity, and of growing weary of the heavenly manna – their proper food. What is needed is, plain decision for Christ; thorough devotedness to Him and to His cause. Where a company of believers are enabled to go on in whole-heartedness for Christ and in marked separation from this present world, there is not so much danger of persons of equivocal character seeking a place among them; though doubtless Satan will always seek to mar the testimony by the introduction of hypocrites. Such persons do obtain an entrance, and then by their evil ways bring reproach on the Lord's name. Satan knew full well what he was doing, when he led the mixed multitude to attach themselves to the congregation of Israel. It was not all at once that the effect of this admixture was made manifest. The people had come forth with a high hand; they had passed through the Red

Sea, and raised the song of victory on its banks. All looked bright and promising; but "the mixed multitude" were there, notwithstanding, and the effect of their presence was very speedily made apparent.

Thus it is ever, in the history of God's people. We may notice, in those great spiritual movements which have taken place from age to age, certain elements of decay which, at the first, were hidden from view by the flowing tide of grace and *energy;* but when that tide began to ebb, then those elements made their appearance.

This is very serious, and calls for much holy watchfulness. It applies to individuals just as forcibly as to the people of God collectively. In our early moments, our young days, when zeal and freshness characterised us, the spring tide of grace rose so blessedly that many things were allowed to escape unjudged, which were, in reality, seeds flung into the ground by the enemy's hand, and which, in due season, are sure to germinate and fructify. Hence it follows that both assemblies of Christians and individual Christians should ever be on the watch tower – ever keeping jealous guard lest the enemy gain an advantage in this matter. Where the heart is true to Christ, all is sure to come right in the end. Our God is so gracious, He takes care of us and preserves us from a thousand snares. May we learn to trust him and to praise Him!

Moses discouraged

But we have further lessons to draw from the weighty section which lies open before us. Not only have we to contemplate failure on the part of the congregation of Israel; but even Moses himself is seen faltering and almost sinking beneath the weight of his responsibility. "And Moses said unto the Lord, Wherefore hast thou afflicted thy servant? and wherefore have I not found favour in thy sight, that thou layest the burden of all this people upon me? Have I conceived all this people? have I begotten them, that thou shouldest say unto me, carry them in thy bosom, as a nursing father beareth the sucking child, unto the land which thou swarest unto their fathers? Whence should I have flesh to give unto all this people? for they weep unto me, saying, Give as flesh, that we may eat. I am not able to bear all this people alone, because it is too heavy for me. And if thou deal thus with me, kill me, I pray thee, out of hand, if I have found favour in thy sight; and let me not see my wretchedness." Verses 11-15.

This is truly wonderful language. It is not that we would think for a moment of dwelling upon the failures and infirmities of so dear and so devoted a servant as Moses. Far be the thought. It would ill become us to comment upon the actings or the sayings of one of whom the Holy Ghost has declared that "he was faithful in all his house" (Heb. 3:2). Moses, like all the Old Testament saints, has taken his place amongst the "spirits of just men made perfect," and every inspired allusion to him throughout the pages of the New Testament tends only to put honour upon him, and to set him forth as a most precious vessel.

But still we are bound to ponder the inspired history now before us – history penned by Moses himself. True it is – blessedly true – that the defects and failures of God's people, in Old Testament times, are not commented upon in the New Testament; yet are they recorded, with faithful accuracy, in the Old; and wherefore? Is it not for our learning? Unquestionably. "Whatsoever things were written aforetime were written for our learning, that we through patience and comfort of the scriptures might have hope." Romans 15:4.

What then are we to learn from the remarkable outburst of feeling recorded in Numbers 11: 11-15? We learn this at least, that it is the wilderness that really brings out what is in the very best of us. It is there we prove what is in our hearts. And, inasmuch as the Book of Numbers is, emphatically, the book of the wilderness, it is just there we might expect to find all sorts of failure and infirmity fully unfolded. The Spirit of God faithfully chronicles everything. He gives us men as they are; and even though it be a Moses that "speaks unadvisedly with his lips," that very unadvised speaking is recorded for our admonition and instruction. Moses "was a man subject to like passions as we are;" and it is very evident that, in the portion of his history now before us, his heart sinks under the tremendous weight of his responsibilities.

Forgetting the divine resources

It will, perhaps, be said, "No wonder his heart should sink." No wonder, surely, for his burden was far too heavy for human shoulders. But the question is, was it too heavy for divine shoulders? Was it really the case that Moses was called to bear the burden alone? Was not the living God with him? And was not He sufficient? What did it matter whether God were pleased to act by one man or by ten thousand? All the power, all the wisdom, all the grace, was in Him. He is the fountain of all blessedness, and, in the judgment of faith, it makes not one whit of difference as to the channel, or whether there is one channel, or a thousand and one.

This is a fine moral principle for all the servants of Christ. It is most needful for all such to remember that whenever the Lord places a man in a position of responsibility, he will both fit him for it and maintain him in it. It is, of course, another thing altogether if a man *will* rush unsent into any field of work, or any post of difficulty or danger. In such a case, we may assuredly look for a thorough break down, sooner or later. But when God calls a man to a certain position, He will endow him with the needed grace to occupy it. He never sends any one a warfare at his own charges; and therefore all we have to do is to draw upon Him for all we need. This holds good in every case. We can never fail if we only cling to the living God. We can never run dry, if we are drawing from the fountain. Our tiny springs will soon dry up; but our Lord Jesus Christ declares that, "He that believeth in me, as the scripture hath said, out of his belly shall flow rivers of living water."

This is a grand lesson for the wilderness. We cannot get on without it. Had Moses fully understood it, he never would have given utterance to such words as these: "Whence should *I* have flesh to give unto all this people" He would have fixed his eye *only* upon God. He would have known that he was but an instrument in the hands of God, whose resources were illimitable. Assuredly, Moses could not supply that vast assembly with food even for a single day; but Jehovah could supply the need of every living thing, and supply it for ever.

Do we really believe this? Does it not sometimes appear as though we doubted it? Do we not sometimes feel as though *we* were to supply instead of God? And then is it any marvel if we quail, and falter, and sink? Well indeed might Moses say, "I am not able to bear all this people alone, because it is too heavy for me." There was only one heart that could bear with such a company, namely, the heart of that blessed One, who, when they were toiling amid the brick-kilns of Egypt, had come down to deliver them, and who, having redeemed them out of the hand of the enemy, had taken up His abode in their midst. He was able to bear them, and He alone. His loving heart and mighty hand were alone adequate to the task; and if Moses had been in the full power of this great truth, He would not and could not have said, "If thou deal thus with me, kill me, I pray thee, out of hand, if I have found favour in thy sight and let we not see my wretchedness."

This surely was a dark moment in the history of this illustrious servant of God. It reminds us somewhat of the prophet Elijah, when he flung himself at the base of the juniper tree and entreated the Lord to take away his life. How wonderful to see those two men together on the mount of transfiguration! It proves, in a very marked way, that God's thoughts are not as ours, nor His ways as ours. He had something better in store for Moses and Elias than anything that they contemplated. Blessed be His name, He rebukes our fears by the riches of His grace, and when our poor hearts would anticipate death and wretchedness, He gives life, victory, and glory.

The seventy elders of Israel

However, we cannot but see, that, in shrinking from a position of weighty responsibility, Moses was really giving up a place of high dignity and holy privilege. This seems most evident from the following passage. "And the Lord said unto Moses, Gather unto me seventy men of the elders of Israel, whom thou knowest to be the elders of the people, and officers over them; and bring them unto the tabernacle of the congregation, *that they may stand there with thee*. And I will come down and talk with thee there; and *I will take of the spirit which is upon thee and will put it upon them;* and they shall bear the burden of the people with thee, that thou bear it not thyself alone." Verses 16, 17.

Was there any additional power gained by the introduction of seventy men? Not spiritual power certainly, inasmuch as it was only the spirit that was upon Moses, after all. True, there were seventy men instead of one; but the multiplication of men was no increase of spiritual power. It saved Moses trouble, but it lost him dignity. He was henceforth to be a joint instrument instead of the sole one. It may be said that Moses – blessed servant as he was! – did not want dignity for himself, but rather sought a shady, retired, humble path. No doubt; but this does not touch the question before us. Moses, as we shall see presently, was the meekest man upon the face of the earth; nor do we mean even to hint that any mere man would have done better under the circumstances. But then we must seek to bear away with us the great practical lesson which our chapter so impressively teaches. The very best of men fail; and it seems exceedingly plain that Moses, in the eleventh chapter of Numbers, was not in the calm elevation of faith. He appears, for the moment, to have lost that even balance of soul which is the sure result of finding one's centre in the living God. We gather this, not merely from the fact of his tottering beneath the weight of his responsibility; but let us ponder the following paragraph.

God's response to unbelief

"And say thou unto the people, Sanctify yourselves against to-morrow, and ye shall eat flesh: for ye have wept in the ears of the Lord, saying, Who shall give us flesh to eat? for it was well with us in Egypt: therefore the Lord will give you flesh, and ye shall eat. Ye shall not eat one day, nor two days, nor five days, neither ten days, nor twenty days; but even a whole month, until it come out at your nostrils, and it be loathsome unto you: because that ye have despised the Lord which is among you, and have wept before him, Saying, Why came we forth out of Egypt? And Moses said, The people, among whom I am, are six hundred thousand footmen; and thou hast said, I will give them flesh, that they may eat a whole month. Shall the flocks and the herds be slain for them to suffice them? or shall all the fish of the sea be gathered together for them, to suffice them? And the Lord said unto Moses, Is the Lord's hand waxed short? thou shalt see now whether my word will come to pass unto thee or not." Verses 18-23.

In all this we see the working of that spirit of unbelief which ever tends to limit the Holy One of Israel. Could not the Almighty God, the Possessor of heaven and earth, the Creator of the ends of the earth – could not He provide flesh for six hundred thousand footmen? Alas! it is just here we all so sadly fail. We do not enter, as we ought, into the reality of having to do with the living God. Faith brings God into the scene, and therefore it knows absolutely nothing of difficulties; yea, it laughs at impossibilities. In the judgment of faith, God is the grand answer to every question – the grand solution of every difficulty. It refers all to Him; and hence, it matters not in the least to faith, whether it be six hundred thousand or six hundred millions; it knows that God is all-sufficient. It finds all its resources in Him. Unbelief says, "*How* can such and such things be?" It is full of "Hows;" but faith has one great answer to ten thousand "hows," and that answer is – GOD.

The Spirit on the seventy elders

"And Moses went out, and told the people the words of the Lord, and gathered the seventy men of the elders of the people, and set them round about the tabernacle. And the Lord came down in a cloud, and spake unto him, *and took of the spirit that was upon him, and gave it unto the seventy elders*; and it came to pass, that when the spirit rested upon them, they prophesied, and did not cease."

The true secret of all ministry is spiritual power. It is not man's genius, or man's intellect, or man's energy; but simply the power of the Spirit of God. This was true in the days of Moses, and it is true now. "Not by might, nor by power, but by my Spirit, saith the Lord of hosts" (Zech. 4:6). It is well for all ministers to bear this ever in mind. It will sustain the heart and give constant freshness to their ministry. A ministry which flows from abiding dependence upon the Holy Ghost can never become barren. If a man is drawing upon his own resources, he will soon run dry. It matters not what his powers may be, or how extensive his reading, or how vast his stores of information; if the Holy Ghost be not the spring and power of his ministry, it must, sooner or later, lose its freshness and its effectiveness.

How important therefore that all who minister, whether in the gospel or in the Church of God, should lean continually and exclusively on the power of the Holy Ghost! He knows what souls need, and He can supply it. But He must be trusted and used. It will not do to lean partly on self and partly on the Spirit of God. If there be anything of self-confidence, it will soon be made apparent. We must really get at the bottom of all that belongs to self, if we are to be the vessels of the Holy Ghost.

It is not – need we say it? – that there should not be holy diligence and earnestness in the study of God's word, and in the study too, of exercises, the trials, the conflicts, and the varied difficulties of souls. Quite the reverse. We feel persuaded that the more absolutely we lean, in self-emptiness, upon the mighty power of the Holy Ghost, the more diligently and earnestly we shall study both *the Book* and *the soul.* It would be a fatal mistake for a man to use professed dependence upon the Spirit as a plea for neglecting prayerful study and meditation. "Meditate upon these things; give thyself *wholly* to them; that thy profiting may appear to all." 1 Timothy 4:15.

But, after all, let it ever be remembered that the Holy Ghost is the ever living, never failing spring of ministry. It is He alone that can bring forth in divine freshness and fullness, the treasures of God's word, and apply them, in heavenly power, to the soul's present need. It is not a question of bringing forth new truth, but simply of unfolding the word itself, and bringing it to bear upon the moral and spiritual condition of the people of God. This is true ministry. A man may speak a hundred times on the same portion of scripture, to the same people, and, on each occasion, he may minister Christ, in spiritual freshness, to their souls. And, on the other hand, a man may rack his brain to find out new subjects, and new modes of handling old themes, and, all the while, there may not be one atom of Christ or of spiritual power in his ministry.

All this holds good in reference to the evangelist, as well as to the teacher or pastor. A man may be called to preach the gospel in the same place for years, and he may, at times, feel burdened by the thought of having to address the same audience, on the same theme, week after week, month after month, year after year. He may feel at a loss for something new, something fresh, some variety. He may wish to get away into some new sphere, where the subjects which are familiar to him will be new to the people. It will greatly help such to remember that the one grand theme of the evangelist is Christ. The power to handle that theme is the Holy Ghost; and the one to whom that theme is to be unfolded is the poor lost sinner. Now, Christ is ever new; the power of the Spirit is ever fresh; the soul's condition and destiny ever intensely interesting. Furthermore, it is well for the evangelist to bear in mind, on every fresh occasion of rising to preach, that those to whom he preaches are really ignorant of the gospel, and hence he should preach as though it were the very first time his audience had ever heard the message, and the first time he had ever delivered it. For, be it remembered, the preaching of the gospel, in the divine acceptation of the phrase, is not a barren statement of mere evangelical doctrine – a certain form of words enunciated over and over again in wearisome routine. Far from it. To preach the gospel is really to unfold the heart of God, the person and work of Christ; and all this by the present energy of the Holy Ghost, from the exhaustless treasury of holy scripture.

May all preachers keep these things before the mind, and then it will not matter whether it be *one* preacher or *seventy,* one man in the same place for fifty years, or the same man in fifty different places in one year. The question is not at all as to new men or new places, but simply and entirely as to the power of the Holy Ghost unfolding Christ to the soul. Thus in the case of Moses, as recorded in our chapter, there was no increase of power. It was the spirit that was upon him given to the seventy elders. God can act by one man just as well as by seventy; and if He does not act, seventy are no more than one. It is of the very utmost importance to keep God ever before the soul. This is the true secret of power and freshness whether for the evangelist, the teacher, or any one else. When a man can say, "All my springs are in God," he need not be troubled as to a sphere of work, or competency to fill it. But when this is not so, we can well understand why a man should sigh for a division of labour and responsibility. We may remember, at the opening of the book of Exodus, how unwilling Moses was to go into Egypt, in simple dependence upon God, and how readily he went in company with Aaron. Thus it is ever. We like something tangible, something that the eye can see, and the hand can handle. We find it hard to endure as seeing Him who is invisible. And yet the very props we lean upon often prove to be broken reeds that pierce the hand. Aaron proved to be a fruitful source of sorrow to Moses;

and those whom we, in our folly, imagine to be indispensable coadjutors, frequently turn out the very reverse. O that we may all learn to lean, with an undivided heart, and unshaken confidence, upon the living God.

Eldad and Medad prophesy in the camp

But we must draw this section to a close, and ere doing so, we shall just glance for a moment at the truly excellent spirit in which Moses meets the new circumstances in which he had placed himself. It is one thing to shrink from the weight of responsibility and care, and it is quite another thing to carry oneself with grace and genuine humility toward those who are called to share that weight with us. The two things are totally different, and we may often see the differences strikingly illustrated. In the scene now before us, Moses manifests that exquisite meekness which so specially characterised him. "But there remained two of the (seventy) men in the camp, the name of the one was Eldad, and the name of the other Medad: and the spirit rested upon them; and they were of them that were written, but went not out unto the tabernacle: and they prophesied in the camp. And there ran a young man, and told Moses, and said, Eldad and Medad do prophesy in the camp. And Joshua the son of Nun, the servant of Moses, one of his young men, answered and said, My lord Moses, forbid them. and Moses said unto him, Enviest thou for my sake? Would God that all the Lord's people were prophets, and that the Lord would put his Spirit upon them!"

This is perfectly beautiful. Moses was far removed from that wretched spirit of envy which would let no one speak but himself. He was prepared, by grace, to rejoice in any and every manifestation of true spiritual power, no matter where or through whom. He knew full well that there could be no right prophesying save by the power of the Spirit of God; and wherever that power was exhibited, who was he that he should seek to quench or hinder?

Would there were more of this excellent spirit! May we

each cultivate it! May we have grace to rejoice unfeignedly in the testimony and service of all the Lord's people, even though we may not see eye to eye with them, and though our mode and our measure may vary. Nothing can be more contemptible than that petty spirit of envy and jealousy which will not permit a man to take an interest in any work but his own. We may rest assured that where the spirit of Christ is in action in the heart, there will be the ability to go out and embrace the wide field of our blessed Master's work and all His beloved workmen: there will be the hearty rejoicing in having the work done, no matter who is the doer of it. A man whose heart is full of Christ will be able to say – and to say it without affectation, "Provided the work is done – provided Christ is glorified – provided souls are saved – provided the Lord's flock is cared for and fed, it matters nothing to me who does the work."

This is the right spirit to cultivate, and it stands out in bright contrast with the narrowness and self-occupation which can only rejoice in work in which "*I, myself*" have a prominent place. May the Lord deliver us from all this, and enable us to cherish that temper of soul expressed by Moses when he said, "Enviest thou for my sake? Would God that all the Lord's people were prophets, and that the Lord would put his spirit upon them?"

The quails

The closing paragraph of our chapter shews us the people in the miserable and fatal enjoyment of that for which their hearts had lusted. "He gave them their request, but sent leanness into their soul." They got what they longed for and found it death. They *would* have flesh; and with the flesh came the judgment of God. This is most solemn. May we heed the warning! The poor heart is full of vain desires and hateful lusts. The heavenly manna fails to satisfy. There must be something else. God allows us to have it. But what then? Leanness – barrenness – judgment! O Lord, keep our hearts fixed on thyself alone and at all times! Be thou the ever satisfying portion of our souls, while we tread this desert, and till we see thy face in glory!

Chapter 12

MIRIAM STRUCK WITH LEPROSY

The brief section of our book to which we now approach may be viewed in two distinct aspects; in the first place, it is typical or dispensational; and, in the second, moral or practical.

The wife of Moses, a type of the Church

In the union of Moses with "the Ethiopian woman," we have a type of that great and marvellous mystery, the union of the Church with Christ her Head. This subject has come before us in our study of the Book of Exodus; but we see it here, in a peculiar light, as that which evokes the enmity of Aaron and Miriam. The sovereign actings of grace draw forth the opposition of those who stand upon the ground of natural relationship and fleshly privilege. We know, from the teaching of the New Testament, that the extension of grace to the Gentiles was that which ever elicited the fiercest and most terrible hatred of the Jews. They would not have it; they would not believe in it; nay, they would not even hear of it. There is a very remarkable allusion to this in the eleventh chapter of Romans, where the apostle, referring to the Gentiles, says, "For as ye in times past have not believed God, yet have now obtained mercy through their unbelief: even so have these [Jews] also now not believed in your mercy [or in mercy to you] that they also may obtain mercy." Verses 30, 31; see Greek.

This is precisely what we have typically presented in the history of Moses. He, first of all, presented himself to Israel, his brethren according to the flesh; but they, in unbelief, rejected him. They thrust him from them, and would not have him. This became, in the sovereignty of God, the occasion of mercy to the stranger, for it was during the period of Moses' rejection by Israel that he formed the mystic and typical union with a Gentile bride. Against this union Miriam and Aaron speak, in the chapter before us; and their opposition brings down the judgment of God. Miriam becomes leprous – a poor defiled thing – a proper subject of mercy, which flows out to her through the intercession of the very one against whom she had spoken.

The type is complete and most striking. The Jews have not believed in the glorious truth of mercy to the Gentiles, and therefore wrath has come upon them to the uttermost. But they will be brought in, by and by, on the ground of simple mercy, just as the Gentiles have come in. This is very humiliating to those who sought to stand on the ground of promise and national privilege; but thus it is in the dispensational wisdom of God, the very thought of which draws forth from the inspired apostle that magnificent doxology, "O the depth of the riches both of the wisdom and knowledge of God! how unsearchable are his judgments, and his ways past finding out! For who hath known the mind of the Lord? or who hath been his counsellor? or who hath first given to him, and it shall be recompensed unto him again? For of him, and through him, and to him, are all things: to whom be glory for ever. Amen."

Thus much as to the typical bearing of our chapter. Let as now look at it in its moral and practical bearing.

Calumny against a servant of God

"And Miriam and Aaron spake against Moses because of the Ethiopian woman whom he had married: for he had married an Ethiopian woman. And they said, Hath the Lord indeed spoken only by Moses? hath he not spoken also by us? And the Lord heard it. (Now the man Moses was very meek, above all the men which were upon the face of the earth.)

And the Lord spake suddenly unto Moses, and unto Aaron, and unto Miriam, Come out ye three unto the tabernacle of the congregation. And they three came out. And the Lord came down in the pillar of the cloud, and stood in the door of the tabernacle, and called Aaron and Miriam: and they both came forth. And he said, Hear now my words: If there be a prophet among you, I the Lord will make myself known unto him in a vision, and will speak unto him in a dream. My servant Moses is not so, who is faithful in all mine house. With him will I speak mouth to mouth, even apparently, and not in dark speeches; and the similitude of the Lord shall he behold: wherefore then were ye not afraid to speak against my servant Moses? And the anger of the Lord was kindled against them; and he departed. And the cloud departed from off the tabernacle; and, behold, Miriam became leprous, white as snow: and Aaron looked upon Miriam, and, behold, she was leprous." Verses 1-10.

It is a most serious thing for any one to speak against the Lord's servant. We may rest assured that God will deal with it, sooner or later. In the case of Miriam, the divine judgment came down suddenly and solemnly. It was a grievous wrong, yea, it was positive rebellion, to speak against the one whom God had so markedly raised up and clothed with a divine commission; and who, moreover, in the very matter of which they complained, had acted in full consonance with the counsels of God, and furnished a type of that glorious mystery which was hidden in His eternal mind, even the union of Christ and the Church.

But, in any case, it is a fatal mistake to speak against the very feeblest and humblest of God's servants. If the servant does wrong – if he is in error, if he has failed in anything – the Lord Himself will deal with him; but let the fellow servants beware how they attempt to take the matter into their hands, lest they be found like Miriam, meddling to their own hurt.

It is very awful to hear, at times, the way in which people allow themselves to speak and write about Christ's servants. True, these latter may give occasion; they may have made mistakes, and manifested a wrong spirit and temper; but we must confess we feel it to be a very dreadful sin against Christ to speak evil of His dear servants. Surely we ought to feel the weight and solemnity of these words, *"Wherefore then were ye not afraid to speak against my servant?"*

May God give us grace to watch against this sore evil! Let us see to it that we be not found doing that which is so offensive to Him, even speaking against those who are dear to His heart. There is not a single one of God's people in whom we cannot find some good thing, provided only we look for it in the right way. Let us be occupied *only* with the good; let us dwell upon that, and seek to strengthen and develop it, in every possible way. And, on the other hand, if we have not been able to discover the good thing in our brother and fellow-servant; if our eye has only detected the crooked thing; if we have not succeeded in finding the vital spark amid the ashes – the precious gem among the surrounding rubbish; if we have only seen what was of mere nature, why then let us, with a loving and delicate hand, draw the curtain of silence around our brother, or speak of him only at the throne of grace.

So also when we happen to be in company with those who indulge in the wicked practice of speaking against the Lord's people, if we cannot succeed in changing the current of the conversation, let us rise and leave the place, thus bearing testimony against that which is so hateful to Christ. Let us never sit by and listen to a backbiter. We may rest assured he is doing the work of the devil, and inflicting positive injury upon three distinct parties, namely, himself, his hearer, and the subject of his censorious remarks.

There is something perfectly beautiful in the way in which Moses carries himself, in the scene before us. Truly he proved himself a meek man, not only in the matter of Eldad and Medad, but also in the more trying matter of Miriam and Aaron. As to the former, instead of being jealous of those who were called to share his dignity and responsibility, he rejoiced in their work, and prayed that all the Lord's people might taste the same holy privilege. And, as to the latter, instead of cherishing any feeling of resentment against his brother and sister, he was ready, at once, to take the place of intercession. "And Aaron said unto Moses, Alas, my lord, I beseech thee, lay not the sin upon us, wherein we have done foolishly, and wherein we have sinned. Let her not be as one dead, of whom the flesh is half consumed when he cometh out of his mother's womb. And Moses cried unto the Lord, saying, Heal her now, O God, I beseech thee." Verses 11-13.

Here Moses breathes the spirit of His Master, and prays for those who had spoken so bitterly against him. This was victory – the victory of a meek man – the victory of grace. A man who knows his right place in the presence of God is able to rise above all evil speaking. He is not troubled by it, save for those who practice it. He can afford to forgive it. He is not touchy, tenacious, or self-occupied. He knows that no one can put him lower than he deserves to be; and, hence, if any speak against him, he can meekly bow his head and pass on, leaving himself and his cause in the hands of Him who judgeth righteously, and who will assuredly reward every man according to his works.

This is true dignity. May we understand it somewhat better, and then we shall not be so ready to take fire if any one thinks proper to speak disparagingly of us or of our work; nay, more, we shall be able to lift up our hearts in earnest prayer for them, and thus draw down blessing on them and on our own souls.

Miriam's seven days outside the camp

The few closing lines of our chapter confirm the typical or dispensational view which we have ventured to suggest. "And the Lord said unto Moses, If her father had but spit in her face, should she not be ashamed seven days? Let her be shut out from the camp seven days, and after that let her be received in again. And Miriam was shut out from the camp seven days: and the people journeyed not till Miriam was brought in again. And afterward the people removed from Hazeroth and pitched in the wilderness of Paran" (ver. 14-16). We may regard Miriam, thus shut out of the camp, as a figure of the present condition of the nation of Israel, who, in consequence of their implacable opposition to the divine thought of mercy to the Gentile, are set aside. But when the "seven days" have run their course, Israel shall be restored, on the ground of sovereign grace exercised toward them through the intercession of Christ.

Chapter 13

SENDING OUT THE SPIES TO CANAAN

The origin of this expedition

"And the Lord spake unto Moses, saying, Send thou men that they may search the land of Canaan, which I give unto the children of Israel: of every tribe of their fathers shall ye send a man, every one a ruler among them. And Moses by the commandment of the Lord sent them from the wilderness of Paran." Verses 1-3.

In order fully to understand the foregoing commandment, we must look at it in connection with a passage in the Book of Deuteronomy, where Moses, in going over the facts of Israel's marvellous history in the wilderness, reminds them of the following important and interesting circumstance: "And when we departed from Horeb, we went through all that great and terrible wilderness, which ye saw by the way of the mountain of the Amorites, as the Lord our God commanded us; and we came to Kadesh-Barnea. And I said unto you, Ye are come unto the mountain of the Amorites, which the Lord our God doth give unto us. Behold, the Lord thy God hath set the land before thee: go up and possess it, as the Lord God of thy fathers hath said unto thee; fear not, neither be discouraged. *And ye came near unto me every one of you,* and said, *We will send men before us,* and they shall search us out the land, and bring us word again by what way we must go up, and into what cities we shall come." Deut. 1:19-22.

Now here we have the moral root of the fact stated in Numbers 13:2. It is evident that the Lord gave the commandment concerning the spies because of the moral condition of the people. Had they been governed by simple faith, they would have acted on those soul-stirring words of Moses, "Behold, the Lord thy God hath set the land before thee: *go up and possess it,* as the Lord God of thy fathers hath said unto thee; *fear not, neither be discouraged."* There is not a single syllable about spies, in this splendid passage. What does faith want of spies, when it has the word and the presence of the living God? If Jehovah had given them a land, it must be worth having. And had He not? Yes, truly; and not only so, but He had borne testimony to the nature and character of that land in the following glowing words, "For the Lord thy God bringeth thee into a good land, a land of brooks of water, of fountains and depths that spring out of valleys and hills; a land of wheat, and barley, and vines, and fig trees, and pomegranates, a land of oil olive and honey; a land wherein thou shalt eat bread without scarceness, thou shalt not lack anything in it; a land whose stones are iron, and out of whose hills thou mayest dig brass." Deut 8:7-9.

Should not all this have sufficed for Israel? Ought they not to have been satisfied with the testimony of God? Had not He spied out the land for them, and told them all about it? And was not this enough? What need of sending men to spy the land? Did not God know all about it? Was there a spot "from Dan to Beersheba" with which he was not perfectly acquainted? Had He not selected this land and allotted it, in His own eternal counsels, for the seed of Abraham His friend? Did He not know all about the difficulties? and was He not able to surmount them? Why, then, did they *"every one of them,* and say, We will send men before us, and they shall search us out the land, and bring us word again"?

Ah! reader, these questions come right home to our hearts. They find us out, and make thoroughly manifest where we are. It is not for us to sit down and coolly animadvert upon the ways of Israel in the wilderness; to point out error here, and failure there. We must take all these things as types set before us for our admonition. They are beacons, erected by a friendly and faithful hand, to warn us off from the dangerous shoals, quicksands, and rocks which lie along our course, and threaten our safety. This, we may be sure, is the true way to read every page of Israel's history, if we would reap the profit which our God has designed for us in penning such a record.

But, it may be the reader is disposed to ask a question here. "Did not the Lord expressly command Moses to send spies? And if so, how was it wrong for Israel to send them? True, the Lord did command Moses to send the spies, in Numbers 13; but this was in consequence of the moral condition of the people, as set forth in Deuteronomy 1. We shall not understand the former unless we read it in the light of the latter. We learn, most distinctly, from Deuteronomy 1:22, that the idea of sending the spies had its origin in the heart of Israel. God saw their moral condition, and He issued a command in full keeping therewith.

If the reader will turn to the opening pages of the first book of Samuel, he will find something similar in the matter of the appointment of a king. The Lord commanded Samuel to hearken to the voice of the people, and make them a king (1 Sam. 8:22). Was it that He approved of the plan? Most surely not; on the contrary, He declares plainly that it was a positive rejection of Himself. Why then command Samuel to appoint a king? The command was given in consequence of Israel's condition. They were growing weary of the position of entire dependence upon an unseen arm; and they longed for an arm of flesh. They desired to be like the nations around them, and to have a king who should go out before them, and fight their battles for them. Well, God gave them their request, and they were very speedily called to prove the worthlessness of their plan. Their king proved a most complete failure, and they had to learn that it was an evil and a bitter thing to forsake the living God and lean on a broken reed of their own selection.

Now, we see the same thing in the matter of the spies. There can be no question, in the mind of any spiritual person who studies the entire subject, as to the fact that the scheme of sending the spies was the fruit of unbelief. A simple heart that trusted God would never have thought of such a thing.

What! are we to send poor mortals to spy out a land which God has graciously given to us, and which He has so fully and faithfully described? Far be the thought; nay, rather let us say, "It is enough; the land is the gift of God, and as such it must be good. His word is enough for our hearts; we want no spies; we seek for no mortal testimony to confirm the word of the living God. He has given; He has spoken; this is enough."

But alas! Israel was not in a condition to adopt such language. They *would* send spies. They wanted them, their hearts craved them: the desire for them lay in the very depths of the soul; Jehovah knew this, and hence He issued a commandment in direct reference to the moral state of the people.

The reader would do well to ponder this subject, in the light of scripture. He will need to compare Deuteronomy 1 with Numbers 13. It is possible he may find difficulty in judging of the true nature and moral roots of the act of sending the spies, from the fact that the thing was ultimately done in pursuance of "the commandment of the Lord." But we must ever remember that the fact of the Lord's commanding the thing to be done does not, by any means, prove that the people were right in seeking it. The giving of the law at Mount Sinai; the sending of the spies; and the appointment of a king, are all proofs of this. No doubt God overruled all these things for His own glory and for man's ultimate blessing; but still the law could not be viewed as the expression of the heart of God; the setting up of a king was a positive rejection of Himself; and we may say that the sending of men to spy out the land of promise proved, very distinctly, that the heart of Israel was not fully satisfied with Jehovah. The whole affair was the fruit of their weakness and unbelief, though acquiesced in by God because of their condition, and overruled by Him, in His infinite goodness and unerring wisdom, for the unfolding of His ways and the display of His glory. All this comes fully out as we pursue the history.

The result of the exploration

"And Moses sent them (the spies) to spy out the land of Canaan, and said unto them, Get you up this way southward, and go up into the mountain: and see the land what it is; and the people that dwelleth therein, whether they be strong or weak, few or many; and what the land is that they dwell in, whether it be good or bad; and what cities they be that they dwell in, whether in tents, or in strong holds; and what the land is, whether it be fat or lean, whether there be wood therein or not. And be ye of good courage, and bring of the fruit of the land. Now the time was the time of the first ripe grapes. So they went up, and searched the land from the wilderness of Zin unto Rehob, as men come to Hamath . . . And they came unto the brook of Eshcol, and cut down from thence a branch with one cluster of grapes, and they bare it between two upon a staff; and they brought of the pomegranates, and of the figs. The place was called the brook Eshcol, because of the cluster of grapes which the children of Israel cut down from thence. And they returned from searching of the land after forty days. And they went and came to Moses, and to Aaron, and to all the congregation of the children of Israel, unto the wilderness of Paran, to Kadesh; and brought back word unto them, and unto all the congregation, and shewed them the fruit of the land. And they told him, and said, We came unto the land whither thou sentest us, and surely it floweth with milk and honey; and this is the fruit of it." Numbers 13:17-27.

Here, then, was the fullest confirmation of all that the Lord had said concerning the land – the testimony of twelve men as to the fact that the land flowed with milk and honey – the testimony of their own senses as to the character of the fruit of the land. Furthermore, there was the telling fact that twelve men had actually been in the land, had spent forty days in travelling up and down therein, had drunk of its springs and eaten of its fruits. And what, according to the judgment of faith, would have been the plain inference to be drawn from such a fact? Why, simply, that the same hand which had conducted twelve men into the land could conduct the whole congregation.

But alas! the people were not governed by faith, but by dark and depressing unbelief; and even the spies themselves – the very men who had been sent for the purpose of assuring and confirming the congregation – even they, with two brilliant exceptions, were under the power of the same God-dishonouring spirit. In short, the whole scheme proved a failure. The issue only made manifest the true condition of the hearts of the people. Unbelief was dominant. The testimony was plain enough: "We came unto the land whither thou sentest us, and surely it floweth with milk and honey; and this is the fruit of it." There was nothing whatever lacking on God's side of the question. The land was all that He had said, the spies themselves being witnesses; but let us hearken to what follows. "Nevertheless the people be strong that dwell in the land, and the cities are walled, and very great: and moreover we saw the children of Anak there." Verse 28.

There is always sure to be a "nevertheless" where man is concerned, and when unbelief is at work. The unbelieving spies *saw* the difficulties – great cities, high walls, tall giants. All these things they saw; but they did not see Jehovah at all. They looked at the things that were seen, rather than at the things that were unseen. Their eye was not fixed upon Him who is invisible. Doubtless, the cities were great; but God was greater. The walls were high; but God was higher. The giants were strong but God was stronger.

Thus it is that faith ever reasons. Faith reasons from God to the difficulties: it begins with Him. Unbelief, on the contrary, reasons from the difficulties to God: it begins with them. This makes all the difference. It is not that we are to be insensible to the difficulties; neither are we to be reckless. Neither insensibility nor yet recklessness is faith. There are some easy-going people who seem to get along through life on the principle of taking things by the smooth handle. This is not faith. Faith looks the difficulties straight in the face; it is fully alive to the roughness of the handle. It is not ignorant, not indifferent – not reckless; but – what? It brings in the living God. It looks to Him; it leans on Him; it draws from Him. Here lies the grand secret of its power. It cherishes the calm and deep conviction that there never was a wall too high for the Almighty God – never a city too great – never a giant too strong. In short, faith is the only thing that gives God His proper place; and, as a consequence, is the only thing that lifts the soul completely above the influences of surrounding circumstances, be they what they may. Of this precious faith, Caleb was the exponent, when he said, "Let us go up at once and possess it; for we are well able to overcome it." These are the pure accents of that lively faith that glorifies God and makes nothing of circumstances.

But alas! the great majority of the spies were no more governed by this lively faith than the men who sent them; and hence, the one believer was talked down by the ten infidels. "The men that went up with him said, We be not able to go up against the people." The language of infidelity was flatly opposed to the language of faith. The latter, looking at God, said," We are *well* able." The former, looking at the difficulties, said, "We are *not* able." Thus it was and thus it is. The eyes of faith are ever covered by the living God, and therefore difficulties are not seen. The eyes of unbelief are covered with the circumstances, and therefore God is not seen. Faith brings in God, and therefore all is bright and easy. Unbelief always shuts God out, and therefore all is dark and difficult.

"And they brought up an evil report of the land which they had searched unto the children of Israel, saying, The land, through which we have gone to search it, is a land that eateth up the inhabitants thereof; and all the people that we saw in it are men of a great stature. And there we saw the giants, the sons of Anak, which come of the giants; and we were in our own sight as grasshoppers, and so we were in their sight." Not a word about God. He is entirely shut out. Had they thought of Him – had they brought the giants into comparison with Him, then it would have made not one whit of difference as to whether they themselves were grasshoppers, or whether they were men. But, in point of fact they, by their shameful unbelief, reduced the God of Israel to the level of a grasshopper.

It is very remarkable, that whenever infidelity is at work, it will always be found characterized by this one fact, namely, it shuts out God. This will be found true in all ages, in all places, and under all circumstances. There is no exception. Infidelity can take account of human affairs,, it can reason upon them, and draw conclusions from them; but all its reasonings and all its conclusions are based upon the exclusion of God. The force of its arguments depends upon shutting Him out, and keeping Him out. Only introduce God, and all the reasonings of infidelity crumble into dust beneath your feet. Thus, in the scene before us, what is faith's reply to all the objections advanced by those ten unbelievers? Its one simple, all-satisfying reply, to which there can be no rejoinder, is – GOD!

Reader, do you know anything of the force and value of this most blessed answer! Do you know God? Does He fill the entire range of your soul's vision? Is He the answer to your every question? the solution of your every difficulty? Do you know the reality of walking, day by day, with the living God? Do you know the tranquillising power of leaning upon Him, "through all the changes and chances of this mortal life?" If not, let me entreat of you not to go on for one hour in your present state. The way is open. God has revealed Himself in the face of Jesus Christ, as the relief, the resource, and the refuge of every needy soul. Look to Him now – even now, "while he may be found; call upon him while he is near." "Whosoever shall call upon the name of the Lord shall be saved;" and "He that believeth shall never be confounded."

But if, on the other hand, you do, through grace, know God as your Saviour – your Father, then seek to glorify Him in all your ways, by a childlike unquestioning confidence in all things. Let Him be a perfect covering for your eyes, under all circumstances, and thus, in spite of all difficulties, your soul shall be kept in perfect peace.

Chapter 14

KADESH: THE REFUSAL TO ENTER THE LAND OF CANAAN

Discouragement and unbelief

"And all the congregation lifted up their voice, and cried; and the people wept that night." Need we wonder? What else could be expected from a people who had nothing before their eyes but mighty giants, lofty walls, and great cities? What but tears and sighs could emanate from a congregation who saw themselves as grasshoppers in the presence of such insuperable difficulties, and having no sense of the divine power that could carry them victoriously through all? The whole assembly was abandoned to the absolute dominion of infidelity. They were surrounded by the dark and chilling clouds of unbelief. God was shut out. There was not so much as a single ray of light to illumine the darkness with which they had surrounded themselves. They were occupied with themselves and their difficulties instead of with God and His resources. What else therefore could they do but lift up the voice of weeping and lamentation?

What a contrast between this and the opening of Exodus 15! In the latter their eyes were only upon Jehovah, and therefore they could sing the song of victory. "Thou in thy mercy hast led forth the people which thou hast redeemed; thou hast guided them in thy strength unto thy holy habitation. *The people shall hear and be afraid: sorrow shall take hold on the inhabitants of Palestina."* Instead of this it was Israel that was afraid, and sorrow took hold upon them. "Then the dukes of Edom shall be amazed; the mighty men of Moab, *trembling shall take hold upon them:* all the inhabitants of Canaan shall melt away. *Fear and dread shall fall upon them.*" In short, it is the most complete reversing of the picture. The sorrow, the trembling, and the fear take hold upon Israel instead of their enemies. And why? Because the One who filled their vision in Exodus 15 is completely shut out in Numbers 14. This makes all the difference. In the one case, faith is in the ascendant; in the other, infidelity. "By the greatness of *thine arm* they shall be as still as a stone; till thy people pass over, O Lord, till the people pass over which thou hast purchased. Thou shalt bring them in, and plant them in the mountain of thine inheritance, in the place, O Lord, which thou hast made for thee to dwell in; in the sanctuary, O Lord, which thy hands have established. The Lord shall reign for ever and ever."

Oh! how do these triumphal accents contrast with the infidel cries and lamentations of Numbers 14! Not a syllable about sons of Anak, lofty walls, and grasshoppers, in Exodus 15. No, no; it is all Jehovah. It is His right hand, His mighty arm, His power, His inheritance, His habitation, His actings on behalf of His ransomed people. And then if the inhabitants of Canaan are referred to, they are only thought of as sorrowing, terror-stricken, trembling, and melting away.

But, on the other hand, when we come to Numbers 14 all is most sadly reversed. The sons of Anak rise into prominence. The towering walls, the giant cities with frowning bulwarks, fill the vision of the people, and we hear not a word about the Almighty Deliverer. There are the difficulties on the one side, and grasshoppers on the other; and one is constrained to cry out, "Can it be possible that the triumphal singers by the Red Sea have become the infidel weepers at Kadesh?"

Alas! it is so; and here we learn a deep and holy lesson. We must continually recur, as we pass along through these wilderness scenes, to those words which tell us that, "All these things happened unto Israel for ensamples: and they are written for our admonition, upon whom the ends of the ages are met" (1 Cor. 10:11; see Greek). Are not we, too, like Israel, prone to look at the difficulties which surround us, rather than at that blessed One who has undertaken to carry us right through them all, and bring us safely into His own everlasting kingdom? Why is it we are sometimes cast down? Why go we mourning? Wherefore are the accents of discontent and impatience heard in our midst, rather than the songs of praise and thanksgiving? Simply because we allow circumstances to shut out God, instead of having God as a perfect covering for our eyes and a perfect object for our hearts.

And, further, let us enquire, wherefore is it that we so sadly fail to make good our position as heavenly men? – to take possession of that which belongs to us as Christians? – to plant the foot upon that spiritual and heavenly inheritance which Christ has purchased for us, and on which He has entered as our forerunner? What answer must be given to these inquiries? Just one word – *Unbelief!*

It is declared, concerning Israel, by the voice of inspiration, that, "They could not enter in [to Canaan] because of unbelief" (Heb. 3). So is it with us. We fail to enter upon our heavenly inheritance – fail to take possession, practically, of our true and proper portion – fail to walk, day by day, as a heavenly people, having no place, no name, no portion in the earth – having nothing to do with this world save to pass through it as pilgrims and strangers, treading in the footsteps of Him who has gone before, and taken His place in the heavens. And why do we fail? Because of unbelief. Faith is not in energy, and therefore the things which are seen have more power over our hearts than the things which are unseen. Oh! may the Holy Spirit strengthen our faith, and energize our souls, and lead us upward and onward, so that we may not merely be found *talking* of heavenly life, but *living* it to the praise of Him who has, in His infinite grace, called us thereto.

A march back

"And all the children of Israel murmured against Moses and against Aaron: and the whole congregation said unto them, Would God that we had died in the land of Egypt! or would

God we had died in this wilderness! And wherefore hath the Lord brought us unto this land, to fall by the sword, that our wives and our children should be a prey? Were it not better for us to return into Egypt? And they said one to another, Let us make a captain, and let us return into Egypt."

There are two melancholy phases of unbelief exhibited in Israel's history in the wilderness; the one at Horeb, the other at Kadesh. At Horeb they made a *calf*, and said, "These be thy gods, O Israel, that brought thee up out of the land of Egypt." At Kadesh, they proposed to make a *captain* to lead them back into Egypt. The former of these is the *superstition* of unbelief; the latter, the wilful *independence* of unbelief; and, most surely, we need not marvel if these who thought that a calf had brought them out of Egypt should seek a captain to lead them back. The poor human mind is tossed like a ball from one to the other of those sore evils. There is no resource save that which faith finds in the living God. In Israel's case God was lost sight of. It was either a calf or a captain; either death in the wilderness, or return into Egypt. Caleb stands in bright contrast with all this. To him it was neither death in the wilderness, nor return into Egypt, but an abundant entrance into the promised land behind the impenetrable shield of Jehovah.

Joshua and Caleb, two faithful witnesses

"And Joshua the son of Nun, and Caleb the son of Jephunneh, which were of them that searched the land, rent their clothes: and they spake unto all the company of the children of Israel, saying, The land, which we passed through to search it, is an exceeding good land. If the Lord delight in us, then he will bring us into this land, and give it us; a land which floweth with milk and honey. Only rebel not ye against the Lord, neither fear ye the people of the land; for they are bread for us: their defence is departed from them, and the Lord is with us: fear them not. But all the congregation bade stone them with stones."

And for what were they to be stoned? Was it for telling lies? was it for blasphemy or evil-doing? No; it was for their bold and earnest testimony to the truth. They had been sent to spy the land, and to furnish a true report concerning it. This they did; and for this "All the congregation bade stone them with stones." The people did not like the truth then any more than now. Truth is never popular. There is no place for it in this world, or in the human heart. Lies will be received; and error in every shape; but truth never. Joshua and Caleb had to encounter, in their day, what all true witnesses, in every age, have experienced and all must expect, namely, the opposition and hatred of the mass of their fellows. There were six hundred thousand voices raised against two men who simply told the truth, and trusted in God. Thus it has been; thus it is; and thus it will be until that glorious moment when "The earth shall be full of the knowledge of the Lord, as the waters cover the sea."

But oh! how important it is to be enabled, like Joshua and Caleb, to bear a full, clear, and uncompromising testimony to the truth of God! How important to maintain the truth as to the proper portion and inheritance of the saints! There is such a tendency to corrupt the truth – to fritter it away – to surrender it – to lower the standard. Hence the urgent need of having the truth in divine power in the soul, of being able, in our little measure, to say, "We speak that we do know, and testify that we have seen." Caleb and Joshua had not only been in the land, but they had been with God about the land. They had looked at it all from faith's point of view. They knew the land was theirs, in the purpose of God; that it was worth having as the gift of God; and that they should yet possess it by the power of God. They were men full of faith, full of courage, full of power.

Blessed men! They were living in the light of the divine presence, while the whole congregation were wrapped in the dark shades of their own unbelief. What a contrast! This it is which ever marks the difference between even the people of God. You may constantly find persons of whom you can have no doubt as to their being children of God; but yet they never seem to rise to the height of divine revelation, as to their standing and portion as saints of God. They are always full of doubts and fears; always overcast with clouds; always at the dark side of things. They are looking at themselves, or at their circumstances, or at their difficulties. They are never bright and happy; never able to exhibit that joyful confidence and courage which become a Christian, and which bring glory to God.

Now all this is truly lamentable; it ought not to be; and we may rest assured there is some grave defect, something radically wrong. The Christian should always be peaceful and happy; always able to praise God, come what may. His joys do not flow from himself, or from the scene through which he is passing; they flow from the living God, and they are beyond the reach of every earthly influence. He can say, "My God, the spring of all my joys." This is the sweet privilege of the very feeblest child of God. But here is just where we so sadly fail and come short. We take our eyes off God, and fix them on ourselves, or on our circumstances, our grievances, or our difficulties; hence all is darkness and discontent, murmuring and complaining. This is not Christianity at all. It is unbelief – dark, deadly, God-dishonouring, heart-depressing unbelief. "God hath not given us the spirit of fear; but of power, and of love, and of a sound mind."

Such is the language of a true spiritual Caleb – language addressed to one whose heart was feeling the pressure of the difficulties and dangers which surrounded him. The Spirit of God fills the soul of the true believer with holy boldness. He gives moral elevation above the chilling and murky atmosphere around, and lifts the soul into the bright sunshine of that region "where storms and tempests never rise."

God ready to execute judgment

"And the glory of the Lord appeared in the tabernacle of the congregation before all the children of Israel. And the

Lord said unto Moses, How long will this people provoke me? and how long will it be ere they believe me, for all the signs which I have showed among them? I will smite them with the pestilence and disinherit them, and will make of thee a greater nation and mightier than they."

What a moment was this in the history of Moses! Here was what nature might well regard as a golden opportunity for him. Never before and never since have we any occasion in the which a mere man had such a door open before him. The enemy and his own heart might say, "Now's your time. You have here an offer of becoming the head and founder of a great and mighty nation – an offer made to you by Jehovah Himself. You have not sought it. It is put before you by the living God, and it would be the very height of folly on your part to reject it."

But, reader, Moses was not a self-seeker. He had drunk too deeply into the spirit of Christ to seek to be anything. He had no unholy ambition, no selfish aspirations. He desired only God's glory and His people's good; and in order to reach those ends, he was ready, through grace, to lay himself and his interests on the altar.

Moses' intercession

Hear his marvellous reply. Instead of jumping at the offer contained in the words, "I will make of thee a greater nation and mightier than they" – instead of eagerly grasping at the golden opportunity of laying the foundation of his personal fame and fortune – he sets himself completely aside, and replies in accents of the most noble disinterestedness: "And Moses said unto the Lord, Then the Egyptians shall hear it, (for thou broughtest up this people in thy might from among them;) and they will tell it to the inhabitants of this land: for they have heard that thou, Lord, art among this people; that thou, Lord, art seen face to face; and that thy cloud standeth over them; and that thou goest before them, by daytime in a pillar of a cloud, and in a pillar of fire by night. Now if thou shalt kill all this people as one man, then the nations which have heard the fame of thee will speak, saying, Because the Lord was not able to bring this people into the land which he sware unto them, therefore he hath slain them in the wilderness." Verses 13-16.

Here Moses takes the very highest ground. He is wholly occupied about the Lord's glory. He cannot endure the thought that the lustre of that glory should be tarnished in the view of the nations of the uncircumcised. What though he should become a head and a founder? What though future millions should look back to him as their illustrious progenitor? If all this personal glory and greatness was only to be purchased by the sacrifice of a single ray of divine glory, – what then? Away with it all. Let the name of Moses be blotted out for ever. He had said as much in the days of the *calf*; and he was ready to repeat it in the days of the *captain*. In the face of the superstition and independence of an unbelieving nation, the heart of Moses throbbed *only* for the glory of God. That must be guarded at all cost. Come what may – cost what it may, the glory of the Lord must be maintained. Moses felt it was impossible for anything to be right if the basis were not laid firmly down in the strict maintenance of the glory of the God of Israel. To think of himself made great at God's expense was perfectly insufferable to the heart of this blessed man of God. He could not endure that the name which he loved so well should be blasphemed among the nations, or that it should ever be said by any one, "The Lord was not able."

But there was another thing which lay near the disinterested heart of Moses. He thought of the people. He loved and cared for them. Jehovah's glory, no doubt, stood uppermost; but Israel's blessing stood next. "And now," he adds, "I beseech thee, let the power of my Lord be great, according as thou hast spoken, saying, The Lord is long-suffering, and of great mercy, forgiving iniquity and transgression, and by no means clearing the guilty; visiting the iniquity of the fathers upon the children unto the third and fourth generation. Pardon, I beseech thee, the iniquity of this people, according unto the greatness of thy mercy, and as thou hast forgiven this people from Egypt even until now." Verses 17-19.

This is uncommonly fine. The order, the tone, and the spirit of this entire appeal are most exquisite. There is, first and chiefest of all, a jealous care for the Lord's glory. This must be fenced round about on every side. But then it is on this very ground, namely, the maintenance of the divine glory, that pardon is sought for the people. The two things are linked together in the most blessed way, in this intercession. "Let the *power* of my Lord be great." To what end? Judgment and destruction? Nay; "The Lord is *long-suffering*." What a thought! The power of God in long-suffering and pardon! How unspeakably precious! How intimate was Moses with the very heart and mind of God when he could speak in such a strain! And how does he stand in contrast with Elijah, on Mount Horeb, when he made intercession *against* Israel! We can have little question as to which of these two honoured men was most in harmony with the mind and spirit of Christ. "Pardon, I beseech thee, the iniquity of this people according unto the greatness of thy mercy." These words were grateful to the ear of Jehovah, who delights in dispensing pardon. "And the Lord said, I have pardoned, according to thy word." And then He adds," But as truly as I live, all the earth shall be filled with the glory of the Lord."

Grace and government

Let the reader carefully note these two statements. They are absolute and unqualified. "I have pardoned." And, "All the earth shall be filled with the glory of the Lord." Nothing could, by any possibility, touch these grand facts. The *pardon* is secured; and the *glory* shall yet shine forth over all the earth. No power of earth or hell, men or devils, can ever interfere with the divine integrity of these two precious statements. Israel shall rejoice in the plenary pardon of their God; and all the earth shall yet bask in the bright sunshine of his glory.

But then there is such a thing as government, as well as

grace. This must never be forgotten; nor must these things ever be confounded. The whole book of God illustrates the distinction between grace and government; and no part of it, perhaps, more forcibly than the section which now lies open before us. Grace will pardon; and grace will fill the earth with the blessed beams of divine glory; but mark the appalling movement of the wheels of government as set forth in the following burning words: "Because all those men which have seen my glory, and my miracles, which I did in Egypt and in the wilderness, have tempted me now these ten times, and have not hearkened to my voice; surely they shall not see the land which I sware unto their fathers, neither shall any of them that provoked me see it. But my servant Caleb, because he had another spirit with him, and hath followed me fully, him will I bring into the land whereinto he went; and his seed shall possess it. (Now the Amalekites and the Canaanites dwelt in the valley.) To-morrow turn you, and get you into the wilderness by the way of the Red Sea." verses 22-25.

This is most solemn. Instead of confiding in God, and going boldly on into the land of promise, in simple dependence upon His omnipotent arm, they provoked him by their unbelief, despised the pleasant land, and were compelled to turn back again into that great and terrible wilderness. "The Lord spake unto Moses and unto Aaron, saying, How long shall I bear with this evil congregation, which murmur against me? I have heard the murmurings of the children of Israel, which they murmur against me. Say unto them, As truly as I live, saith the Lord, as ye have spoken in mine ears, so will I do to you: your carcasses shall fall in this wilderness; and all that were numbered of you, according to your whole number, from twenty years old and upward, which have murmured against me, doubtless ye shall not come into the land concerning which I sware to make you dwell therein, save Caleb the son of Jephunneh, and Joshua the son of Nun. But your little ones which ye said should be a prey, them will I bring in, and they shall know the land which ye have despised. But as for you, your carcasses, they shall fall in this wilderness.

And your children shall wander in the wilderness forty years, and bear your whoredoms, until your carcasses be wasted in the wilderness. After the number of the days in which ye searched the land, even forty days, each day for a year, shall ye bear your iniquities, even forty years; and ye shall know my breach of promise. I the Lord have said, I will surely do it unto all this evil congregation, that are gathered together against me; in this wilderness they shall be consumed, and there they shall die." Verses 26-35.

Such, then, was the fruit of unbelief, and such the governmental dealings of God with a people that had provoked Him by their murmurings and hardness of heart.

It is of the utmost importance to note here that it was unbelief that kept Israel out of Canaan, on the occasion now before us. The inspired commentary in Hebrews 3 places this beyond all question. "So we see that they could not enter in because of unbelief." It might, perhaps, be said that the time was not come for Israel's entrance upon the land of Canaan. The iniquity of the Amorites had not yet reached its culminating point. But this is not the reason why Israel refused to cross the Jordan. They knew nothing and thought nothing about the iniquity of the Amorites. Scripture is as plain as possible: "They could not enter in" – not because of the iniquity of the Amorites; not because the time was not come – but simply "because of unbelief." They ought to have entered. They were responsible to do so; and they were judged for not doing so. The way was open. The judgment of faith, as uttered by faithful Caleb, was clear and unhesitating: "Let us go up *at once* and possess it; for we are well able to overcome it." They were as well able, at that moment, as they could ever be at any moment, inasmuch as the One who had given them the land was the spring of their ability to enter upon it and possess it.

It is well to see this; and to ponder it deeply. There is a certain style of speaking of the counsels, purposes, and decrees of God – of the enactments of His moral government; and of the times and seasons which he has put in His own power – which goes far to sweep away the very foundations of human responsibility. This must be carefully guarded against. We must ever bear in mind that man's responsibility rests on what is *revealed*, not on what is *secret*. Israel was responsible to go up at once and take possession of the land; and they were judged for not doing so. Their carcasses fell in the wilderness, because they had not faith to enter the land.

The typical significance of the entry into Canaan

And does not this convey a solemn lesson to us? Most surely. How is it that we, as Christians, so fail in making good, practically, our heavenly position? We are delivered from judgment by the *blood* of the Lamb; we are delivered from this present world by the *death* of Christ; but we do not, in spirit and by faith, cross the Jordan, and take possession of our heavenly inheritance. It is generally believed that Jordan is a type of death, as the end of our natural life in this world. This, in one sense, is true. But how was it that when Israel did, at length cross the Jordan, they had to begin to fight? Assuredly, we shall not have any fighting when we actually get to heaven. The spirits of those who have departed in the faith of Christ are not fighting in heaven. They are not in conflict in any shape or form. They are at rest. They are waiting for the morning of the resurrection; but they wait in rest, not in conflict.

Hence, therefore, there is something more typified in Jordan than the end of an individual's life in this world. We must view it as the figure of the death of Christ, in one grand aspect; just as the Red Sea is a figure of it, in another; and the blood of the paschal lamb, in another. The blood of the lamb sheltered Israel from the judgment of God upon Egypt. The waters of the Red Sea delivered Israel from Egypt itself and all its power. But they had to cross the Jordan; they had to plant the sole of their foot upon the land of promise, and make good their place there in spite of every foe. They had to fight for every inch of Canaan.

And what is the meaning of this latter? Have we to fight for heaven? When a Christian falls asleep, and his spirit goes to be with Christ in paradise, is there any question of fighting? Clearly not. What then are we to learn from the crossing of Jordan, and the wars of Canaan? Simply this, Jesus has died. He has passed away out of this world. He has not only died for our sins, but He has broken every link which connected us with this world; so that we are dead to the world, as well as dead to sin, and dead to the law. We have, in God's sight, and in the judgment of faith, as little to do with this world as a man lying dead on the floor. We are called to reckon ourselves dead to it all, and alive to God through Jesus Christ our Lord. We live in the power of the new life which we possess in union with Christ risen. We belong to heaven; and it is in making good our position as heavenly men that we have to fight with wicked spirits in the heavenlies – in the very sphere which belongs to us, and from which they have not yet been expelled. If we are satisfied to "walk as men" – to live as those who belong to this world – to stop short of Jordan – if we are satisfied to live as "dwellers upon the earth" – if we do not aim at our proper heavenly portion and position – then we shall not know anything of the conflict of Ephesians 6:12. It is seeking to live as heavenly men now on earth, that we shall enter into the meaning of that conflict which is the antitype of Israel's wars in Canaan. We shall not have to fight when we get to heaven, but if we want to live a heavenly life, on the earth, if we seek to carry ourselves as those who are dead to the world, and alive to Him who went down into Jordan's cold flood for us, then, assuredly, we must fight. Satan will leave no stone unturned to hinder our living in the power of our heavenly life; and hence the conflict. He will seek to make us walk as those who have an earthly standing, to be citizens of this world, to contend for our rights, to maintain our rank and dignity, to give the lie, practically, to that great foundation Christian truth, that we are dead and risen with and in Christ.

If the reader will turn for a moment to Ephesians 6 he will

see how this interesting subject is presented by the inspired writer. "Finally, my brethren, be strong in the Lord, and in the power of his might. Put on the whole armour of God, that ye may be able to stand against *the wiles* of the devil. For we wrestle not against flesh and blood (as Israel had to do in Canaan); but against principalities, against powers, against the rulers of the darkness of this world, against wicked spirits in heavenly places. Wherefore take unto you the whole armour of God, that ye may be able to withstand in the evil day, and having done all, to stand." Verses 10-13.

Here we have proper Christian conflict. It is not here a question of the lusts of the flesh, or the fascinations of the world – though surely we have to watch against these – but "the wiles of the devil." Not his power, which is forever broken, but those subtle devices and snares by which he seeks to keep Christians from realizing their heavenly position and inheritance.

Now, it is in carrying on this conflict, that we so signally fail. We do not aim at apprehending that for which we have been apprehended. Many of us are satisfied with knowing that we are delivered from judgment by the blood of the Lamb. We do not enter into the deep significance of the Red Sea and the river Jordan; we do not practically seize their spiritual import. We walk as men, the very thing for which the apostle blamed the Corinthians. We live and act as if we belonged to this world, whereas scripture teaches and our baptism expresses that we are dead to the world, even as Jesus is dead to it; and that we are risen in Him, through the faith of the operation of God, who hath raised Him from the dead. Colossians 2:12.

May the Holy Spirit lead our souls into the reality of these things. May He so present to us the precious fruits of that heavenly land which is ours in Christ, and so strengthen us with His own might in the inner man, that we may boldly cross the Jordan and plant the foot upon the spiritual Canaan. We live far below our privileges as Christians. We allow the things that are seen to rob us of the enjoyment of those things that are unseen. Oh! for a stronger faith, to take possession of all that God has freely given to us in Christ!

Faith and unbelief

We must now proceed with our history.

"And the men which Moses sent to search the land, who returned, and made all the congregation to murmur against him, by bringing up a slander upon the land, even those men that did bring up the evil report upon the land, died by the plague before the Lord. But Joshua the son of Nun, and Caleb the son of Jephunneh, which were of the men that went to search the land, lived still." Verses 36-38.

It is wonderful to think that out of that vast assembly of six hundred thousand men, besides women and children, there were only two that had faith in the living God. We do not, of course, speak of Moses, but merely of the congregation. The whole assembly, with two very brilliant exceptions indeed, was governed by a spirit of unbelief. They could not trust God to bring them into the land; nay, they thought He had brought them into the wilderness to die there; and surely we may say, they reaped according to their dark unbelief. The ten false witnesses died by the plague; and the many thousands who received their false witness were compelled to turn back into the wilderness, there to wander up and down for forty years, and then die and be buried.

But Joshua and Caleb stood on the blessed ground of faith in the living God – that faith which fills the soul with the most joyful confidence and courage. And of them we may say, they reaped according to their faith. God must always honour the faith which He has implanted in the soul. It is His own gift, and He cannot, we may say with reverence, but own it wherever it exists. Joshua and Caleb were enabled, in the simple power of faith, to withstand a tremendous tide of infidelity. They held fast their confidence in God in the face of every difficulty; and he signally honoured their faith in the end, for while the carcasses of their brethren were mouldering in the dust of the wilderness, their feet were treading the vine-clad hills and fertile valleys of the land of Canaan. The former declared that God had brought them forth to die in the wilderness; and they were taken at their word. The latter declared that God was able to bring them into the land, and they were taken at their word.

This is a most weighty principle, "According to your faith so be it unto you." Let us remember this, God delights in faith. He loves to be trusted, and He will ever put honour on those who trust Him. On the contrary, unbelief is grievous to Him. It provokes and dishonours Him, and brings darkness and death over the soul. It is a most terrible sin to doubt the living God who cannot lie, and to harbour questions when He has spoken. The devil is the author of all doubtful questions. He delights in shaking the confidence of the soul, but he has no power whatever against a soul that simply confides in God. His fiery darts can never reach one who is hidden behind the shield of faith. And oh, how precious it is to live a life of childlike trust in God! It makes the heart so happy, and fills the mouth with praise and thanksgiving. It chases away every cloud and mist, and brightens our path with the blessed beams of our Father's countenance. On the other hand, unbelief fills the heart with all manner of questions, throws us in upon ourselves, darkens our path and makes us truly miserable. Caleb's heart was full of joyful confidence, while the hearts of his brethren were filled with bitter murmurings and complaints. Thus it must ever be. If we want to be happy, we must be occupied with God and His surroundings. If we want to be miserable, we have only to be occupied with self and its surroundings. Look, for a moment, at the first chapter of Luke. What was it that shut up Zacharias in dumb silence? It was unbelief. What was it that filled the heart and opened the lips of Mary and Elizabeth? Faith. Here lay the difference. Zacharias might have joined those pious women in their songs of praise, were it not that dark unbelief sealed his lips in melancholy silence. What a picture! What a lesson! Oh that we may learn to trust God more simply. May the doubtful mind be far from us. May it be ours, in the midst of an infidel scene, to be strong in faith giving glory to God.

Confidence in their own strength

The closing paragraph of our chapter teaches us another holy lesson – let us apply our hearts to it with all diligence. "And Moses told these sayings unto all the children of Israel: and the people mourned greatly. And they rose up early in the morning, and gat them up into the top of the mountain, saying, Lo, we be here, and will go up unto the place which the Lord hath promised: for we have sinned. And Moses said, Wherefore now do ye transgress the commandment of the Lord? but it shall not prosper. Go not up, for the Lord is not among you; that ye be not smitten before your enemies. For the Amalekites, and the Canaanites are there before you, and ye shall fall by the sword; because ye are turned away from the Lord, therefore the Lord will not be with you. But they presumed to go up unto the hill top; nevertheless, the ark of the covenant of the Lord and Moses, departed not out of the camp. The Amalekites came down, and the Canaanites which dwelt in that hill, and smote them, and discomfited them, even unto Hormah.

What a mass of contradictions is the human heart! When exhorted to go up, at once, in the energy of faith, and possess the land, they shrank back and refused to go. They fell down and wept when they ought to have gone up and conquered. In vain did the faithful Caleb assure them that the Lord would bring them in and plant them in the mountain of His inheritance – that He was able to do it. They would not go up, because they could not trust God. But now, instead of bowing their heads and accepting the governmental dealings of God, they *would* go up presumptuously, trusting in themselves.

But ah! how vain to move without the living God in their midst! Without Him, they could do nothing. And yet, when they might have had Him, they were afraid of the Amalekites; but now they presume to face those very people without Him.

"Lo, we be here, and *will* go up unto the place which the Lord hath promised." This was more easily said than done. An Israelite without God was no match for an Amalekite; and it is very remarkable that, when Israel refused to act in the energy of faith, when they fell under the power of a God-dishonouring unbelief, Moses points out to them the very difficulties to which they themselves had referred. He tells them *"The Amalekites and the Canaanites are there before you."*

This is full of instruction. They, by their unbelief, had shut out God; and therefore it was obviously a question between Israel and the Canaanites. Faith would have made it a question between God and the Canaanites. This was precisely the way in which Joshua and Caleb viewed the matter when they said, "If the Lord delight in us, then He will bring us into this land, and give it us; a land which floweth with milk and honey. Only rebel not ye against the Lord, *neither fear ye the people of the land,* for they are bread for us: their defence is departed from them, and *the Lord is with us: fear them not."*

Here lay the grand secret. The Lord's pleasure with His people secures victory over every foe. But if He be not with them, they are as water poured upon the ground. The ten unbelieving spies had declared themselves to be as grasshoppers in the presence of the giants; and Moses, taking them at their word, tells them, as it were, that grasshoppers are no match for giants. If on the one hand, it be true that "according to your faith, so be it unto you;" it is also true, on the other hand, that according to your unbelief, so be it unto you.

But the people presumed. They affected to be something when they were nothing. And, oh! how miserable to presume to move in our own strength! What defeat and confusion! what exposure and contempt! what humbling and smashing to pieces! It must be so. They abandoned God in their unbelief; and He abandoned them in their vain presumption. They would not go with Him in faith; and He would not go with them in their unbelief. "Nevertheless the ark of the covenant of the Lord, and Moses, departed not out of the camp." They went without God, and hence they fled before their enemies.

Thus it must ever be. It is of no possible use to affect strength, to put forth lofty pretensions, to presume to be anything. Assumption and affectation are worse than worthless. If God be not with us, we are as the vapour of the morning. But this must be learnt practically. We must be brought down to the very bottom of all that is in self, so as to prove its utter worthlessness. And truly it is the wilderness, with all its varied scenes, and its thousand and one exercises, that leads to this practical result. There we learn what flesh is. There nature comes fully out, in all its phases; sometimes full of cowardly unbelief; at other times, full of false confidence. At Kadesh, refusing to go up when told to go; at Hormah, persisting in going when told not. Thus it is that extremes meet in that evil nature which the writer and reader bear about, from day to day.

Submission to the consequences of their faults

But there is one special lesson, beloved Christian reader, which we should seek to learn thoroughly, ere we take our departure from Hormah; and it is this: There is immense difficulty in walking humbly and patiently in the path which our own failure has rendered necessary for us. Israel's unbelief, in refusing to go up into the land, rendered it needful, in the governmental dealings of God, that they should turn about and wander in the wilderness for forty years. To this they were unwilling to submit. They kicked against it. They could not bow their necks to the necessary yoke.

How often is this the case with us! We fail; we take some false step; we get into trying circumstances in consequence; and, then, instead of meekly bowing down under the hand of God, and seeking to walk with Him, in humbleness and brokenness of spirit, we grow restive and rebellious; we quarrel with the circumstances instead of judging ourselves; and we seek, in self-will, to escape from the circumstances, instead of accepting them as the just and necessary consequence of our own conduct.

Again, it may happen that through weakness or failure, of one kind or another, we refuse to enter a position or path of spiritual privilege, and thereby we are thrown back in our course, and put upon a lower form in the school. Then, instead of carrying ourselves humbly, and submitting, in meekness and contrition, to the hand of God, we presume to force ourselves into the position, and affect to enjoy the privilege, and put forth pretensions to power, and it all issues in the most humiliating defeat and confusion.

These things demand our most profound consideration. It is a great thing to cultivate a lowly spirit, a heart content with a place of weakness and contempt. God resisteth the proud, but He giveth grace to the lowly. A pretentious spirit must, sooner or later, be brought down; and all hollow assumption of power must be exposed. If there be not faith to take possession of the promised land, there is nothing for it but to tread the wilderness in meekness and lowliness.

And, blessed be God, we shall have Him with us in that wilderness journey, though we shall not and cannot have Him with us in our self-chosen path of pride and assumption. Jehovah refused to accompany Israel into the mountain of the Amorites; but He was ready to turn about, in patient grace, and accompany them through all their desert wanderings. If Israel would not enter Canaan with Jehovah, He would go back into the wilderness with Israel. Nothing can exceed the grace that shines in this. Had they been dealt with according to their deserts, they might, at least, have been left to wander alone through the desert. But, blessed for ever be His great name, He does not deal with us after our sins, or reward us according to our iniquities. His thoughts are not as our thoughts; nor are His ways as our ways. Notwithstanding all the unbelief, the ingratitude, and the provocation exhibited by the people; notwithstanding that their return back into the desert was the fruit of their own conduct, yet did Jehovah, in condescending grace and patient love, turn back with them to be their travelling companion for forty long and dreary years in the wilderness.

Thus, if the wilderness proves what man is, it also proves what God is; and, further, it proves what faith is; for Joshua and Caleb had to return with the whole congregation of their unbelieving brethren, and remain for forty years out of their inheritance, though they themselves were quite prepared, through grace, to go up into the land. This might seem a great hardship. Nature might judge it unreasonable that two men of faith should have to suffer on account of the unbelief of other people. But faith can afford to wait patiently. And besides, how could Joshua and Caleb complain of the protracted march, when they saw Jehovah about to share it with them? Impossible. They were prepared to wait for God's time; for faith is never in a hurry. The faith of the servants might well be sustained by the grace of the Master.

Chapter 15

VARIOUS INSTRUCTIONS

When you have entered

The words with which our chapter opens are peculiarly striking, when taken in connection with the contents of chapter 14. There all seemed dark and hopeless. Moses had to say to the people, "*Go not up*, for the Lord is not among you; that ye be not smitten before your enemies." And, again, the Lord had said to them, "As truly as I live, as ye have spoken in mine ears, so will I do to you. Your carcasses shall fall in this wilderness . . . Doubtless *ye shall not come into the land* concerning which I sware to make you dwell therein . . . As for you, your carcasses, they shall fall in this wilderness."

Thus much as to chapter 14. But no sooner do we open the section now before us, than, just as though nothing had happened, and though all were as calm, as bright, and as certain as God could make it, we read such words as these, "The Lord spake unto Moses, saying, Speak unto the children of Israel, and say unto them, *when ye be come into the land of your habitations, which I give unto you*," &c. This is one of the most remarkable passages in the entire of this most wonderful book. Indeed there is not, in the whole compass of the book, a passage more thoroughly characteristic, not only of Numbers, but of the entire volume of God. When we read the solemn sentence, "Ye shall not come into the land," what is the plain lesson which it reads out to us? The lesson, which we are so slow to learn, of man's utter worthlessness. "All flesh is grass."

And, on the other hand, when we read such words as these, "When ye be come into the land of your habitations, which I give unto you," what is the precious lesson which they read out to us? This, assuredly, that salvation is of the Lord. In the one, we learn man's failure; in the other, God's faithfulness. If we look at man's side of the question, the sentence is, "Doubtless *ye shall not* come into the land." But if we look at God's side of the question, we can reverse the matter, and say, "Doubtless *ye shall.*"

Thus it stands in the scene now before us; and thus it stands in the whole volume of inspiration, from beginning to end. Man fails; but God is faithful. Man forfeits everything; but God makes good all. "The things which are impossible with man are possible with God." Need we travel through the inspired canon in order to illustrate and prove this? Need we refer the reader to the history of Adam, in paradise? or the history of Noah, after the flood? or the history of Israel, in the wilderness? Israel, in the land? Israel, under the law? Israel, under the Levitical ceremonial? Shall we dwell upon the record of man's failure in the prophetic, priestly, and kingly office? Shall we point out the failure of the professing church as a responsible vessel on the earth? Has not man failed always and in everything? Alas! it is so.

This is one side of the picture – the dark and humbling side. But, blessed be God, there is the bright and encouraging side also. If there is the "Doubtless ye shall not;" there is also the "Doubtless ye shall." And why? Because Christ has entered the scene, and in Him all is infallibly secured for the glory of God and the eternal blessing of man. It is God's eternal purpose to "head up all things in Christ." There is not a single thing in which the first man has failed, that the second Man will not make good. All is set up on a new footing in Christ. He is the Head of the new creation; Heir of all the promises made to Abraham, Isaac, and Jacob, touching the land; Heir of all the promises made to David concerning the throne. The government shall be upon His shoulders. He shall bear the glory. He is the Prophet, Priest, and King. In a word, Christ makes good all that Adam lost, and brings in much more beside than Adam ever had. Hence, when we look at the first

Adam and his doings, whenever and however viewed, the sentence is "Doubtless *ye shall not.*" Ye shall not remain in Paradise – ye shall not retain the government – ye shall not inherit the promises – ye shall not enter the land – ye shall not occupy the throne – ye shall not enter the kingdom.

But, on the other hand, when we look at the last Adam and His doings, wherever and however viewed, the entire category must be gloriously reversed; the "not" must be for ever elided from the sentence, for in Christ Jesus "all the promises of God are yea and Amen, to the glory of God by us." There is no "nay" in the matter when Christ is concerned. All is "yea" – all is divinely settled and established; and because it is so, God has set His seal to it, even the seal of His Spirit, which all believers now possess. "For the Son of God, Jesus Christ, who was preached among you by us, even by me and Silvanus and Timotheus, was not yea and nay, but in him was yea. For all the promises of God in him are yea, and in him Amen, unto the glory of God by us. Now He which stablisheth us with you in Christ, and hath anointed us, is God; who hath also sealed us, and given the earnest of the Spirit in our hearts." 2 Cor. 1:19-22.

Thus, then, the opening lines of Numbers 15 must be read in the light of the whole volume of God. It falls in with the entire history of the ways of God with man, in this world. Israel had forfeited all title to the land. They deserved nothing better than that their carcasses should fall in the wilderness. And yet such is the large and precious grace of God, that He could speak to them of their coming into the land, and instruct them as to their ways and works therein.

Nothing can be more blessed or more establishing than all this. God rises above all human failure and sin. It is utterly impossible that a single promise of God can fail of its accomplishment. Could it be that the conduct of Abraham's seed in the wilderness should frustrate God's eternal purpose, or hinder the fulfilment of the absolute and unconditional promise made to the fathers? Impossible; and, therefore, if the generation which came up out of Egypt refused to go into

Canaan, Jehovah would, of the very stones, raise up a seed to whom His promise should be made good. This will help to explain the opening sentence of our chapter, which comes in with such remarkable force and beauty after the humiliating scenes of chapter 14. In this latter, Israel's sun seems to go down amid dark and angry clouds; but in the former, it rises with serene brightness, revealing and establishing that great truth that "The gifts and calling of God are without repentance." God never repents of His call or His gift; and hence, though an unbelieving generation should murmur and rebel ten thousand times over, He will make good all that He has promised.

Here is the divine resting place of faith at all times – the sure and safe haven for the soul amid the wreck of all human schemes and undertakings. Everything goes to pieces in man's hands; but God in Christ remains. Let man be set up in business again and again, under the most favourable circumstances, and he is sure to become a bankrupt; but God has set up Christ in resurrection, and all who believe in Him are placed on a new footing altogether, they are taken into partnership with the risen and glorified Head, and there they stand for ever. That wondrous partnership can never be dissolved. All is secured on a basis that no power of earth or hell can ever touch.

Reader, say, Dost thou understand the application of all this to thyself? Hast thou discovered, in the light of God's presence, that thou art, in very deed, a bankrupt; that thou hast made shipwreck of everything; that thou hast not a single plea to urge? Hast thou been led to make a personal application of those two sentences upon which we have been dwelling, namely, "Doubtless thou shalt not," and "Doubtless thou shalt"? Hast thou learnt the force of these words, "Thou hast destroyed thyself; but in me is thy help"? In one word, hast thou come to Jesus as a lost, guilty, self-destroyed sinner, and found redemption, pardon, and peace in Him?

Do pause, dear friend, and seriously consider these things. We can never lose sight of the weighty fact that we have something more to do than to write "Notes on the Book of Numbers." We have to consider the soul of the reader. We have a most solemn responsibility to discharge to him or to her; and therefore it is that, from time to time, we feel constrained to turn, for a moment, from the page on which we are meditating, in order to make an appeal to the heart and conscience of the reader, and entreat him, most earnestly, that if he be as yet unconverted, undecided, he would lay aside this volume, and apply his heart seriously to the great question of his present condition and eternal destiny. In comparison with this, all other questions dwindle into utter insignificance. What are all the schemes and undertakings which begin, continue, and end in time, when compared with eternity and the salvation of your never-dying soul? They are as the small dust of the balance. "What shall it profit a man if he shall gain the whole world and lose his own soul?" If you had the wealth of a Rothschild, the money king – if you stood on the loftiest pinnacle of literary fame or political ambition – if your name were adorned with all the honours which the universities of this world could bestow – if your brow were wreathed with the laurels and your breast covered with the medals of a hundred victories – what would it profit you? You must leave all – you must pass through the narrow arch of time into the boundless ocean of eternity. Men of princely wealth, men of literary fame, men who have ruled by their intellectual power the House of Lords and Commons – men who have held thousands hanging entranced upon their lips – men who have reached the very highest point of naval, military, and forensic distinction – have passed away into eternity; and the awful question as to such is, "Where is the soul?"

Beloved reader, we beseech thee, by the most weighty arguments that can possibly be urged upon the soul of man, not to turn away from this subject until thou hast come to a right conclusion. By God's great love – by the cross and passion of Christ – by the powerful testimony of God the Holy Ghost – by the awful solemnity of a never-ending eternity

– by the unspeakable value of thy immortal soul – by all the joys of heaven – by all the horrors of hell – by these seven weighty arguments, we urge thee, this moment, to come to Jesus. Delay not! Argue not! Reason not! But come now, just as you are, with all your sins, with all your misery, with your misspent life, with your dreadful record of mercies slighted, advantages abused, opportunities neglected – come to Jesus who stands, with open arms and loving heart, ready to receive you, and points to those wounds which attest the reality of His atoning death upon the cross, and tells you to put your trust in Him, and assures you you will never be confounded. May God's Spirit carry home this appeal to thy heart, this moment, and give thee no rest until thou art savingly converted to Christ, reconciled to God, and sealed with the Holy Spirit of promise!

A picture of Israel restored

We shall now return, for a moment, to our chapter.

Nothing can be more lovely than the picture here presented. We have vows and freewill offerings, sacrifices of righteousness, and the wine of the Kingdom, all based upon the sovereign grace which shines in the very first verse. It is a fair sample, a beauteous foreshadowing of the future condition of Israel. It reminds us of the marvellous visions which close the book of the prophet Ezekiel. The unbelief, the murmuring, the rebellion, are all over and all forgotten. God retires into His own eternal counsels, and from thence looks forward to the time when His people shall offer an offering in righteousness and pay their vows to Him, and the joy of His kingdom shall fill their hearts for ever. Verses 3-13.

But there is one very striking feature in this chapter, and that is the place which "the stranger" gets. It is most thoroughly characteristic. "And if a stranger sojourn with you, or whosoever be among you in your generations, and will offer an offering made by fire, of a sweet savour unto the Lord; as ye do, so he shall do. One ordinance shall be both for you of the congregation, and also for the stranger that sojourneth with you, *an ordinance for ever* in your generations: *as ye are, so shall the stranger be before the Lord.* One law and one manner shall be for you, and for the stranger that sojourneth with you."

What a place for the stranger! What a lesson for Israel! What a standing testimony on the page of their favourite and boasted Moses! The stranger is placed on the very same platform with Israel! "*As* ye are, *so* shall the stranger be," and this, too, "before the Lord." In Exodus 12:48 we read, "And when a stranger shall sojourn with thee, and will keep the passover to the Lord, let all his males be circumcised, and then let him come near and keep it." But in Numbers 15 there is no allusion to circumcision at all. And why? Is it that such a point could ever be waived? No; but we believe the omission here is full of meaning. Israel had forfeited everything. The rebellious generation was to be set aside and cut off; but God's eternal purpose of grace must stand, and all His promises be fulfilled. All Israel shall be saved; they shall possess the land; they shall offer pure offerings, pay their vows, and taste the joy of the kingdom. On what ground? On the ground of sovereign mercy. Well, it is on the selfsame ground that "the stranger" shall be brought in; and not only brought in, but "*As* ye are, *so* shall the stranger be before the Lord."

Will the Jew quarrel with this? Let him go and study Numbers 13 and 14. And when he has drunk into his inmost soul the wholesome lesson, then let him meditate on Numbers 15; and we feel assured he will not seek to push "the stranger" off the platform, for he will be ready to confess himself a debtor to mercy alone, and to acknowledge that the same mercy which has reached him can reach the stranger, and he will rejoice to go in company with that stranger to drink of the wells of salvation thrown open by the sovereign grace of the God of Jacob.

Are we not forcibly reminded, by the teaching of this part of our book, of that profound section of dispensational truth presented in Romans 9-11, particularly of its magnificent close? "The gifts and calling of God are without repentance. For as ye [strangers] in times past have not believed God, yet have now obtained mercy through their unbelief: even so have these also now not believed in your mercy [i.e., mercy shown to the Gentiles, see Greek], that they also may obtain mercy [i.e., come in on the ground of mercy like the stranger]. For God hath concluded them all in unbelief, that he might have mercy upon all [Jews and Gentiles – Israel and the stranger]. O the depth of the riches both of the wisdom and knowledge of God! how unsearchable are his judgments, and his ways past finding out! For who hath known the mind of the Lord? or who hath been his counsellor? Or who hath first given to him, and it shall be recompensed unto him again? For of him, and through him, and to him, are all things: to whom be glory for ever. Amen." Romans 11:29-36.

Sins of ignorance and presumptuous sins

From verse 22-31 of our chapter, we have instructions as to sins of ignorance and presumptuous sins – a very grave and important distinction. For the former, ample provision is made, in the goodness and mercy of God. The *death* of Christ is presented, in this portion of the chapter, in its two grand aspects, namely, the burnt offering, and the sin offering; that is, its aspect to Godward, and its aspect to usward; and we have also all the preciousness, fragrance, and joy of His perfect *life* and service, as a man in this world, as typified by the meat offering and drink offering. In the burnt offering, we see atonement wrought according to the measure of Christ's devotedness to God, and of God's delight in Him. In the sin offering, we see atonement wrought according to the measure of the sinner's necessities and the hatefulness of sin in God's sight. The two offerings, taken together, present the atoning death of Christ in all its fullness. Then, in the meat offering, we have Christ's perfect life and the reality of His human nature, as manifested in all the details of His path and service in this world. While the drink offering typifies

His complete surrender of Himself to God.

Into the rich and marvellous instruction conveyed in the different classes of sacrifices, presented in this passage, we do not attempt to enter now. The reader who desires to study the subject more fully, is referred to a little volume entitled "Notes on the Book of Leviticus" (pages 17–129). We merely state here, in the very briefest manner, what we judge to be the main import of each offering; to go into details would only be to repeat what we have already written.

We would merely add that the claims of God demand that sins of ignorance should be taken cognizance of. We might feel disposed to say, or at least to think, that such sins ought to be passed over. But God does not think so. His holiness must not be reduced to the standard of our intelligence. *Grace* has made provision for sins of ignorance; but *holiness* demands that such sins should be judged and confessed. Every true heart will bless God for this. For what would become of us if the provisions of divine grace were not adequate to meet the claims of divine holiness? And adequate they most surely could not be, if they travelled not beyond the range of our intelligence.

And yet, while all this will, generally speaking, be fully admitted, it is often very sorrowful to hear professing Christians making excuses for ignorance, and justifying unfaithfulness and error on the ground of ignorance. But very often, in such cases, the question may, very cogently, be urged, why are we ignorant, in reference to any point of conduct, or the claims of Christ upon us? Suppose a question comes before us, demanding a positive judgment, and calling for a certain line of action; we plead ignorance. Is this right? Will it avail? Will it dispose of our responsibility! Will God allow us to shirk the question after such a fashion? Nay, reader, we may rest assured it will not do. Why are we ignorant? Have we put forth all our energies, have we adopted every available means, have we made every possible effort, to get at the root of the matter and reach a just conclusion? Let us bear in mind that the claims of truth and holiness demand all this of us;

nor should we be satisfied with anything less. We cannot but admit that, were it a question involving, in any measure, *our own* interests, *our* name, *our* reputation, *our* property, we should leave no stone unturned in order to make ourselves fully acquainted with all the facts of the case. We should not long plead ignorance in such matters. If information were to be had, we should have it. We should do our very utmost to know all the ins and outs, the *pros* and *cons* of the question, so that we might form a sound judgment in the matter.

Is this not so, reader? Well, then, why should we plead ignorance when the claims of Christ are in question? Does it not prove that while we are quick, earnest, energetic, all alive, when *self* is concerned, we are indifferent, sluggish, slow-paced, when Christ is concerned? Alas! alas! this is the plain humbling truth. May we be humbled under a sense of it! May the Spirit of God make us more thoroughly in earnest in things which concern our Lord Jesus Christ. May self and its interests sink, and may Christ and His interests rise in our estimation, every day! And may we at least cordially own our holy responsibility to go diligently into every question in the which the glory of our Lord and Saviour Jesus Christ may, even in the most remote degree, be involved, however we may fail practically in our research. Let us not dare to say, or think, or act, as though we thought that anything that concerns Him is a matter of indifference to us. God, in His mercy, forbid! Let us esteem all that merely concerns ourselves to be, comparatively, non-essential; but the claims of Christ to be of paramount authority.

We have said thus much on the subject of ignorance, in the sense of our responsibility, to the truth of God, and to the soul of the reader. We feel its immense practical importance. We believe we very often plead *ignorance*, when *indifference* would be the truer term to use. This is very sad. Surely if our God, in His infinite goodness, has made ample provision even for sins of ignorance, that is no reason why we should coolly shelter ourselves behind the plea of ignorance when there is the most abundant information within our reach, had we only the energy to make use of it.

We might not, perhaps, have dwelt at such length upon this point, were it not for the conviction which becomes, each day, more strengthened in the soul, that we have reached a serious moment in our history as Christians. We are not given to croaking. We have no sympathy whatever with it. We believe it is our privilege to be filled with the most joyful confidence, and to have our hearts and minds ever garrisoned by the peace of God that passeth all understanding. "God hath not given us the spirit of fear; but of power, and of love, and of a sound mind." 2 Timothy 1:7.

But it is impossible to close our eyes to the startling fact that the claims of Christ – the value of truth – the authority of holy scripture, are being, more and more, set aside, each day, each week, each year. We believe we are approaching a moment in the which there will be toleration for anything and everything save the truth of God. It behoves us therefore to look well to it, that God's word has its own proper place in the heart; and that the conscience is governed, in all things, by its holy authority. A tender conscience is a most precious treasure to carry about with us, from day to day – a conscience that ever yields a true response to the action of the word of God – that bows down, without a question, to its plain statements. When the conscience is in this fine condition, there is always a regulating power wherewith to act upon one's practical course and character. Conscience may be compared to the regulator of a watch. It may happen that the hands of the watch get astray; but so long as the regulator has power over the spring, there is always the means of correcting the hands. If that power be gone, the entire watch must be taken to pieces. So with the conscience. So long as it continues true to the touch of scripture, as applied by the Holy Ghost, there is always a safe and sure regulating power; but if it becomes sluggish, hardened, or perverted, if it refuses to yield a true response to "Thus saith the Lord," there is little if any hope. It then becomes a case similar to that referred to in our chapter, "But the soul that doeth anything *presumptuously*, whether he be born in the land, or a stranger, *the same reproacheth the Lord;* and that soul shall be cut off from among his people. *Because he hath despised the word of the Lord,* and hath broken his commandment, that soul shall utterly be cut off; his iniquity shall be upon him." Verses 30, 31.

This is no sin of ignorance, but a presumptuous, wilful sin, for which nothing remained but the unmitigated judgment of God. "Rebellion is as the sin of witchcraft, and stubbornness is as iniquity and idolatry" (1 Sam. 15:23). These are weighty words for a moment like the present, when man's will is developing itself with such extraordinary force. It is deemed manly to assert our will; but scripture teaches the direct opposite. The two grand elements of human perfection – of perfect manhood – are these, namely, *dependence* and *obedience*. In proportion as any one departs from these, he departs from the true spirit and attitude of a man. Hence, when we turn our eyes to Him who was *the* perfect Man – the Man Christ Jesus, we see these two grand features perfectly adjusted and perfectly developed, from first to last. That blessed One was never, for a single moment, out of the attitude of perfect dependence and absolute obedience. To prove and illustrate this fact would take us through the entire gospel narrative. But take the scene of the temptation, and there you will find a sample of the whole of that blessed life. His one unvarying reply to the tempter was, *"It is written."* No reasonings, no arguments, no questions. He lived by the word of God. He conquered Satan by holding fast the *only* true position of a man – dependence and obedience. He *could* depend upon God; and He *would* obey Him. What could Satan do in such a case? Absolutely nothing.

Well, then, this is our example. We, as having the life of Christ, are called to live in habitual dependence and obedience. This is walking in the Spirit. This is the safe and happy path of the Christian. Independence and disobedience go together. They are utterly unchristian and unmanly. We find these two things in the first man, as we find the two opposites in the Second. Adam in the garden sought to be independent. He was not content with being a man, and abiding in the only true place and spirit of a man, and he became disobedient. Here lies the secret of fallen humanity – these are the two elements which make up fallen manhood. Trace it where you will – before the flood, after the flood; without law, under the law; Heathen, Pagan, Jew, Turk, or nominal Christian; analyze it as closely as you please – and you will see that it resolves itself into these two component parts – independence and disobedience. And when you reach the close of man's history in this world, when you view him in that last sad sphere in which he is to figure, how do you see him? in what character does he appear? As "the wilful king," and the "lawless man."

May we have grace to ponder these things aright. Let us cultivate a lowly and an obedient spirit. God has said, "To this man will I look, even to him who is of a contrite spirit and trembleth at my word." May these words sink down into our ears and into our hearts; and let the constant breathing of our souls be, "Keep back thy servant, O Lord, from presumptuous sins, and let them not have dominion over him."[11]

Profaning the Sabbath

It only remains for us, ere closing this section, to notice the case of the Sabbath-breaker and the institution of "the riband of blue."

"And while the children of Israel were in the wilderness, they found a man that gathered sticks upon the sabbath day. And they that found him gathering sticks brought him to Moses and Aaron, and to all the congregation. And they put him in ward, because it was not declared what should be done to him. And the Lord said unto Moses, The man shall be surely put to death: all the congregation shall stone him with stones without the camp. And all the congregation brought him without the camp, and stoned him with stones, and he died; as the Lord commanded Moses." Verses 32-36.

This surely was a presumptuous sin – it was flying in the face of a most plain and positive commandment of God. It is this that specially marks a presumptuous sin, and leaves it utterly inexcusable. Ignorance cannot be pleaded in the face of a divine command.

But why, it may be asked, had they to put the man in ward? Because, although the commandment was explicit, yet the breach of it had not been anticipated, nor had any penalty been enacted. To speak after the manner of men, Jehovah had not contemplated such folly on man's part, as the interruption of His rest, and therefore He had not formally provided for such an occurrence. We need not say that God knows the end from the beginning; but in the matter now before us, He purposely left the case unnoticed until occasion required. But alas! occasion did require, for man is capable of anything. He has no heart for God's rest. To kindle a fire on the Sabbath day was not only a positive breach of the law, but it evidenced the most complete alienation from the mind of the Lawgiver, inasmuch as it introduced into the day of *rest* that which is the apt symbol of *judgment*. Fire is emblematic of judgment, and as such it was wholly out of keeping with the repose of the Sabbath. Nothing therefore remained but to visit the Sabbath-breaker with judgment, for "whatsoever a man soweth, that shall he also reap."

A fringe and a riband of blue

"And the Lord spake unto Moses, saying, Speak unto the children of Israel, and bid them that they make them fringes in the borders of their garments, throughout their generations, and that they put upon the fringe of the borders a ribband of blue. And it shall be unto you for a fringe, that ye may look upon it, and remember all the commandments of the Lord, and do them; and that ye seek not after your own heart, and your own eyes . . . that ye may remember, and do all my commandments, and be holy unto your God. I am the Lord your God, which brought you out of the land of Egypt, to be your God: I am the Lord your God." Verses 37-41.

The God of Israel would keep His people in continual

remembrance of His holy commandments. Hence the beautiful institution of "the ribband of *blue*" which was designed to be a *heavenly* memorial attached to the very borders of their garments, so that the word of God might ever be held fast in the remembrance of the thoughts of their hearts. Whenever an Israelite cast his eyes upon the blue ribband, he was to think of Jehovah, and yield a hearty obedience to all His statutes.

Such was the great practical intention of "the ribband of blue." But when we turn to Matthew 23:5, we learn the sad use which man had made of the divine institution: "But all their works they do for to be seen of men: they make broad their phylacteries, and *enlarge the borders of their garments.*" Thus the very thing which had been instituted for the purpose of leading them to remember Jehovah, and to yield a lowly obedience to His precious word, was turned into an occasion of self-exaltation and religious pride. Instead of thinking of God, and His word, they thought of themselves, and of the place which they held in the estimation of their fellows. *"All their works they do to be seen of men."* Not a thought of God. The spirit of the original institution was completely lost, while the outward form was kept up for selfish ends. Can we not see something like this around us and among us? Let us think of it – think deeply and seriously. Let us see to it that we do not turn the heavenly memorial into an earthly badge, and that which ought to lead to lowly obedience into an occasion of self-exaltation.

---

[11] We would remind the young Christian reader, especially, that the true safeguard against sins of ignorance is the study of the word; and the true safeguard against presumptuous sins, is subjection to the word. We all need to bear these things in mind; but our younger brethren particularly. There is a strong tendency amongst young Christians to get into the current of this present age, and to drink in its spirit. Hence the independence, the strong will, the impatience of control, the disobedience to parents, the headiness, high-mindedness, and self-confidence, the pretentious style, the assumption, the setting up to be wiser than their elders – all these things so hateful in the sight of God, and so entirely opposed to the spirit of Christianity. We would most earnestly and lovingly entreat all our young friends to guard against these things, and to cultivate a lowly mind. Let them remember that "God resisteth the proud, but giveth grace to the lowly."

Chapter 16

THE REBELLION OF KORAH, DATHAN AND ABIRAM

Jealousy

The chapter on which we have just been dwelling, is what may be called a digression from the history of Israel's wilderness life, except indeed the short paragraph respecting the Sabbath-breaker, It looks forward into the future, when, spite of all their sin and folly, their murmuring and rebellion, Israel shall possess the land of Canaan, and offer sacrifices of righteousness and songs of praise to the God of their salvation. In it we have seen Jehovah rising far above all the unbelief and disobedience, the pride and wilfulness exhibited in chapters 13 and 14, and looking on to the full and final accomplishment of His own eternal purpose, and the fulfilment of His promise to Abraham, Isaac, and Jacob.

But in chapter 16 the wilderness story is resumed – that sad and humbling story, so far as man is concerned; but a bright and blessed story of the exhaustless patience and boundless grace of God. These are the two grand lessons of the wilderness. We learn what man is, and we learn what God is. The two things lie side by side on the pages of the Book of Numbers. Thus in chapter 14 we have man and his ways. In chapter 15 we have God and His ways. And now, in the chapter which opens before us, we come back to man and his ways again. May we reap much deep and solid instruction from the double lesson!

"Now Korah, the son of Izhar, the son of Kohath, the son of Levi, and Dathan and Abiram, the sons of Eliab, and On, the son of Peleth, sons of Reuben, took men: and they rose up before Moses, with certain of the children of Israel, two hundred and fifty princes of the assembly, famous in the congregation, men of renown: and they gathered themselves together against Moses and against Aaron, and said unto them, Ye take too much upon you, seeing all the congregation are holy, every one of them, and the Lord is among them: wherefore then lift ye up yourselves above the congregation of the Lord?" Verses 1-3.

Here then we enter upon the solemn history of what the Holy Ghost, by the Apostle Jude, terms "The gainsaying of Core." The rebellion is attributed to Korah, inasmuch as he was the religious leader in it. He seems to have possessed sufficient influence to gather around him a large number of influential men – "princes, famous men, and men of renown." In short, it was a very formidable and serious rebellion; and we shall do well to look closely at its source and moral features.

It is always a most critical moment in the history of an assembly when a spirit of disaffection displays itself; for, if it be not met in the right way, the most disastrous consequences are sure to follow. There are materials in every assembly capable of being acted upon, and it only needs some restless master spirit to arise, in order to work on such materials, and fan into a devouring flame the fire that has been smouldering in secret. There are hundreds and thousands ready to flock around the standard of revolt, when once it has been raised, who have neither the vigour nor the courage to raise it themselves. It is not every one that Satan will take up as an instrument in such work. It needs a shrewd, clever, energetic man – a man of moral power – one possessing influence over the minds of his fellows, and an iron will to carry forward his schemes. No doubt Satan infuses much of all these into the men whom he uses in his diabolical undertakings. At all events, we know, as a fact, that the great leaders in all rebellious movements are generally men of master minds, capable of swaying, according to their own will, the fickle multitude, which, like the ocean, is acted upon by every stormy mind that blows. Such men know how, in the first place, to stir the passions of the people; and, in the second place, how to wield them, when stirred. Their most potent agency – the lever with which they can most effectually raise the masses – is some question as to their liberty and their rights. If they can only succeed in persuading people that their liberty is curtailed, and their *rights* infringed, they are sure to gather a number of restless spirits around them, and do a vast deal of serious mischief.

Thus it was in the matter of Korah and his coadjutors. They sought to make it appear that Moses and Aaron were lording it over their brethren, and interfering with their rights and privileges as members of a holy congregation, in which, according to their judgment, all were on a dead level, and one had as much right to be active as another.

"Ye take too much upon you." Such was their charge against "the meekest man in all the earth." But what had Moses taken upon him? Surely the most cursory glance back at the history of that dear and honoured servant would have been sufficient to convince any impartial person that, so far from taking dignity and responsibility upon him, he had shown himself only too ready to shrink from them when presented, and sink under them when imposed. Hence, therefore, any one who could think of accusing Moses of taking upon him, only proved himself totally ignorant of the man's real spirit and character. Assuredly the one who could say to Joshua, "Enviest thou for my sake? Would God that all the Lord's people were prophets, and that the Lord would put His spirit upon them!" was not very likely to take much upon him.

But, on the other hand, if God calls one a man into prominence – if he qualifies him for work – if He fills and fits the vessel for special service – if He assigns a man his position – then of what possible use can it be for any one to quarrel with divine gift, and divine appointment? In truth, nothing can be more absurd. "A man can receive nothing except it be given him from heaven." And therefore it must prove worse than useless for any one to assume to be or have anything, for all such assumption must prove hollow in the end. Men will, sooner or later, find their level; and nothing will stand but what is of God.

Korah and his company, therefore, were quarrelling with God and not with Moses and Aaron. These latter had been called of God to occupy a certain position, and to do a certain work, and woe be to them if they refused. It was not they who had aimed at the position or assumed the work; they were ordained of God. This ought to have settled the question; and it would have settled it for all save restless, self-occupied rebels, who sought to undermine the true servants of God in order to exalt themselves. This is always the way with the promoters of sedition or disaffection. Their real object is to make themselves somebody. They talk loudly and very plausibly about the common rights and privileges of God's people; But, in reality, they themselves are aiming at a position for which they are in no way qualified; and at privileges to which they have no right.

In point of fact, the matter is as simple as possible. Has God given a man his place to fill – his work to do? Who will question this? Well, then, let each one know his place and fill it – know his work and do it. It is the most senseless thing in the world for one to attempt to occupy another's post or do another's work. We were led to see this, very distinctly, when meditating on chapters 3 and 4 of this book. It must ever hold good. Korah had his work; Moses had his. Why should one envy another? It would be quite as reasonable to charge the sun, moon, and stars with taking too much upon them, when they shine in their appointed spheres, as to charge any gifted servant of Christ therewith, when he seeks to discharge the responsibility which his gift, most surely, imposes upon him. These luminaries serve in the place assigned them by the hand of the Almighty Creator; and so long as Christ's servants do the same, it is charging them falsely to say that they take too much upon them.

Now this principle is of immense importance, in every assembly, large or small – under all circumstances where

Christians are called to work together. It is a mistake to suppose that all the members of the body of Christ are called to places of prominence; or that any member can select his place in the body. It is wholly and absolutely a matter of divine appointment.

This is the clear teaching of 1 Corinthians 12. "The body is not one member, but many. If the foot shall say, Because I am not the hand, I am not of the body; is it therefore not of the body? And if the ear shall say, Because I am not the eye, I am not of the body; is it therefore not of the body? If the whole body were an eye, where were the hearing? If the whole were hearing, where were the smelling? But now *hath God set the members every one of them in the body as it hath pleased him.*" Verses 14-18.

Here lies the true, the *only* true source of ministry in the Church of God – the body of Christ. "God hath set the members." It is not one man appointing another; still less is it a man appointing himself. It is divine appointment or nothing, yea, worse than nothing, a daring usurpation of divine rights.

Now, looking at the subject in the light of that marvellous illustration of 1 Corinthians 12, what sense would there be in the feet charging the hands, or the ears charging the eyes, with taking too much upon them? Would not the notion be preposterous in the extreme? True, those members occupy a prominent place in the body; but why do they? Because "God has set them there, as it pleased him." And what are they doing in that prominent place? They are doing the work which God has given them to do. And to what end? The good of the whole body. There is not a single member, however obscure, that does not derive positive benefit from the duly discharged functions of the prominent member. And, on the other hand, the prominent member is a debtor to the duly discharged functions of the obscure one. Let the eyes lose their power of vision, and every member will feel it. Let there be functional derangement in the most trivial member, and the most honourable member will suffer.

Hence, therefore, it is not a question of taking upon us much or little, but of doing our appointed work, and filling our appointed place. It is by the effectual working of all the members, according to the measure of every part, that the edification of the whole body is promoted. If this great truth be not seized and carried out, edification, so far from being promoted, is most positively hindered; the Holy Ghost is quenched and grieved; the sovereign rights of Christ are denied; and God is dishonoured. Every Christian is responsible to act on this divine principle, and to testify against everything that practically denies it. The fact of the ruin of the professing Church is no reason whatever for abandoning the truth of God, or sanctioning any denial of it. The Christian is always solemnly bound to submit himself to the revealed mind of God. To plead circumstances as an excuse for doing wrong, or for neglecting any truth of God, is simply flying in the face of divine authority, and making God the Author of our disobedience.

But we cannot pursue this subject further. We have merely referred to it here in connection with our chapter, with which we must now proceed. It is undoubtedly a most solemn page of Israel's wilderness story.

Moses' attitude

Korah and his company were very speedily taught the folly and sin of their rebellious movement. They were awfully wrong in daring to set themselves up against the true servants of the living God. As to Moses, the man against whom they were gathered together, when he heard their seditious words, "he fell upon his face." This was a very good way to meet rebels. We have seen this beloved servant of God on his face when he ought to have been on his feet (Exod. 14). But here it was about the best and safest thing he could do. There is never much use in contending with restless and disaffected people; better far leave them in the Lord's hands; for with Him, in reality, is their controversy. If God sets a man in a certain position, and gives him a certain work to do, and his fellows think proper to quarrel with him, simply on the score of his doing that work, and filling that position, then is their quarrel really with God, who knows how to settle it, and will do it in His own way. The assurance of this gives holy calmness and moral elevation to the Lord's servant, in moments when envious and turbulent spirits rise up against him. It is hardly possible for any one to occupy a prominent place of service, or to be pre-eminently used of God, without, at some time or another, having to encounter the attacks of certain radical and discontented men, who cannot bear to see any one more honoured than themselves. But the true way to meet such is to take the place of utter prostration and nothingness, and allow the tide of disaffection to roll over one.

"And when Moses heard it, he fell upon his face. And he spake unto Korah and all his company, saying, Even to-morrow *the Lord will shew* [not Moses will shew] who are his, and who is holy; and will cause him to come near unto him: even him *whom he hath chosen* will he cause to come near unto him. This do; take you censers, Korah and all his company; and put fire therein, and put incense in them *before the Lord* tomorrow: and it shall be that the man whom *the Lord doth choose,* he shall be holy: ye take too much upon you, ye sons of Levi." Verses 4-7.

This was placing the matter in the proper hands. Moses gives great prominence to the sovereign rights of Jehovah. "The Lord will shew" and "The Lord will choose." There is not a syllable about himself or Aaron. The whole question hinges upon the Lord's choice and the Lord's appointment. The two hundred and fifty rebels are brought face to face with the living God. They are summoned into His presence, with their censers in their hands, in order that the whole matter may be thoroughly gone into, and definitely settled before that grand tribunal from which there can be no appeal. It would, obviously, have been of no possible use for Moses and Aaron to attempt to give judgment, inasmuch as they were defendants in the cause. But Moses was blessedly willing to have all parties summoned into the divine presence, there to have their matters judged and determined.

This was true humility and true wisdom. It is always well, when people are seeking a place, to let them have it, to their hearts content; for most assuredly, the very place after which they have foolishly aspired will be the scene of their signal defeat and deplorable confusion. You may sometimes see men envying others in a certain sphere of service, and longing to occupy that sphere themselves. Let them try it; and they are sure, in the end, to break down and retire covered with shame and confusion of face. The Lord will surely confound all such. There is no use in man trying to do it; and hence it is always best for such as may happen to be the objects of envious attack just to fall on their faces before God, and let Him settle the question with the malcontents. It is most sad when such scenes occur in the history of God's people; but they have occurred; they do occur; and they may occur again and again; and we feel assured that the very best plan is to let men of a restless, ambitions, disaffected spirit run to the full length of their tether, and then they are sure to be pulled up. It is, in point of fact, to leave them in the hands of God, who will most surely deal with them in His own perfect way.

"And Moses said unto *Korah*, hear, I pray you, ye sons of Levi: seemeth it but a small thing unto you, that the God of Israel hath separated you from the congregation of Israel, to bring you near to Himself to do the service of the tabernacle of the Lord, and to stand before the congregation to minister unto them? And he hath brought *thee* near unto him, and all thy brethren the sons of Levi with thee: and *seek ye the priesthood also?* For which cause both thou and all thy company are gathered together against the Lord: and what is Aaron, that ye murmur against Him?" Verses 8-11.

Here we are conducted to the very root of this terrible conspiracy. We see the man who originated it, and the object at which he aimed. Moses addresses Korah, and charges him with aiming at the priesthood. Let the reader carefully note this. It is important that he should have this point clearly before his mind, according to the teaching of scripture. He must see what Korah was – what his work was – and what the object of his restless ambition was. He must see all these things if he would understand the true force and meaning of Jude's expression, "The gainsaying of Core."

What then was Korah? He was a Levite, and, as such, he was entitled to minister and to teach: "They shall teach Jacob thy judgments, and Israel thy law." "The God of Israel hath brought you near to himself, to do the service of the tabernacle of the Lord, and to stand before the congregation to minister unto them." Such was Korah, and such his sphere of work. At what did he aim? *At the priesthood.* "Seek ye the priesthood also?"

Now, to a cursory observer it might not have appeared that Korah was seeking anything for himself. He seemed to be contending for the rights of the whole assembly. But Moses, by the Spirit of God, unmasks the man, and shows that, under the plausible pretext of standing up for the common rights of the congregation, he was audaciously seeking the priesthood for himself. It is well to note this. It will most generally be found that loud talkers about the liberties, rights, and privileges of God's people are, in reality, seeking their own exaltation and advantage. Not content with doing their proper work, they are seeking an improper place. This is not always apparent; but God is sure to make it manifest sooner or later, for "by him actions are weighed." Nothing can be more worthless than seeking a place for oneself. It is sure to end in disappointment and confusion. The grand thing for each one is to be found filling his appointed place and doing his appointed work; and the more humbly, quietly, and unpretendingly, the better.

But Korah had not learnt this simple but wholesome principle. He was not content with his divinely appointed place and service, but aimed at something which did not belong to him at all. He aimed at being a priest. His sin was the sin of rebellion against God's high priest. This was "the gainsaying of Core."

It is important to seize this fact in Korah's history. It is not generally understood; and hence it is that his sin is charged, now-a-days, upon those who seek to exercise any gift which may have been bestowed upon them by the Head of the Church. But a moment's calm reflection upon the subject in the light of scripture would be quite sufficient to show how utterly baseless is such a charge. Take, for example, a man to whom Christ has manifestly given the gift of an evangelist. Are we to suppose him guilty of the sin of Korah because, in pursuance of the divine gift and the divine commission, he goes forth to preach the gospel? Should he preach? or should he not preach? Is the divine gift – the divine call – sufficient? Is he acting as a rebel when he preaches the gospel?

So also as regards a pastor or teacher. Is he guilty of the sin of Korah, because he exercises the special gift imparted to him by the Head of the Church? Does not Christ's gift make a man a minister? Is anything further necessary? Is it not plain to any unprejudiced mind – to any one willing to be taught by scripture – that the possession of a divinely imparted gift makes a man a minister, without anything further whatsoever? And is it not equally plain that, though a man had everything else that could be had, and yet had no gift from the Head of the Church, he is no minister? We confess we do not see how these plain propositions can be called in question.

Ministers and priests

We are speaking, be it remembered, of special gifts of ministry in the Church. No doubt, every member in the body of Christ has some ministry to fulfil, some work to do. This is understood by every well-instructed Christian; and, moreover, it is clear that the edification of the body is carried on, not merely by some special prominent gifts, but by the effectual working of all the members in their respective places, as we read in the Epistle to the Ephesians: "But speaking the truth in love, may grow up into him in all things, which is the head, even Christ: from whom the whole body fitly joined together, and compacted by that which *every joint supplieth* according to *the effectual working in the measure of every part,* maketh increase of the body unto the edifying of itself in love." Chapter 4:15, 16.

All this is as plain as scripture can make it. But, as to any special gifts, such as that of evangelist, pastor, prophet, or teacher, it must be received from Christ alone; and the possession of it makes a man a minister, without anything further. And, on the other hand, all the education and all the human authority under the sun could not make a man an evangelist, a pastor, or teacher, unless he has a *bona fide* gift from the Head of the Church.

Thus much as to ministry in the Church of God. We trust enough has been said to prove to the reader that it is a very grave mistake indeed to charge men with the awful sin of Korah because they exercise those gifts which have been imparted to them by the great Head of the Church. In point of fact it would be a sin not to exercise them.

But there is a very material difference between ministry and priesthood. Korah did not aim at being a minister, for that he was. He aimed at being a priest, which he could not be. The priesthood was vested in Aaron and his family; and it was a daring usurpation for any one else, no matter who, to attempt to offer sacrifice, or discharge any other priestly function. Now, Aaron was a type of our great High Priest who is passed into the heavens – Jesus the Son of God. Heaven is the sphere of His ministry. "If he were on earth he should not be a priest" (Heb. 8:4). "Our Lord sprang out of Juda; of which tribe Moses spake nothing concerning priesthood." There is no such thing as a priest on earth now, save in the sense in which all believers are priests. Thus we read in Peter, "But ye are a chosen generation, a royal priesthood" (1 Peter 2:9). Every Christian is a priest in this sense of the term. The very feeblest saint in the Church of God is as much a priest as Paul was. It is not a question of capacity or spiritual power, but simply of position. All believers are priests, and they are called to offer spiritual sacrifices, according to Hebrews 13:15, 16: "By him therefore let us offer the *sacrifice of praise* to God continually, that is, the fruit of our lips, giving thanks to his name. But to do good, and to communicate, forget not: for with *such sacrifices* God is well pleased."

This is the Christian priesthood. And let the reader note it carefully, that to aim at any other form of priesthood than this – to assume any other priestly function – to set up a certain priestly class – a sacerdotal *caste* – a number of men to act on behalf of their fellows – or discharge priestly service for them before God – this is, in principle, the sin of Korah. We only speak of the principle; not of persons. The germ of the sin is as distinct as possible. By and by there will be the full blown fruit.

The reader cannot possibly be too simple in apprehending this entire subject. It is, we may truly say, of capital importance, at this moment. Let him examine it only in the light of Holy Scripture. Tradition will not do. Ecclesiastical history will not do. It must be God's word alone. In the light of that word let the question be asked and answered, "Who are justly chargeable with the sin of Korah? Is it those who seek to exercise whatever gifts the Head of the Church has bestowed; or those who assume a priestly office and work which only belong to Christ Himself?" This is a very weighty and solemn question. May it be calmly pondered, in the divine presence; and may we seek grace to be faithful to Him who is not only our gracious Saviour but our sovereign Lord!

The judgment of God

The remainder of our chapter presents a most solemn picture of divine judgment executed upon Korah and his company. The Lord very speedily settled the question raised by those rebellious men. The very record of it is appalling beyond expression. What must the fact have been? The earth opened her mouth and swallowed up the three principal movers in the rebellion; and the fire of the Lord went forth and consumed the two hundred and fifty men who undertook to offer incense.

"And Moses said, Hereby ye shall know that the Lord hath sent me to do all these works; for *I have not done them of mine own mind*. If these men die the common death of all men, or if they be visited after the visitation of all men; then the Lord hath not sent me. But if the Lord make a new thing, and the earth open her mouth, and swallow them up, with all that appertain unto them, and they go down quick into the pit; then ye shall understand that these men have provoked the Lord." Verses 28-30.

Moses, in these words, makes it a question simply between Jehovah and the rebels. He can appeal to God, and leave all in His hands. This is the true secret of moral power. A man who has nothing of his own to seek – no aim or object but the divine glory – can confidently wait the issue of things. But in order to do this, the eye must be single, the heart upright, the purpose pure. It will not do to assume or affect anything. If God is going to judge, He most assuredly will expose all assumption and affectation. These things can have no place when the earth is opening her mouth, and the fire of the Lord is devouring all around. It is all very well to swagger, and boast, and speak great swelling words, when all is at rest. But when God enters the scene, in terrible judgment, the aspect of things is speedily changed.

"And it came to pass, as he had made an end of speaking all these words, that the ground clave asunder that was under them; and the earth opened her mouth, and swallowed them up, and their houses, and all the men that appertained unto Korah, and all their goods. They, and all that appertained to them, went down alive into the pit, and the earth closed upon them; and they perished from among the congregation. And all Israel that were round about them fled at the cry of them: for they said, Lest the earth swallow us up also." Verses 31-34.

Truly, "It is a fearful thing to fall into the hands of the living God." "God is greatly to be feared in the assembly of his saints; and to be had in reverence of all them that are round about Him." "Our God is a consuming fire." How much better it would have been for Korah had he rested content with his Levite service which was of the very highest order. His work as a Kohathite was to carry some of the most precious vessels of the sanctuary but he aimed at the priesthood, and fell into the pit.

Nor was this all. Hardly had the ground closed over the rebels, when "there came out a fire from the Lord, and consumed the two hundred and fifty men that offered incense." It was a most terrific scene altogether – a signal and soul-subduing exhibition of divine judgment upon human pride and pretension. It is vain for man to exalt himself against God, for He resisteth the proud, but giveth grace to the humble. What consummate folly for worms of the dust to lift themselves up against the Almighty God! Poor man! He is more silly by far than the moth that rushes against the blaze that consumes it.

Oh! to walk humbly with our God! to be content with His will; to be satisfied to fill a very humble niche, and to do the most unpretending work! This is true dignity, and true happiness. If God gives us a crossing to sweep, let us sweep it, as under His eye, and to His praise. The grand and all-essential point is to be found doing the very work which he gives us to do, and occupying the very post to which He appoints us. Had Korah and his company learnt this, their piercing wail would never have terrified the hearts of their brethren. But, no; they would be something when they were nothing, and hence they went down into the pit. Pride and destruction are inseparably linked together in the moral government of God. This principle always holds good, however the measure may vary. Let us remember it. Let us seek to rise from the study of Numbers 16 with a deepened sense of the value of an humble and contrite spirit. We live at a moment in the which man is pushing himself upward and onward. *"Excelsior"* is a very popular motto just now. Let us look well to our mode of interpreting and applying it. "He that exalteth himself shall be abased." If we are to be governed by the rule of God's kingdom, we shall find that the only way to get up is to go down. The One who now occupies the very highest place in heaven is the One who voluntarily took the very lowest place on earth. See Philippians 2:5-11.

Here is our example, as Christians; and here, too, the divine antidote against the pride and restless ambition of the men of this world. Nothing is more sad than to witness a pushing, bustling, forward, self-confident spirit and style in those who profess to be followers of Him who was meek and lowly in heart. It is such a flagrant contradiction of the spirit and precepts of Christianity, and is a sure accompaniment of an unbroken condition of soul. It is utterly impossible for any one to indulge in a boastful, pretentious, self-confident spirit, if ever he has really measured himself in the presence of God. To be much alone with God is the sovereign remedy for pride and self-complacency. May we know the reality of this in the secret of our own souls! May the good Lord keep us truly humble, in all our ways, simply leaning on Himself, and very very little in our own eyes!

The next day

The closing paragraph of our chapter illustrates, in a most striking manner, the incorrigible evil of the natural heart. One might fondly hope that after the impressive scenes enacted in the presence of the congregation, deep and permanent lessons would be learnt. Having seen the earth open her mouth – having heard the heart-rending cry of the rebels as they descended into the pit – having seen the fire of the Lord coming forth and consuming, as in a moment, two hundred and fifty princes of the congregation – having witnessed such tokens of the divine judgment – such a display of divine power and majesty – one might suppose that the people would henceforth walk softly and humbly; and that the accents of discontent and rebellion would no more be heard in their tents.

Alas! alas! man is not to be so taught. The flesh is utterly incurable. This truth is taught in every section and on every page of the volume of God. It is illustrated in the closing lines of Numbers 16. "But on the morrow." Think of that! It was not in a year, or a month, or even a week after the appalling scenes on which we have been dwelling, "But, on the morrow, *all the congregation* (no longer a few daring spirits merely) murmured against Moses and against Aaron, saying, Ye have killed the people of the Lord. And it came to pass, when the congregation was gathered against Moses and against Aaron, that they looked toward the tabernacle of the congregation: and, behold, the cloud covered it, and the glory of the Lord appeared. And Moses and Aaron came before the tabernacle of the congregation. And the Lord spake unto Moses saying, Get you up from among this congregation, that I may consume them as in a moment." Verses 41-45.

Here is another opportunity for Moses. The whole congregation is again threatened with immediate destruction. All seems hopeless. The divine long-suffering seems at an end, and the sword of judgment is about to fall on the whole assembly. And now it appears that in that very priesthood which the rebels had despised lies the only hope for the people; and that the very men whom they had charged with killing the Lord's people, were God's instruments in saving their lives. "And Moses and Aaron fell upon their faces. And Moses said unto Aaron, Take a censer, and put fire therein from off the altar, and put on incense, and go quickly unto the congregation, and make an atonement for them: for there is wrath gone out from the Lord; the plague is begun. And Aaron took as Moses commanded, and ran into the midst of the congregation; and, behold, the plague had begun among the people: and he put on incense, and made an atonement for the people. and he stood between the dead and the living; and the plague was stayed." Verses 46-48.

It is here made very apparent that nothing but priesthood – even that very priesthood which had been so despised – could avail for a rebellious and stiff-necked people. There is something unspeakably blessed in this closing paragraph. There stands Aaron, God's high priest, between the dead and the living, and from his censer a cloud of incense goes up before God – impressive type of One greater than Aaron, who having made a full and perfect atonement for the sins of His people, is ever before God in all the fragrance of His Person and work. Priesthood alone could bring the people through the wilderness. It was the rich and suited provision of divine grace. The people were indebted to intercession for their preservation from the just consequences of their rebellious murmurings. Had they been dealt with merely on the ground of justice, all that could be said was, "Let me alone that I may consume them in a moment."

This is the language of pure and inflexible justice. Immediate destruction is the work of justice. Full and final preservation is the glorious and vital characteristic work of divine grace – grace reigning through righteousness. Had God dealt in mere justice with the people, His name would not have been declared, inasmuch as there is far more in His name than justice. There is love, mercy, goodness, kindness, long-suffering, deep and unfailing compassion. But none of these things could be seen had the people been consumed in a moment, and hence the name of Jehovah would not have been declared or glorified. "For my name's sake will I defer mine anger, and for my praise will I refrain from thee, that I cut thee not off. . . . For mine own sake, even for mine own sake, will I do it: for how should my name be polluted? and I will not give my glory unto another." Isaiah 48:9, 11.

How well it is for us that God acts towards us, and for us, and in us, for the glory of His own name! How wonderful too that His glory should most fully shine – yea, could only be seen in that vast plan which His own heart has devised, in which He is revealed as "A just God and a Saviour." Precious title for a poor lost sinner! In it is wrapped up all that such an one can possibly need for time and eternity. It meets him in the depth of his need, as a guilty hell-deserving one, bears him along through all the varied exigencies, trials, and sorrows of the wilderness; and, finally, conducts him to that bright and blessed world above, where sin and sorrow can never enter.

Chapters 17 & 18

THE PRIESTHOOD

These two chapters form a distinct section in which we have presented to us the source, the responsibilities, and the privileges of priesthood. Priesthood is a divine institution. "No man taketh this honour unto Himself, but he that is called of God, as was Aaron." This is made manifest, in a most striking manner, in chapter 17.

The rod that budded

"The Lord spake unto Moses, saying, speak unto the children of Israel, and take of every one of them a rod according to the house of their fathers, of all their princes according to the house of their fathers twelve rods: write thou every man's name upon his rod. And thou shalt write Aaron's name upon the rod of Levi: for one rod shall be for the head of the house of their fathers. And thou shalt lay them up in the tabernacle of the congregation before the testimony, where I will meet with you. And it shall come to pass, that the man's rod, whom I shall choose, shall blossom: and I will make to cease from me the murmurings of the children of Israel, whereby they murmur against you. And Moses spake unto the children of Israel, and every one of their princes gave him a rod apiece, for each prince one, according to their father's houses, even twelve rods: and the rod of Aaron was among their rods." Verses 1-6.

What matchless wisdom shines in this arrangement! How completely is the matter taken out of man's hands and placed where alone it ought to be, namely, in the hands of the living God! It was not to be a man appointing himself, or a man appointing his fellow; but God appointing the man of His own selection. In a word, the question was to be definitively settled by God Himself, so that all murmurings might be silenced for ever, and no one be able again to charge God's high priest with taking too much upon him. The human will had nothing whatever to do with this solemn matter. The twelve rods, all in a like condition, were laid up before the Lord; man retired and left God to act. There was no room, no opportunity, because there was no occasion, for human management. In the profound retirement of the sanctuary, far away from all man's thinkings, was the grand question of priesthood settled by divine decision; and, being thus settled, it could never again be raised.

"And Moses laid up the rods before the Lord in the tabernacle of witness. And it came to pass that on the morrow Moses went into the tabernacle of witness; and, behold, the rod of Aaron for the house of Levi was budded, and brought forth buds, and bloomed blossoms, and yielded almonds." Striking and beautiful figure of Him who was "declared to be the Son of God with power by resurrection from the dead!" The twelve rods were all alike lifeless; but God, the living God, entered the scene, and, by that power peculiar to Himself, infused life into Aaron's rod, and brought it forth to view, bearing upon it the fragrant fruits of resurrection.

Who could gainsay this? The rationalist may sneer at it, and raise a thousand questions. Faith gazes on that fruit-bearing rod, and sees in it a lovely figure of the new creation in the which all things are of God. Infidelity may argue on the ground of the apparent impossibility of a dry stick budding, blossoming, and bearing fruit in the course of one night. But to whom does it appear impossible? To the infidel – the rationalist – the sceptic. And why? Because he always shuts out God. Let us remember this. *Infidelity invariably shuts out God.* Its reasonings are carried on and its conclusions reached in midnight darkness. There is not so much as a single ray of true light in the whole of that sphere in which infidelity operates. It excludes the only source of light, and leaves the soul wrapped in the shades and deep gloom of a darkness that may be felt.

It is well for the young reader to pause here, and deeply ponder this solemn fact. Let him calmly and seriously reflect on this special feature of infidelity – rationalism – or scepticism. It begins, continues, and ends with shutting out God. It would approach the mystery of Aaron's budding, blossoming, fruit bearing rod with a godless, audacious "*How*?" This is the infidel's great argument. He can raise ten thousand questions; but never settle one. He will teach you how to doubt, but never how to believe. He will lead you to doubt everything; but gives you nothing to believe.

Such, beloved reader, is infidelity. It is of Satan who ever has been, is, and will be, the great question raiser. Wherever you trace Satan, you will always find him raising questions. He fills the heart with all sorts of "ifs" and "hows," and thus plunges the soul in thick darkness. If he can only succeed in raising a question, he has gained his point. But he is perfectly powerless with a simple soul that just believes that GOD IS, and GOD HAS SPOKEN. Here is faith's noble answer to the infidel's questions – its divine solution of all the infidel's difficulties. Faith always brings in the very One that infidelity always shuts out. It thinks with God; infidelity thinks without Him.

Hence, then, we would say to the Christian reader, and specially to the young Christian, never admit questions when God has spoken. If you do, Satan will have you under his foot in a moment. Your only security against him is found in that one impregnable, immortal sentence, "It is written." It will never do to argue with him on the ground of experience, of feeling, or of observation; it must be absolutely and exclusively on the ground of this – that God is, and that God has spoken. Satan can make no hand of this weighty argument at all. It is invincible. Everything else he can shiver to pieces; but this confounds him and puts him to flight at once.

We see this very strikingly illustrated in the temptation of our Lord. The enemy, according to his usual way, approached the blessed One with *a question* – "*If* thou be the Son of God."

How did the Lord answer Him? Did He say, "I know I am the Son of God – I have had a testimony from the opened heavens, and from the descending and anointing Spirit – I feel, and believe, and realise that I am the Son of God?" No; such was not His mode of answering the tempter. How then? *"It is written."* Such was the thrice repeated answer of the obedient and dependent Man; and such must be the answer of every one who will overcome the tempter.

Thus, in reference to Aaron's budding rod, if any inquire, "How can such a thing be? It is contrary to the laws of nature; and how could God traverse the established principles of natural philosophy?" Faith's reply is sublimely simple. God can do as He pleases. The One who called worlds into existence, could make a rod to bud, blossom, and bear fruit in a moment. Bring God in, and all is simple and plain as possible. Leave God out, and all is plunged in hopeless confusion. The attempt to tie up – we speak with reverence – the Almighty Creator of the vast universe, by certain laws of nature, or certain principles of natural philosophy, is nothing short of impious blasphemy. It is almost worse than denying His existence altogether. It is hard to say which is the worse, the atheist who says there is no God, or the rationalist who maintains that He cannot do as He pleases.

We feel the immense importance of being able to see the real roots of all the plausible theories which are afloat at the present moment. The mind of man is busy forming systems, drawing conclusions, and reasoning in such a manner as virtually to exclude the testimony of holy scripture altogether, and to shut out God from His own creation. Our young people must be solemnly warned as to this. They must be taught the immense difference between the facts of science, and the conclusions of scientific men. A fact is a fact wherever you meet it, whether in geology, astronomy, or any other department of science; but men's reasonings, conclusions, and systems are another thing altogether. Now, scripture will never touch the facts of science; but the reasonings of scientific man are constantly found in collision with scripture. Alas! alas! for such men! And when such is the case we must, with plain decision, denounce such reasonings altogether, and exclaim with the apostle, "Let God be true, and every man a liar."

Gladly would we dwell upon this point though it be a digression, for we deeply feel its seriousness. But we must, for the present, be content with solemnly urging upon the reader the necessity of giving to holy scripture the supreme place in his heart and mind. We must bow down, with absolute submission, to the authority of, not "Thus saith the Church" – "Thus say the fathers" – "Thus say the doctors;" but *"Thus saith the Lord" – "It is written."* This is our *only* security against the rising tide of infidelity which threatens to sweep away the foundations of religious thought and feeling throughout the length and breadth of Christendom. None will escape save those who are taught and governed by the word of the Lord. May God increase the number of such!

A witness to the grace of God

We shall now proceed with our chapter.

"And Moses brought out all the rods from before the Lord unto all the children of Israel: and they looked, and took every man his rod. And the Lord said unto Moses, Bring Aaron's rod again before the testimony, to be kept for a token against the rebels; and thou shalt quite take away their murmurings from me, that they die not. And Moses did so: as the Lord commanded Him, so did he." Verses 9-11.

Thus the question was divinely settled. Priesthood is founded upon that precious grace of God which brings life out of death. This is the source of priesthood. It could be of no possible use for man to take any one of the eleven dead rods and make it the badge of the priestly office. All the human authority under the sun could not infuse life into a dead stick, or make that stick the channel of blessing to souls. And so of all the eleven rods put together; there was not so much as a single bud or blossom throughout the whole. But where there were precious evidences of quickening power – refreshing traces of divine life and blessing – fragrant fruits of efficacious grace – there and there alone was to be found the source of that priestly ministry which could carry not only a needy but murmuring and rebellious people through the wilderness.

And here we may naturally inquire, "What about Moses' rod? Why was it not amongst the twelve?" The reason is blessedly simple. Moses rod was the expression of power and authority. Aaron's rod was the lovely expression of that grace that quickens the dead, and calls those things that be not as though they were. Now, mere power or authority could not conduct the congregation through the wilderness. Power could crush the rebel; authority might strike the sinner; but only mercy and grace could avail for an assembly of needy, helpless, sinful men, women, and children. The grace that could bring almonds out of a dead stick, could bring Israel through the wilderness. It was only in connection with Aaron's budding rod that Jehovah could say, "Thou shalt *quite* take away the murmurings of the children of Israel from me, that they die not." The rod of *authority* could take away *the murmurers*; but the rod of *grace* could take away the *murmurs*.

The reader may refer, with interest and profit, to a passage in the opening of Hebrews 9 in connection with the subject of Aaron's rod. The apostle, in speaking of the ark of the covenant, says, "Wherein was the golden pot that had manna, and Aaron's rod that budded, and the tables of the covenant." This was in the wilderness. The rod and the manna were the provisions of divine grace for Israel's desert wanderings and desert need. But, when we turn to 1 Kings 8:9, we read, "There was nothing in the ark save the two tables of stone, which Moses put there at Horeb, when the Lord made a covenant with the children of Israel, when they came out of the land of Egypt." The wilderness wanderings were over, the glory of Solomon's day was sending forth its beams over the land, and hence the budding rod and the pot of manna are omitted, and nothing remains save that law of God, which was the foundation of His righteous government in the midst of His people.

Now, in this we have an illustration, not only of the divine accuracy of scripture, as a whole, but also of the special character and object of the Book of Numbers. Aaron's rod was in the ark during its wilderness wanderings. Precious fact! Let the reader seek to lay hold of its deep and blessed significance. Let him ponder the difference between the rod of Moses and the rod of Aaron. We have seen the former doing its characteristic work in other days and amid other scenes. We have seen the land of Egypt trembling beneath the heavy strokes of that rod. Plague after plague fell upon that devoted scene, in answer to that outstretched rod. We have seen the waters of the sea divided in answer to that rod. In short, the rod of Moses was a rod of power, a rod of authority. But it could not avail to hush the murmurings of the children of Israel; nor yet to bring the people through the desert. Grace alone could do that; and we have the expression of pure grace – free, sovereign grace – in the budding of Aaron's rod.

Nothing can be more forcible, nothing more lovely. That dry, dead stick was the apt figure of Israel's condition, and indeed of the condition of every one of us by nature. There was no sap, no life, no power. One might well say, "What good can ever come of it?" None whatever, had not grace come in and displayed its quickening power. So was it with Israel, in the wilderness; and so is it with us now. How were they to be led along from day to day? How were they to be sustained in all their weakness and need? How were they to he borne with in all their sin and folly? The answer is found in Aaron's budding rod. If the dry dead stick was the expression of nature's barren and worthless condition; the buds, blossoms, and fruit set forth that living and life-giving grace and power of God on which was based the priestly ministry that alone could bear the congregation through the wilderness. Grace alone could answer the ten thousand necessities of the militant host. Power could not suffice. Authority could not avail. Priesthood alone could supply what was needed; and this priesthood was instituted on the foundation of that efficacious grace which could bring fruit out of a dry rod.

Priesthood and ministry

Thus it was as to priesthood of old; and thus it is as to ministry now. All ministry in the Church of God is the fruit of divine grace – the gift of Christ, the Church's Head. There is no other source of ministry whatsoever. From apostles down to the very lowest gifts, all proceed from Christ. The grand root principle of all ministry is embodied in those words of Paul to the Galatians in which he speaks of himself as "An apostle, not of man, neither by man, but by Jesus Christ, and God the Father, who raised him from the dead." Galatians 1:1.

Here, be it noted, is the sublime source from whence all ministry emanates. It is not of man, or by man, in any shape or form. Man may take up dry sticks and shape and fashion them according to his own will; and he may ordain and appoint, and call them by certain high-sounding, official titles. But of what use is it? They are only dry, dead sticks. We may justly say, "Where is there a single cluster of fruit? Where is there a single blossom? Nay, where is there one solitary bud?" Even one bud will suffice to prove that there is something divine. But in the absence of this there can be no living ministry in the Church of God: it is the gift of Christ and that alone that makes a man a minister. Without this it is an empty assumption for any one to set himself up, or be set up by others to be a minister.

Does the reader thoroughly own this great principle? Is it as clear as a sunbeam to his soul? Has he any difficulty respecting it? If so, we entreat him to seek to divest his mind of all preconceived thoughts, from what source soever derived; let him rise above the hazy mists of traditional religion; let him take the New Testament, and study, as in the immediate presence of God, 1 Corinthians 12 and 14; and also Ephesians 4:7-12. In these passages he will find the whole subject of ministry unfolded; and from them he will learn that all true ministry, whether it be apostles, prophets, teachers, pastors, or evangelists, all is of God – all flows down from Christ the exalted Head of the Church. If a man be not possessed of a *bonâ fide* gift from Christ he is not a minister. Every member of the body has a work to do. The edification of the body is promoted by the proper action of all the members, whether prominent or obscure, "comely" or "uncomely." In short, all ministry is from God, and not from man; it is by God, and not by man. There is no such thing in scripture as a humanly-ordained ministry. All is of God.

We must not confound ministerial gifts with office or local charge. We find the apostles, or their delegates, ordaining elders and appointing deacons; but this was quite a distinct thing from ministerial gifts. Those elders and deacons might possess and exercise some specific gift in the body; the apostle did not ordain them to exercise such gift, but only to fulfil the local charge. The spiritual gift was from the Head of the Church, and was independent of the local charge altogether.

It is most necessary to be clear as to the distinction between gift and local charge. There is the utmost confusion of the two things throughout the entire professing church, and the consequence is that ministry is not understood. The members of the body of Christ do not understand their place or their functions. Human election, or human authority in some shape or another, is deemed essential to the exercise of ministry in the Church. But there is really no such thing in scripture. If there be, nothing is easier than to produce it. We ask the reader to find a single line, from cover to cover of the New Testament in which a human call, human appointment, or human authority, has anything whatsoever to do with the exercise of ministry in its very fullest range. We boldly assert there is no such thing.[12] Ah, no; blessed be God, ministry in His Church is "not of men, neither by man, but by Jesus Christ, and God the Father, who raised Him from the dead." "*God hath set* the members *every one of them* in the body, *as it hath pleased Him.*" (1 Cor. 12:18) "But unto every one of us is given grace according to the measure of the gift of Christ. Wherefore he saith, When he ascended up on high, he led captivity captive, and gave gifts unto men . . . And he gave some, apostles; and some, prophets; and some, evangelists; and some, pastors and teachers; for the perfecting of the saints, for the work of the ministry, for the edifying of the body of Christ: till we all come in the unity of the faith, and of the knowledge of the Son of God, unto a perfect man, unto the measure of the stature of the fulness of Christ." Ephesians 4:7-13.

Here all the grades of ministerial gift are placed on one and the same ground, from apostles down to evangelists and teachers. They are all given by the Head of the Church and, when bestowed, they render the possessors responsible, at once, to the Head in heaven, and to the members on earth. The idea of any possessor of a positive gift from God waiting for human authority, is as great an insult to the Divine Majesty as if Aaron had gone with his blooming rod in his hand, to be ordained to the priesthood by some of his fellows. Aaron knew better. He was called of God, and that was quite enough for him. And so now, all who possess a divine gift are called of God to the ministry, and they need nothing more save to wait on their ministry, and cultivate their gift.

Need we add that it is vain for men to set up to be ministers unless they really do possess the gift? A man may fancy he has a gift, and it may be only a vain conceit of his own mind. It is quite as bad, if not worse, for one man to go to work on the strength of his own foolish imagination, as for another to go on the strength of the unwarrantable authority of his fellows. What we contend for is this – ministry is of God as to its source, power, and responsibility. We do not think that this statement will be called in question by any who are disposed to be taught exclusively by scripture. Every minister, whatever be his gift, should be able, in his measure, to say, "God has put me into the ministry." But for a man to use this language without possessing any gift, is, to say the least of it, worse than worthless. The people of God can easily tell where there is real spiritual gift. Power is sure to be felt. But if men pretend to gift or power without the reality, their folly shall speedily be manifest to all. All pretenders are sure to find their true level, sooner or later.

Thus much as to ministry and priesthood. The source of each is divine. The true foundation of each lies in the budding rod. Let this be ever borne in mind. Aaron could say," God put me into the priesthood;" and if challenged for his proof, he could point to the fruit-bearing rod. Paul could say, "God put me into the ministry;" and when challenged for his proof, could point to the thousands of living seals to his work. Thus it must ever be in principle, whatever be the measure. Ministry must not be merely in word or in tongue; but in deed and in truth. God will not know the speech, but the power.

But, ere we turn from this subject, we deem it most necessary to impress upon the reader the importance of distinguishing between ministry and priesthood. The sin of Korah consisted in this, that, not content with being a minister, he aimed at being a priest; and the sin of Christendom is of the same character. Instead of allowing ministry to rest upon its own proper New Testament basis, to exhibit its proper characteristics, and discharge its proper functions, it is exalted into a priesthood, a sacerdotal caste, the members of which are distinguished from their brethren by their style of dress and certain titles. There is no foundation whatsoever for these things in the New Testament. According to the plain teaching of that blessed book, all believers are priests. Thus, in Peter we read, "But *ye* [not merely the apostles, but all believers] are a chosen generation, a *royal priesthood*" (1 Peter 2:9). So also in Revelation, "Unto him that loved us, and washed us from our sins in his own blood, and hath made us kings and *priests* unto God and his Father" (chap. 1:5, 6). And, in pursuance of the truth set forth in the foregoing passages, we find the Apostle Paul, by the Holy Ghost, exhorting the Hebrew believers to draw nigh, and enter with boldness into the very holiest of all (Heb. 10:19-22). And further on he says, "By him therefore [i.e., Jesus] let us *offer the sacrifice* of praise to God continually, that is, the fruit of our lips, giving thanks to his name. But to do good, and to communicate, forget not: for with *such sacrifices* God is well pleased." Hebrews 13:15,16.

How marvellous it must have appeared to Jewish saints – to those trained amid the institutions of the Mosaic economy, to be exhorted to enter into a place to which the very highest functionary in Israel could only approach once a year, and that but for a moment! And then to be told that they were to offer sacrifice, that they were to discharge the peculiar functions of the priesthood. All this was wonderful. But thus it is, if we are to be taught by scripture, and not by the commandments, the doctrines, and the traditions of men. All Christians are priests. They are not all apostles, prophets, teachers, pastors, or evangelists; but they are all priests. The very feeblest member of the Church was as much a priest as Peter, Paul, James, or John. We speak not of capacity or spiritual power, but of the position which all occupy in virtue of the blood of Christ. There is no such thing in the New Testament as a certain class of men, a certain privileged caste, brought into a higher or nearer position than their brethren. All this is flatly opposed to Christianity – a bold traversing of all the precepts of the word of God, and the special teachings of our blessed Lord and Master.

Let no one suppose that these things are unimportant. Far from it. They affect the very foundations of Christianity. We have only to open our eyes and look around us in order to see the practical results of this confounding of ministry and priesthood. And we may rest assured that the moment is rapidly approaching when these results will all assume a far more awful character, and bring down the very heaviest judgments from the living God. We have not yet seen the full antitype of "the gainsaying of Core;" but it will soon be manifested: and we solemnly warn the Christian reader to take heed how he lends his sanction to the serious error of mixing up two things so entirely distinct as ministry and priesthood. We would exhort him to take this whole subject up in the light of scripture. We want him to submit to the authority of God's word, and to abandon everything that is not founded thereon. It matters not what it is; it may be a time-honoured institution; an expedient arrangement; a decent ceremony supported by tradition, and countenanced by thousands of the very best of men. It matters not. If the thing has no foundation in holy scripture, it is an error, and an evil, and a snare of the devil, to entrap our souls, and lead us away from the simplicity that is in Christ. For example, if we are taught that there is, in the Church of God, a sacerdotal caste, a class of men, more holy, more elevated, nearer to God, than their brethren – than ordinary Christians; what is this but Judaism revived and tacked on to Christian forms? And what must be the effect of this, but to rob the children of God of their proper privileges as such, and to put them at a distance from Him, and place them under bondage?

We shall not pursue this subject any further just now. Enough, we trust, has been suggested to lead the reflecting reader to follow it up for himself. We only add, and that with special emphasis, let him follow it up *only* in that light of scripture. Let him resolve, by the grace of God, to lay aside everything which rests not upon the solid and sacred basis of the written word. Thus, and thus alone, can he be preserved from every form of error, and led to a sound conclusion on this most important and interesting question.

Misplaced fear

The closing lines of chapter 17 furnish a remarkable illustration of how quickly the human mind passes from one extreme to another. "The children of Israel spake unto Moses, saying, Behold, we die, we perish, we all perish. Whosoever cometh anything near unto the tabernacle of the Lord shall die: shall we be consumed with dying?" In the preceding chapter, we see bold presumption in the very presence of the majesty of Jehovah, where there should have been profound humility. Here, in the presence of divine grace and its provisions, we observe legal fear and distrust. Thus it is ever. Mere nature neither understands holiness nor grace. At one moment we hearken to such accents as these, "*All* the congregation are holy;" and the next moment, the word is, "Behold we die, we perish, we all perish." The carnal mind presumes where it ought to retire; it distrusts where it ought to confide.

However, all this becomes the occasion, through the goodness of God, of unfolding to us, in a very full and blessed manner, the holy responsibility as well as the precious privileges of the priesthood. How gracious it is – how like our God, to turn His people's mistakes into an occasion of furnishing deeper instruction as to His ways! It is His prerogative, blessed be His name, to bring good out of evil; to make the eater yield meat, and the strong, sweetness. Thus "the gainsaying of Core" gives occasion for the copious volume of instruction furnished by Aaron's rod; and the closing lines of chapter 17 call forth an elaborate statement of the functions of Aaron's priesthood. To this latter we shall now proceed to direct the reader's attention.

The Levites, servants of Aaron

"And the Lord said unto Aaron, Thou and thy sons, and thy father's house with thee, shall bear the iniquity of the sanctuary; and thou and thy sons with thee shall bear the iniquity of your priesthood. And thy brethren also of the tribe of Levi, the tribe of thy father, bring thou with thee, that they may be joined unto thee, and minister unto thee: but thou and thy sons with thee shall minister before the tabernacle of witness. And they shall keep thy charge, and the charge of all the tabernacle: only they shall not come nigh the vessels of the sanctuary and the altar, that neither they, nor ye also, die. And they shall be joined unto thee, and keep the charge of the tabernacle of the congregation, for all the service of the tabernacle: and a stranger shall not come nigh unto you. And ye shall keep the charge of the sanctuary, and the charge of the altar: *that there be no wrath any more upon the children of Israel.* And I, behold, I have taken your brethren the Levites from among the children of Israel: to you they are given as a gift for the Lord, to do the service of the tabernacle of the congregation. Therefore thou and thy sons with thee shall keep your priest's office for every thing of the altar, and within the vail; and ye shall serve: I have given your priest's office unto you as a service of gift: and the stranger that cometh nigh shall be put to death." Chap. 18:1-7.

Here we have a divine answer to the question raised by the children of Israel, "Shall we be consumed with dying?" "No," says the God of all grace and mercy. And why not? Because "Aaron and his sons with him shall keep the charge of the sanctuary, and the charge of the altar; that there be *no wrath any more* upon the children of Israel." Thus the people are taught that in that very priesthood which had been so despised and spoken against, they were to find their security.

But we have to notice particularly that Aaron's sons, and his father's house are associated with him in his high and holy privileges and responsibilities. The Levites were given as a gift to Aaron, to do the service of the tabernacle of the congregation. They were to serve under Aaron, the head of the priestly house. This teaches us a fine lesson, and one much needed by Christians at the present moment. We all want to bear in mind that service, to be intelligent and acceptable, must be rendered in subjection to priestly authority and guidance. "And thy brethren also of the tribe of Levi, the tribe of thy father, bring thou with thee, that they may be *joined unto thee,* and *minister unto thee."* This stamped its distinct character upon the entire range of Levite service. The whole tribe of workers were associated with and subject to the great high priest. All was under his immediate control and guidance. So must it be now, in reference to all God's workers. All Christian service must be rendered in fellowship with our great High Priest, and in holy subjection to His authority. It is of no value otherwise. There may be a great deal of work done, there may be a great deal of activity; but if Christ be not the immediate object before the heart, if His guidance and authority be not fully owned, the work must go for nothing.

But, on the other hand, the smallest act of service, the meanest work done under the eye of Christ, done with direct reference to Him, has its value in God's estimation, and shall, most assuredly, receive its due reward. This is truly encouraging, and consolatory to the heart of every earnest worker. The Levites had to work under Aaron. Christians have to work under Christ. We are responsible to Him. It is very well and very beautiful to walk in fellowship with our dear fellow-workmen, and to be subject one to another, in the fear of the Lord. Nothing is further from our thoughts than to foster or countenance a spirit of haughty independence, or that temper of soul which would hinder our genial and hearty co-operation with our brethren in every good work. All the Levites were "joined unto Aaron," in their work, and therefore they were joined one to another. Hence, they had to work together. If a Levite had turned his back upon his brethren, he would have turned his back upon Aaron. We may imagine a Levite, taking offence at something or other in the conduct of his fellows, and saying to himself, "I cannot get on with my brethren. I must walk alone. I can serve God, and work under Aaron; but I must keep aloof from my brethren inasmuch as I find it impossible to agree with them as to the mode of working." But we can easily see through the fallacy of all this. For a Levite to adopt such a line of action would have produced nothing but confusion. All were called to work together, how varied soever their work might be.

Workers subject to their head

Still, be it ever borne in mind, their work did vary and, moreover, each was called to work under Aaron. There was individual responsibility with the most harmonious corporate action. We certainly desire, in every possible way, to promote unity in action; but this must never be suffered to trench upon the domain of personal service, or to interfere with the direct reference of the individual workman to his Lord. The Church of God affords a very extensive platform to the Lord's workers. There is ample space thereon for all sorts of labourers. We must not attempt to reduce all to a dead level, or cramp the varied energies of Christ's servants by confining them to certain old ruts of our own formation. This will never do. We must, all of us, diligently seek to combine the most cordial unanimity with the greatest possible variety in action. Both will be healthfully promoted by each and all remembering that we are called to serve together under Christ.

Here lies the grand secret. *Together, under Christ!* May we bear this in mind. It will help us to recognise and appreciate another's line of work though it may differ from our own; and, on the other hand, it will preserve us from an overweening sense of our own department of service, inasmuch as we shall see that we are, one and all, but co-workers in the one wide field; and that the great object before the Master's heart can only be attained by each worker pursuing his own special line, and pursuing it in happy fellowship with all.

There is a pernicious tendency in some minds to depreciate every line of work save their own. This must be carefully guarded against. If all were to pursue the same line, where were that lovely variety which characterises the Lord's work and workmen in the world? Nor is it merely a question of the line of work, but actually of the peculiar style of each workman. You may find two evangelists, each marked by an intense desire for the salvation of souls, each preaching, substantially, the same truth; and yet there may be the greatest possible variety in the mode in which each one seeks to gain the self-same object. We should be prepared for this. Indeed we should fully expect it. And the same holds good in reference to every other branch of Christian service. We should strongly suspect the ground occupied by a Christian assembly if there were not ample space allowed for every branch and style of Christian service – for every line of work capable of being taken up in individual responsibility to the great Head of the priestly house. We ought to do nothing which we cannot do under Christ, and in fellowship with Him. And all that can be done in fellowship with Christ can surely be done in fellowship with those who are walking with Him.

The priestly service

Thus much as to the special manner in which the Levites are introduced in our chapter, in connection with Aaron and his sons. To these latter we shall now turn for a few moments, and meditate on the rich provision made for them, in the goodness of God, as well as the solemn functions devolving upon them, in their priestly place.

"And the Lord spake unto Aaron, Behold, I also have given thee the charge of mine heave-offerings of all the hallowed things of the children of Israel; unto thee have I given them, *by reason of the anointing,* and to thy sons, by an ordinance for ever. This shall be thine of the most holy things, reserved from the fire: every oblation of theirs, every meat-offering of theirs, and every sin-offering of theirs, and every trespass offering of theirs, which they shall render unto me, shall be most holy for thee and for thy sons. In the most holy place shalt thou eat it; *every male* shall eat it: it shall be holy unto thee." Verses 8-10.

Here we have a type of the people of God looked at in another aspect. They are here presented, not as workers, but as worshippers; not as Levites, but as priests. All believers – all Christians – all the children of God, are priests. There is, according to the teaching of the New Testament, no such thing as a priest upon earth, save in the sense in which all believers are priests. A special priestly caste – a certain class of men set apart as priests, is a thing not only unknown in Christianity, but most positively hostile to the spirit and principles thereof. We have already referred to this subject, and quoted the various passages of scripture bearing upon it. We have a great High Priest who has passed into the heavens, for if He were on earth He should not be a priest. (Compare Heb. 4:14 and 8:4.) "Our Lord sprang out of Juda; of which tribe Moses spake nothing concerning priesthood." Hence, therefore, a sacrificing priest on the earth is a direct denial of the truth of scripture, and a complete setting aside of the glorious fact on which Christianity is based, namely, accomplished redemption. If there is any need of a priest now, to offer sacrifice for sins, then, most assuredly, redemption is not an accomplished fact. But scripture, in hundreds of places, declares that it is, and therefore we need no more offering for sin. "But Christ being come an high priest of good things to come, by a greater and more perfect tabernacle, *not made with hands,* that is to say, not of this building; neither by the blood of goats and calves, but by his own blood, he entered in once into the holy place, *having obtained eternal redemption"* (Heb. 9:11, 12). So also, in chapter 10 we read, "By one offering he hath perfected for ever them that are sanctified." And again, "Their sins and iniquities will I remember no more. Now where remission of these is, there is no more offering for sin."

This settles the great question as to priesthood and sacrifice for sin. Christians cannot be too clear or decided in reference to it. It lies at the very foundation of true Christianity, and demands the deep and serious attention of all who desire to walk in the clear light of a full salvation, and to occupy the true Christian position. There is a strong tendency towards Judaism – a vigorous effort to engraft Christian forms upon the old Jewish stem. This is nothing new; but, just now, the enemy seems peculiarly busy. We can perceive a great leaning towards Romanism, throughout the length and breadth of Christendom; and in nothing is the leaning more strikingly apparent than in the institutions of a special priestly order in the Church of God. We believe it to be a thoroughly antichristian institution. It is the denial of the common priesthood of all believers. If a certain set of men are ordained to occupy a place of peculiar nearness and sanctity, then where are the great mass of Christians to stand?

This is the question. It is precisely here that the great importance and gravity of this whole subject are made apparent. Let not the reader suppose that we are contending for some peculiar theory of any particular class or sect of Christians. Nothing is further from our thoughts. It is because we are convinced that the very foundations of the Christian faith are involved in this question of priesthood that we urge its consideration upon all with whom we have to do. We believe it will invariably be found that in proportion as Christians become clear and settled on the divine ground of accomplished redemption, they get further and further away from the Romanism and Judaism of an order of priests in the Church of God. And, on the other hand, where souls are not clear, not settled, not spiritual; where there is legality, carnality and worldliness, there you will find a hankering after a humanly appointed priesthood. Nor is it difficult to see the reason of this. If a man is not himself in a fit state to draw nigh to God, it will be a relief to him to employ another to draw nigh for him. And, most certainly, no man is in a fit state to draw nigh to a holy God who does not know that his sins are forgiven – has not got a perfectly purged conscience – is in a dark, doubting, legal state of soul. In order to come boldly into the holiest of all, we must know what the blood of Christ has done for us; we must know that we ourselves are made priests to God; and that, in virtue of the atoning death of Christ, we are brought so near to God that it is impossible for any order of men to come between. "He hath loved us, and washed us from our sins in his own blood, and made us priests unto God and his Father" (Rev. 1). "But ye are a chosen generation, *a royal priesthood,* an holy nation, a peculiar people; that ye should show forth the praises of him who hath called you out of darkness into his marvellous light." And again, "Ye also, as lively stones, are built up a spiritual house, *an holy priesthood,* to offer up *spiritual sacrifices,* acceptable to God by Jesus Christ" (1 Peter 2:5, 9). "By him therefore let us offer the *sacrifice of praise* to God continually, that is, the fruit of our lips, giving thanks to his name. But to do good and to communicate, forget not: for with such sacrifices God is well pleased." Hebrews 13:15, 16.

 Here we have the two great branches of spiritual sacrifice which, as priests, we are privileged to offer, namely, praise to God, doing good to men. The very youngest, the most inexperienced, the most unlettered Christian is capable of understanding these things. Who is there in all the family of God – in all the priestly household of our divine High Priest, who cannot, with his *heart*, say, "The Lord be praised"? And who cannot, with his *hand*, do good to his fellow? And this is priestly worship, and priestly service – the common worship and service of all true Christians. True, the measure of spiritual power may vary; but all the children of God are constituted priests, one as much as another.

Now in Numbers 18 we are presented with a very full statement of the provision made for Aaron and his house; and, in that provision, a type of the spiritual portion of the Christian priesthood. And surely we cannot read the record without seeing what a royal portion is ours. "Every oblation of theirs, every meat offering of theirs, and every sin offering of theirs, and every trespass offering of theirs, which they shall render unto me, shall be most holy for thee and for *thy sons. In the most holy place* shalt thou eat it; *every male* shall eat it: it shall be holy unto thee."

Eating the sin offering

It demands a very large measure of spiritual capacity to enter into the depth and meaning of this marvellous passage. To eat the sin offering, or the trespass offering is, in figure, to make another's sin or trespass one's own. This is very holy work. It is not every one who can, in spirit, identify himself with the sin of his brother. To do so in fact, in the way of atonement, is, we need hardly say, wholly out of question. There was but one who could do this; and He – adored for ever be His name! – has done it perfectly.

But there is such a thing as making my brother's sin my own, and bearing it in spirit before God, as though it were my own. This is shadowed forth by Aaron's sons eating the sin offering, in the most holy place. It was only the *sons* who did so. "Every *male* shall eat it."[13] It was the very highest order of priestly service. "In the most holy place shalt thou eat it." We need to be very near to Christ in order to enter into the spiritual meaning and application of all this. It is a wonderfully blessed and holy exercise; and it can only be known in the immediate presence of God. How little we really know of this the heart can testify. Our tendency is, when a brother has sinned, to sit in judgment upon him; to take the place of a severe censor, to look upon his sin as a something with which we have nothing whatever to do. This is to fail sadly in our priestly functions. It is refusing to eat the sin offering in the most holy place. It is a most precious fruit of grace to be able so to identify oneself with an erring brother as to make his sin one's own – to bear it in spirit before God. This truly is a very high order of priestly service, and demands a large measure of the spirit and mind of Christ. It is only the spiritual who really enter into this; and alas! how few of us are truly spiritual! "Brethren, if a man be overtaken in a fault, *ye which are spiritual* restore such an one in the spirit of meekness; considering thyself, lest thou also be tempted. Bear ye one another's burdens, and so fulfil the law of Christ" (Gal. 6:1, 2). May the Lord give us grace to fulfil this blessed "law!" How unlike it is to everything in us! How it rebukes our harshness and selfishness! Oh! to be more like Christ in this as in all beside!

The heave offerings

But there was another order of priestly privilege, not so high as that which we have been considering. "And this is thine: the heave offering of their *gift,* with all the wave offerings of the children of Israel: I have given them unto thee, and to thy sons, and to thy *daughters* with thee, by a statute for ever: *every one that is clean* in thy house shall eat of it." Verse 11.

The daughters of Aaron were not to eat of the sin offerings or the trespass offerings. They were provided for according to the utmost limit of their capacity; but there were certain functions which they could not discharge – certain privileges which lay beyond their range – certain responsibilities too weighty for them to sustain. It is far easier to have fellowship with another in the presentation of a thank offering than it is to make his sin our own. This matter demands a measure of priestly energy which finds its type in Aaron's "sons," not in his "daughters." We must be prepared for those varied measures amongst the members of the priestly household. We are all, blessed be God, on the same ground; we all stand in the same title; we are all in the same relationship; but our capacities vary; and while we should all aim at the very highest standard of priestly service, and the very highest measure of priestly capacity, it is of no possible use to pretend to what we do not possess.

One thing, however, is clearly taught in verse 11 and that is, we must be "*clean*" in order to enjoy any priestly privilege, or eat of any priestly food – clean, through the precious blood of Christ applied to our conscience – clean, through the application of the word, by the Spirit, to our habits, associations, and ways. When thus clean, whatever be our capacity, we have the richest provision made for our souls, through the precious grace of God. Hearken to the following words: "*All the best* of the oil, and *all the best* of the wine, and of the wheat, the firstfruits of them which they shall offer unto the Lord, them have I given thee. And whatsoever is *first ripe* in the land, which they shall bring unto the Lord, shall be thine; *every one who is clean* in thy house shall eat of it." Verses 12, 13.[14]

Here, assuredly, we have a princely portion provided for those who are made priests unto God. They were to have the very best, and the very first of everything which the Lord's land produced. There was "The wine which maketh glad the heart of man, and oil to make his face to shine, and bread which strengtheneth man's heart." Psalm 104:15.

What a figure have we, in all this, of our portion in Christ! The olive, the grape, and the finest of the wheat were pressed and bruised, in order to feed and gladden the priests of God; and the blessed Antitype of all these has, in infinite grace, been bruised and crushed in death, in order that by His flesh and blood, He might minister life, strength, and gladness to

His household. He, the precious corn of wheat, fell into the ground and died, that we might live; and the juices of the living vine were pressed to fill that cup of salvation of which we drink, now, and shall drink for ever, in the presence of our God.

What, therefore, remains? What do we want, save an enlarged capacity to enjoy the fullness and blessedness of our portion in a crucified, risen, and glorified Saviour? We may well say, "We have all and abound." God has given us all that even He could give – the very best He had. He has given us His own portion. He has called us to sit down with Himself, in holy, happy fellowship, and feast upon the fatted calf. He has caused our ears to hear, and our hearts, in some small degree, to enter into these most marvellous words, "Let *us* eat and be merry."

How wonderful to think that nothing could satisfy the heart and mind of God but to gather His people round Himself and feed them with that in which He Himself delights! "Truly our fellowship is with the Father, and with his Son, Jesus Christ" (1 John 1). What more could even the love of God do for us than this? And for whom has He done it? For those who were dead in trespasses and sins – for aliens, enemies, guilty rebels – for dogs of the Gentiles – for those who were far from Him, having no hope, and without God in the world – for those who, had we our deserts, should lie now burning in the eternal flames of hell. Oh! what wondrous grace! What profound depths of sovereign mercy! And, we must add, what a divinely precious atoning sacrifice, to bring poor self-destroyed, guilty, hell-deserving sinners into such ineffable blessedness! – to pluck us as brands from everlasting burnings, and make us priests to God! – to take away all our "filthy garments" from us, and cleanse, clothe, and crown us, in His own presence, and to His own praise! May we praise Him! May our hearts and lives praise Him! May we know how to enjoy our priestly place and portion, and to wear our mitre well! We can do nothing better than praise God – nothing higher than to present to Him, by Jesus Christ, the fruit of our lips giving thanks to His name.

This shall be our everlasting employment in that bright and blessed world to which we are hastening, and where we shall soon be, to dwell for ever with Him who has loved us and given Himself for us – our own blessed Saviour God – to go no more out for evermore.

The redemption of the firstborn

In verses 14-19 of our chapter we have instruction as to "The firstborn of man and beast." We may remark that man is placed on a level with the unclean beast. Both had to be redeemed. The unclean beast was unfit for God; and so was man, unless redeemed by blood. The clean animal was not to be redeemed. It was fit for God's use, and was given to be the food of the entire priestly household – sons and daughters alike. In this we have a type of Christ in whom God can find His perfect delight – the full joy of His heart – the only object, throughout the wide universe, in which He could find perfect rest and satisfaction. And – wondrous thought – He has given Him to us, His priestly household, to be our food, our light, our joy, our all in all for ever.[15]

> "Jesus, of thee we ne'er would tire:
> The new and living food
> Can satisfy our heart's desire,
> And life is in thy blood."

No earthly heritage for the Levites

The reader will notice, in this chapter, as elsewhere, that every fresh subject is introduced by the words, "And the Lord spake unto Moses," or "unto Aaron." Thus, from verses 20-32, we are taught that the priests and Levites – God's worshippers and workers, were to have no inheritance among the children of Israel, but were to be absolutely shut up to God Himself, for the supply of all their need. Most blessed position. Nothing can be more lovely than the picture here presented. The children of Israel were to bring their offerings, and lay them down at the feet of Jehovah, and He, in His infinite grace, commanded His workers to pick up these precious offerings – the fruit of His people's devotedness – and feed upon them, in His own blessed presence, with thankful hearts. Thus the circle of blessing went round. God ministered to all the wants of His people; His people were privileged to have the rich fruits of His bounty with the priests and Levites; and these latter were permitted to taste the rare and exquisite pleasure of giving back to God of that which had flown from Him to them.

All this is divine. It is a striking figure of that which we should look for in the Church of God now. As we have already remarked, God's people are presented, in this book, under three distinct phases, namely, as warriors, workers, and worshippers; and in all three they are viewed as in the attitude of the most absolute dependence upon the living God. In our warfare, in our work, and in our worship, we are *shut up to God.* Precious fact! "All our springs are in Him." What more do we want? Shall we turn to man or to this world for relief or resource? God forbid! Nay, rather let it be our one grand object to prove, in our entire history, in every phase of our character, and in every department of our work, that God is enough for our hearts.

It is truly deplorable to find God's people, and Christ's servants, looking to the world for support, and trembling at the thought of that support being withheld. Only let us try to imagine the Church of God, in the days of Paul, relying upon the Roman government for the support of its bishops, teachers, and evangelists. Ah! no, dear reader; the Church looked to its divine Head in the heavens, and to the divine Spirit upon earth, for all its need. Why should it be otherwise now? The world is the world still; and the Church is not of the world, and should not look for the world's gold and silver. God will take care of His people and of His servants, if they will only trust Him. We may depend upon it, the *divinum donum* (God's gift) is far better for the Church than the *regium donum* (government gift) – no comparison in the estimation of a spiritual mind.

May all the saints of God, and all the servants of Christ, in every place, apply their hearts, earnestly, to the consideration of these things! And may we have grace to confess, practically, in the face of a godless, Christless, infidel world, that the living God is amply sufficient for our every need, not only while passing through the narrow archway of time, but also for the boundless ocean of eternity! God grant it for Christ's sake!

---

[12] Even in the matter of appointing deacons, in Acts 6, we see it was an apostolic act. "Wherefore, brethren, look ye out among you seven men of honest report, full of the Holy Ghost and wisdom, whom *we may appoint* over this business." The brethren were allowed to *select* the men, inasmuch as it was their money that was in question. But the *appointment* was divine. And this, be it remembered, had reference merely to the business of deacons who were to manage the Church's temporal affairs. But as regards the work of evangelists, pastors, and teachers, it is wholly independent of human choice and human authority, and rests simply upon the gift of Christ, Ephesians 4:11.

[13] As a general principle, the "son" presents the divine idea; the "daughter," the human apprehension thereof: the "male" sets forth the thing as God gives it; the "female" as we realise and exhibit it.

[14] Let the reader consider what the moral effect must be of taking the above passage literally and applying it to a certain priestly class in the Church of God. Take it typically and spiritually, and you have a striking and beautiful figure of the spiritual food provided for all the members of the priestly family, which is, in one word, Christ in all His preciousness and fullness.

[15] For further remarks on the subject presented to Numbers 18:14-19, the reader is referred to "Notes on Exodus," chapter 13. We are anxious to avoid, as much as possible, any repetition of what has been gone into in previous volume.

THE RED HEIFER

A picture of the perfection of Christ

One of the most important sections of the book of Numbers now lies open before us, presenting for our consideration the deeply interesting and instructive ordinance of "The Red Heifer." A thoughtful student of scripture would naturally feel disposed to inquire why it is that we get this type in Numbers and not in Leviticus. In the first seven chapters of the latter book, we have a very elaborate statement of the doctrine of sacrifice; and yet we have no allusion whatever to the red heifer. Why is this? What are we to learn from the fact that this beautiful ordinance is presented in the Book of Numbers and nowhere else? We believe it furnishes another striking illustration of the distinctive character of our book. The red heifer is, pre-eminently, a wilderness type. It was God's provision for defilements by the way, and it prefigures the death of Christ as a purification for sin, to meet our need in passing through a defiling world, home to our eternal rest above. It is a most instructive figure, and unfolds most precious and needed truth. May the holy Ghost, who has penned the record, be graciously pleased to expound and apply it to our souls!

"And the Lord spake unto Moses and unto Aaron, saying, This is the ordinance of the law which the Lord hath commanded, saying, Speak unto the children of Israel that they bring thee a red heifer without spot, wherein is no blemish, and upon which never came yoke." Verses 1, 2.

When, with the eye of faith, we gaze upon the Lord Jesus, we not only see Him to be the spotless One, in His own holy

Person, but also One who never bore the yoke of sin. The Holy Ghost is ever the jealous guardian of the person of Christ, and He delights to present Him to the soul in all His excellency and preciousness. Hence it is that every type and every shadow, designed to set Him forth, exhibits the same careful guardianship. Thus, in the red heifer, we are taught that, not only was our blessed Saviour, as to His human nature, intrinsically and inherently pure and spotless, but that, as to His birth and relationships, He stood perfectly clear from every mark and trace of sin. No yoke of sin ever came upon His sacred neck. When He speaks of "my yoke" (Matt. 11:29), it was the yoke of implicit subjection to the Father's will, in all things. This was the only yoke He ever wore; and this yoke was never off, for one moment, during the entire of His spotless and perfect career – from the manger, where He lay a helpless babe, to the cross, where He expired as a victim.

But He wore no yoke of sin. Let this be distinctly understood. He went to the cross to expiate our sins, to lay the groundwork of our perfect purification from all sin; but He did this as One who had never, at any time during His blessed life, worn the yoke of sin. He was "without sin;" and, as such, was perfectly fitted to do the great and glorious work of expiation. To think of him as bearing the yoke of sin in His life, would be to think of him as unfit to atone for it in His death. "*Wherein* is no blemish, and *whereon* never came yoke." It is quite as needful to remember and weigh the force of the word "whereon," as of the word "wherein." Both expressions are designed by the Holy Ghost to set forth the perfection of our Lord and Saviour Jesus Christ, who was not only internally spotless, but also externally free from every trace of sin. Neither in His Person, nor yet in His relationships, was He, in anywise, obnoxious to the claims of sin or death. He – adored for ever be His name! – entered into all the reality of our circumstances and condition; but *in* Him was no sin, and *on* Him no yoke of sin.

> "Touched with a sympathy within,
> He knows our feeble frame;
> He knows what sore temptations mean,
> For He has felt the same.
>
> "But spotless, undefiled, and pure,
> The great Redeemer stood,
> While Satan's fiery darts He bore,
> And did resist to blood."

Christ as victim and then as priest

"And ye shall give her unto Eleazar the priest, that he may bring her forth without the camp, and one shall slay her before his face." Verse 3.

The thoughtful reader of scripture will not pass over any expression, how trivial soever it may seem to be. Such an one will ever bear in mind that the book which lies open before him is from God, and therefore perfect – perfect as a whole – perfect in all its parts. Every little word is pregnant with meaning. Each little point, feature, and circumstance contains some spiritual teaching for the soul. No doubt, infidels and rationalists altogether fail in seizing this weighty fact, and, as a consequence, when they approach the divine volume, they make the saddest havoc. They see flaws where the spiritual student sees only gems. They see incongruities and contradictions where the devout, self-distrusting, Spirit-taught disciple beholds divine harmonies and moral glories.

This is only what we might expect; and it is well to remember it now-a-days. "God is His own interpreter," in scripture, as well as in providence; and if we wait on Him, He will assuredly make it plain. But, as in providence, "Blind unbelief is sure to err, and scan His ways in vain," so in scripture, it is sure to err, and scan His lines in vain. And the devout poet might have gone farther; for, most surely, unbelief will not only scan God's ways and God's word in vain, but turn both the one and the other into an occasion of making a blasphemous attack upon God Himself, upon His nature, and upon His character, as well as upon the revelation which He has been pleased to give us. The infidel would rudely smash the lamp of inspiration, quench its heavenly light, and involve us all in the deep gloom and moral darkness which entrap his own misguided mind.

We have been led into the foregoing train of thought while meditating upon the third verse of our chapter. We are exceedingly desirous to cultivate the habit of profound and careful study of holy scripture. It is of immense importance. To say or to think that there is so much as a single clause, or a single expression, from cover to cover of the inspired volume, unworthy of our prayerful meditation, is to imply that God the Holy Ghost has thought it worth His while to write what we do not think it worth our while to study. "All scripture is given by inspiration of God" (2 Tim. 3:16). This commands our reverence. "Whatsoever things were written aforetime were written for our learning" (Rom 15:4). This awakens our personal interest. The former of these quotations proves that scripture comes *from God*; the latter proves that it comes *to us*. That and this, taken together, bind us to God by the divine link of holy scripture – a link which the devil, in this our day, is doing his very utmost to snap; and that, too, by means of agents of acknowledged moral worth and intellectual power. The devil does not select an ignorant or immoral man to make his grand and special attacks upon the Bible, for he knows full well that the former could not speak, and the latter would not get a hearing. But he craftily takes up some amiable, benevolent, and popular person – some one of blameless morals – a laborious student, a profound scholar, a deep and original thinker. Thus he throws dust in the eyes of the simple, the unlearned, and the unwary.

Christian reader, we pray you to remember this. If we can deepen in your soul the sense of the unspeakable value of your Bible; if we can warn you off from the dangerous rocks and quicksands of rationalism and infidelity; if we are made the means of stablishing and strengthening you in the assurance that when you are hanging over the sacred page of scripture, you are drinking at a fountain every drop of which has flowed into it from the very bosom of God Himself; if we can reach all or any of these results, we shall not regret the digression from our chapter, to which we now return.

"And ye shall give her unto Eleazar the priest, that he may bring her forth without the camp, and one shall slay her before his face." We have, in the priest and the victim, a joint type of the Person of Christ. He was, at once, the Victim and the Priest. But He did not enter upon His priestly functions until His work as a victim was accomplished. This will explain the expression in the last clause of the third verse, *"one shall slay her before his face"*. The death of Christ was accomplished on earth, and could not, therefore, be represented as the act of priesthood. Heaven, not earth, is the sphere of His priestly service. The apostle, in the Epistle to the Hebrews, expressly declares, as the sum of a most elaborate and amazing piece of argument, that "We have such an high priest, who is set on the right hand of the throne of the Majesty in the heavens; a minister of the sanctuary, and of the true tabernacle which the Lord pitched, and not man. For every high priest is ordained to offer gifts and sacrifices: wherefore it is of necessity that this man have somewhat also to offer. *For if he were on earth, he should not be a priest,* seeing that there are priests that offer gifts according to the law" (Heb. 8:1-4). "But Christ being come an high priest of good things to come, by a greater and more perfect tabernacle, not made with hands, that is to say, not of this building; neither by the blood of goats and calves, but by his own blood he entered in once into the holy place, having obtained eternal redemption." "For Christ is not entered into the holy places made with hands, the figures of the true; *but into heaven itself,* now to appear in the presence of God for us" (Heb. 9:11, 12, 24). "But this man, after he had offered one sacrifice for sins, for ever *sat down on the right hand of God."* Heb. 10:12.

From all these passages, taken in connection with Numbers 19:3, we learn two things, namely, that the death of Christ is not presented as the proper, ordinary act of priesthood; and, further, that heaven, not earth, is the sphere of His priestly ministry. There is nothing new in these statements; others have advanced them repeatedly; but it is important to notice everything tending to illustrate the divine perfection and precision of holy scripture. It is deeply interesting to find a truth, which shines brightly in the pages of the New Testament, wrapped up in some ordinance or ceremony of Old Testament times. Such discoveries are ever welcome to the intelligent reader of the word. The truth, no doubt, is the same wherever it is found; but when it bursts upon us, with meridian brightness, in the New Testament scriptures, and is divinely shadowed forth in the Old, we not only have the truth established, but the unity of the volume illustrated and enforced.

Outside the camp

But we must not pass over, unnoticed, the place where the death of the victim was accomplished. "That he may bring her forth without the camp." As has already been remarked, the priest and the victim are identified, and form a joint type of Christ; but it is added, "one shall slay her before his face," simply because the death of Christ could not be represented as the act of priesthood. What marvellous accuracy! And yet it is not marvellous, for what else should we look for in a book every line of which is from God Himself? Had it been said, "He shall slay her," then Numbers 19 would be at variance with the Epistle to the Hebrews. But no; the harmonies of the volume shine forth among its brightest glories. May we have grace to discern and appreciate them!

Jesus, then, suffered without the gate. "Wherefore Jesus also, that he might sanctify the people with his own blood, suffered without the gate" (Heb. 13:12). He took the outside place, and His voice falls on the ear from thence. Do we listen to it? Do we understand it? Should we not consider more seriously the place where Jesus died? Are we to rest satisfied with reaping the benefits of Christ's death, without seeking fellowship with Him in His rejection? God forbid! "Let us *go forth* therefore unto him without the camp, bearing his reproach."[16] There is immense power in these words. They should rouse our whole moral being to seek more complete identification with a rejected Saviour. Shall we see Him die outside, while we reap the benefits of His death and remain within? Shall we seek a home, and a place, and a name, and a portion, in that world from which our Lord and Master is an outcast? Shall we aim at getting on in a world which could not tolerate that blessed One to whom we owe our present and everlasting felicity? Shall we aspire after honour, position, and wealth, where our Master found only a manger, a cross, a borrowed grave? May the language of our *hearts* be, "Far be the *thought!*" And may the language of our *lives* be, "Far be the *thing!*" May we, by the grace of God, yield a more hearty response to the Spirit's call to *"Go forth!"*

Christian reader, let us never forget that, when we look at the death of Christ, we see two things, namely, the death of a victim, and the death of a martyr – a victim for sin, a martyr for righteousness – a victim, under the hand of God, a martyr, under the hand of man. He suffered for sin, that we might never suffer. Blessed be His name for evermore! But then, His martyr sufferings, His sufferings for righteousness under the hand of man, these we may know. "For unto you *it is given,* in the behalf of Christ, not only to believe on him, but also to *suffer* for his sake" (Phil. 1:29). It is a positive *gift* to be allowed to suffer with Christ. Do we so esteem it?

In contemplating the death of Christ, as typified by the ordinance of the red heifer, we see not only the complete putting away of sin, but also the judgment of this present evil world. "He gave himself for our sins that he might deliver us from this present evil world, according to the will of God and our Father" (Gal 1:4). Here the two things are put together by God; and, most surely, they should never be separated by us. We have the judgment of sin, root and branch; and the judgment of this world. The former should give perfect repose to the exercised conscience; while the latter should deliver the heart from the ensnaring influence of the world, in all its multiplied forms. That purges the conscience from all sense of guilt; this snaps the link which binds the heart and the world together.

Now, it is most needful for the reader to understand and enter experimentally into the connection existing between these two things. It is quite possible to miss this grand link, even while holding and contending for a vast amount of evangelical truth; and it may be confidently affirmed that where this link is missing, there must be a very serious defect in the Christian character. We frequently meet with earnest souls who have been brought under the convicting and awakening power of the Holy Spirit, but who have not yet known, for the ease of their troubled consciences, the full value of the atoning death of Christ, as putting away, for ever, all their sins, and bringing them nigh to God, without a stain upon the soul, or a sting in the conscience. If this be the present actual condition of the reader, he would need to consider the first clause of the verse just quoted. "He gave himself for our sins." This is a most blessed statement for a troubled soul. It settles the whole question of sin. If it be true that Christ gave Himself for my sins, what remains for me but to rejoice in the precious fact that my sins are all gone? The One who took my place, who stood charged with my sins, who suffered in my room and stead, is now at the right hand of God, crowned with glory and honour. This is enough. My sins are all gone for ever. If they were not, *He* could not be where He now is. The crown of glory which wreathes His blessed brow is the proof that my sins are perfectly atoned for, and therefore perfect peace is my portion – a peace as perfect as the work of Christ can make it.

But then, let us never forget that the very same work that has for ever put away our sins has delivered us from this present evil world. The two things go together. Christ has not only delivered me from the consequences of my sins, but also from the present power of sin, and from the claims and influences of that thing which scripture calls "the world." All this, however, will come more fully out as we proceed with our chapter.

Purification by the blood of Christ

"And Eleazar the priest shall take of her blood with His finger, and sprinkle of her blood directly before the tabernacle of the congregation seven times." Here we have the solid groundwork of all real purification. We know that, in the type before us, it is only, as the inspired apostle tells us, a question of "sanctifying to the purifying of the flesh" (Heb. 9:13). But we have to look beyond the type to the antitype – beyond the shadow to the substance. In the sevenfold sprinkling of the blood of the red heifer, before the tabernacle of the congregation, we have a figure of the perfect presentation of the blood of Christ to God, as the only ground of the meeting-place between God and the conscience. The number "seven," as has frequently been observed, is expressive of perfection; and, in the figure before us, we see the perfection attaching to the death of Christ, as an atonement for sin, presented to, and accepted by God. All rests upon this divine ground. The blood has been shed, and presented to a holy God, as a perfect atonement for sin. This, when simply received by faith, must relieve the conscience from all sense of guilt and all fear of condemnation. There is nothing before God save the perfection of the atoning work of Christ. Sin has been judged and our sins put away. They have been completely obliterated by the precious blood of Christ. To believe this is to enter into perfect repose of conscience.

And here let the reader carefully note that there is no further allusion to the sprinkling of blood throughout the entire of this singularly interesting chapter. This is precisely in keeping with the doctrine of Hebrews 9, 10. It is but another illustration of the divine harmony of the Volume. The sacrifice of Christ, being divinely perfect, needs not to be repeated. Its efficacy is divine and eternal. "But Christ being come an high priest of good things to come, by a greater and more perfect tabernacle, not made with hands, that is to say, not of this building; neither by the blood of goats and calves, but by his own blood, he entered in once into the holy place, having obtained *eternal* redemption. For if the blood of bulls and of goats, and *the ashes of an heifer,* sprinkling the unclean, sanctifieth to the purifying of the flesh; how much more shall the blood of Christ, who through the eternal Spirit offered himself without spot to God, purge your conscience from dead works to serve the living God?" (Heb. 9: 11-14). Observe the force of these two words, "*once*" and "*eternal.*" See how they set forth the completeness and divine efficacy of the sacrifice of Christ. The blood was shed once and for ever. To think of a repetition of that great work would be to deny its everlasting and all-sufficient value, and reduce it to the level of the blood of bulls and goats.

But, further, "It was therefore necessary that the patterns of things in the heavens should be purified with these; but the heavenly things themselves with better sacrifices than these. For Christ is not entered into the holy places made with hands, which are the figures of the true; but into heaven itself, now to appear in the presence of God for us; nor yet *that he should offer himself often,* as the high priest entereth into the holy place every year with blood of others; for then *must he often have suffered* since the foundation of the world; but now *once* in the end of the world hath he appeared to *put away sin* by the sacrifice of himself." Sin therefore, has been put away. It cannot be put away, and, at the same time, be on the believer's conscience. This is plain. It must either be admitted that the believer's sins are blotted out, and his conscience perfectly purged, or that Christ must die over again. But this latter is not only needless, but wholly out of the question; for, as the apostle goes on to say, "As it is appointed unto men *once* to die, but after this the judgment; so Christ was once offered to bear the sins of many; and unto them that look for him shall he appear the second time, without sin, unto salvation."

There is something most marvellous in the patient

elaborateness with which the Holy Ghost argues out this entire subject. He expounds, illustrates, and enforces the great doctrine of the completeness of the sacrifice in such a way, as to carry conviction to the soul, and relieve the conscience of its heavy burden. Such is the exceeding grace of God that He has not only accomplished the work of eternal redemption for us, but, in the most patient and painstaking manner, has argued and reasoned, and proved the whole point in question, so as not to leave one hair's breadth of ground on which to base an objection. Let us hearken to His further powerful reasonings, and may the Spirit apply them in power to the heart of the anxious reader!

"For the law having a shadow of good things to come, and not the very image of the things, can never with those sacrifices which they offered year by year continually, make the comers thereunto *perfect*. For then would they not have *ceased to be offered?* because that the worshippers *once purged* should have had *no more conscience of sins*. But in these sacrifices there is a remembrance again made of sins every year. For it is not possible that the blood of bulls and of goats should take away sins." But that which the blood of bulls could never do, the blood of Jesus has for ever done. This makes all the difference. All the blood that ever flowed around Israel's altars – the millions of sacrifices, offered according to the requirements of the Mosaic ritual – could not blot out one stain from the conscience, or justify a sin-hating God in receiving a sinner to Himself. "It is not possible that the blood of bulls and of goats should take away sins." "Wherefore when he cometh into the world he saith, sacrifice and offering thou wouldest not, but a body hast thou prepared me. In burnt offerings and sacrifices for sin thou hast had no pleasure. Then said I, Lo, I come (in the volume of the book it is written of me) to do thy will, O God . . . By the which will we are sanctified through the offering of the body of Jesus Christ *once*." Mark the contrast. God had no pleasure in the endless round of sacrifices under the law. They did not please Him. They left wholly unaccomplished that which He had in

His loving heart to do for His people, namely, to rid them completely of sin's heavy load, and bring them unto Himself, in perfect peace of conscience and liberty of heart. This, Jesus, by the one offering of His blessed body, did. He did the will of God; and, blessed for ever be His name, He has not to do His work over again. We may refuse to believe that the work is done – refuse to commit our souls to its efficacy – to enter into the rest which it is calculated to impart – to enjoy the holy liberty of spirit which it is fitted to yield; but there stands the work in its own imperishable virtue; and there, too, stand the Spirit's arguments respecting that work, in their own unanswerable force and clearness; and neither Satan's dark suggestions, nor our own unbelieving reasonings can ever touch either the one or the other. They may, and alas! they do, most sadly interfere with our soul's enjoyment of the truth; but the truth itself remains ever the same.

"And every priest *standeth daily* ministering, and *offering oftentimes the same sacrifices, which can never take away sins;* but this man, after he had offered *one sacrifice* for sins, *for ever sat down* on the right hand of God; from henceforth expecting till his enemies be made his footstool. For *by one offering* he hath perfected for ever them that are sanctified." It is due to the blood of Christ that it should impart eternal perfection; and, we may surely add, it is due to it likewise that our souls should taste that perfection. No one need ever imagine that he is doing honour to the work of Christ, or to the Spirit's testimony respecting that work, when he refuses to accept that perfect remission of sins which is proclaimed to him through the blood of the cross. It is no sign of true piety, or of pure religion, to deny what the grace of God has done for us in Christ, and what the record of the Eternal Spirit has presented to our souls on the page of inspiration.

Christian reader, anxious inquirer, does it not seem strange that, when the word of God presents to our view Christ seated at the right hand of God, in virtue of accomplished redemption, we should be, virtually, in no wise better off than those who had merely a human priest standing daily ministering, and offering the same round of sacrifices? We have a divine Priest who has sat down for ever. They had a merely human priest, who could never, in his official capacity, sit down at all; and yet are we, in the state of the mind, in the apprehension of the soul, in the actual condition of the conscience, in no respect better off than they? Can it be possible that, with a perfect work to rest upon, our souls should never know perfect rest? The Holy Ghost, as we have seen in these various quotations taken from the Epistle to the Hebrews, has left nothing unsaid to satisfy our souls as to the question of the complete putting away of sin by the precious blood of Christ. Why then should you not, this moment, enjoy full, settled peace of conscience? Has the blood of Jesus done nothing more for you than the blood of a bullock did for a Jewish worshipper?

It may be, however, that the reader is ready to say, in reply to all that we have been seeking to urge upon him, "I do not, in the least, doubt the efficacy of the blood of Jesus. I believe it cleanseth from all sin. I believe, most thoroughly, that all who simply put their trust in that blood are perfectly safe, and will be eternally happy. My difficulty does not lie here at all. What troubles me is, not the efficacy of the blood, in which I fully believe, but *my own personal interest in that blood,* of which I have no satisfactory evidence. This is the secret of all my trouble. The doctrine of the blood is as clear as a sunbeam; but the question of *my* interest therein is involved in hopeless obscurity."

Now if this be at all the embodiment of the reader's feelings on this momentous subject, it only proves the necessity of his deeply pondering the fourth verse of the nineteenth of Numbers. There he will see that the true basis of all purification is found in this, that the blood of atonement has been presented to God, and accepted by Him. This is a most precious truth, but one little understood. It is of all importance that the really anxious soul should have a clear view of the subject of atonement. It is so natural to us all to be occupied with our thoughts and feelings about the blood of Christ, rather than with the blood itself, and with

God's thoughts respecting it. If the blood has been perfectly presented to God, if He has accepted it, if He has glorified Himself in the putting away of sin, then what remains for the divinely exercised conscience but to find perfect repose in that which has met all the claims of God, harmonised His attributes, and laid the foundations of that marvellous platform whereon a sin-hating God and a poor sin-destroyed sinner can meet? Why introduce the question of my interest in the blood of Christ, as though that work were not complete without anything of mine, call it what you will, my interest, my feelings, my experience, my appreciation, my appropriation, my anything? Why not rest in Christ alone? This would be really having an interest in Him. But the very moment the heart gets occupied with the question of its own interest – the moment the eye is withdrawn from that divine object which the word of God and the Holy Ghost present – then spiritual darkness and perplexity must ensue; and the soul, instead of rejoicing in the perfection of the work of Christ, is tormented by looking at its own poor, imperfect feelings.

> "The atoning work is done,
> The Victim's blood is shed;
> And Jesus now is gone,
> *His* people's cause to plead.
> He stands in heaven their Great High Priest,
> And bears their names upon His breast."

Here, blessed be God, we have the stable groundwork of "purification for sin," and of perfect peace for the conscience. "The atoning work is done." All is finished. The great Antitype of the red heifer has been slain. He gave himself up to death, under the wrath and judgment of a righteous God, that all who simply put their trust in Him might know, in the deep secret of their own souls, divine purification and perfect peace. We are purified as to the conscience, not by our thoughts about the blood, but by the blood itself. We must insist upon this. God Himself has made out our title for us, and that title is found in the blood *alone*. Oh! that most precious blood of Jesus that speaks profound peace to every troubled soul that will simply lean upon its eternal efficacy. Why, we may ask, is it that the blessed doctrine of the blood is so little understood and appreciated? Why will people persist in looking to anything else, or in mingling anything else with it? May the Holy Ghost lead the anxious reader, as he reads these lines, to stay his heart and conscience upon the atoning sacrifice of the Lamb of God.

The ashes of the heifer

Having thus endeavoured to present to the reader the precious truth unfolded to us in the *death* of the red heifer, we shall now ask him to meditate, for a few moments, upon the *burning* of the heifer. We have looked at the *blood*, let us now gaze upon the *ashes*. In the former, we have the sacrificial death of Christ, as the only purification for sin. In the latter, we have the remembrance of that death applied to the heart by the Spirit, through the word, in order to remove any defilement contracted in our walk from day to day. This gives great completeness and beauty to this most interesting type. God has not only made provision for past sins, but also for present defilement, so that we may be ever before Him in all the value and credit of the perfect work of Christ. He would have us treading the courts of His sanctuary, the holy precincts of His presence, "Clean every whit.' And not only does He Himself see us thus; but, blessed for ever be His name, He would have us thus in our own inward self-consciousness. He would give us, by His Spirit, through the word, the deep inward sense of cleanness in His sight, so that the current of our communion with Him may flow on without a ripple and without a curve. "If we walk in the light as He is in the light, we have fellowship one with another, and the blood of Jesus Christ his Son cleanseth us from all sin" (1 John 1). But if we fail to walk in the light – if we forget, and, in our forgetfulness, touch the unclean thing, how is our communion to be restored? Only by the removal of the defilement. And how is this to be effected? By the application to our hearts and consciences of the precious truth of the death of Christ. The Holy Ghost produces self-judgment, and brings to our remembrance the precious truth that Christ suffered death for that defilement which we so lightly and indifferently contract. It is not a fresh sprinkling of the blood of Christ – a thing unknown in scripture; but the remembrance of His death brought home, in fresh power, to the contrite heart, by the ministry of the Holy Ghost.

"And one shall burn the heifer in his sight . . . And the priest shall take cedar wood, and hyssop, and scarlet, and cast it into the midst of the burning of the heifer . . . And a man that is clean shall gather up the ashes of the heifer, and lay them up without the camp in a clean place, and it shall be kept for the congregation of the children of Israel for a water of separation: it is a purification for sin."

It is the purpose of God that His children should be purified from all iniquity, and that they should walk in separation from this present evil world, where all is death and defilement. This separation is effected by the action of the word on the heart, by the power of the Holy Ghost. "Grace to you and peace from God the Father, and our Lord Jesus Christ, who gave Himself for our sins, that he might deliver us from this present evil world, according to the will of God and our Father" (Gal. 1:4). And again, "Looking for that blessed hope, and the glorious appearing of the great God and our Saviour Jesus Christ; who gave himself for us, that he might *redeem* us from all iniquity, and *purify* unto himself a peculiar people, zealous of good works." Titus 2:13, 14.

It is remarkable how constantly the Spirit of God presents, in intimate connection, the full relief of the conscience from all sense of guilt, and the deliverance of the heart from the moral influence of this present evil world. Now, it should be our care, beloved Christian reader, to maintain the integrity of this connection. Of course, it is only by the gracious energy of the Holy Ghost that we can do so; but we ought to seek earnestly to understand and practically carry out the blessed link of connection between the death of Christ as an atonement for sin, and as the moral power of separation from this world. Many of the people of God never get beyond the former, if they even get that length. Many seem to be quite satisfied with the knowledge of the forgiveness of sins through the atoning work of Christ, while, at the same time, they fail to realise deadness to the world in virtue of the death of Christ, and their identification with Him therein.

Now, when we stand and gaze upon the burning of the red heifer, in Numbers 19 – when we examine that mystic heap of ashes, what do we find? It may be said, in reply, "We find our sins there." True, thanks be to God, and to the Son of His love, we do indeed find our sins, our iniquities, our trespasses, our deep crimson guilt, all reduced to ashes. But is there nothing more? Can we not, by a careful analysis, discover more? Unquestionably. We find nature there, in every stage of its existence – from the highest to the lowest point in its history. Moreover, we find all the glory of this world there. The cedar and the hyssop represent nature in its widest extremes; and, in giving its extremes, they take in all that lies between. "Solomon spake of trees, from the cedar tree that is in Lebanon even unto the hyssop that springeth out of the wall."

"Scarlet" is viewed, by those who have carefully examined scripture on the point, as the type or expression of human splendour, worldly grandeur, the glory of this world, the glory of man. Hence, therefore, we see in the burning of the heifer, the end of all worldly greatness, human glory, and the complete setting aside of the flesh, with all its belongings. This renders the burning of the heifer deeply significant. It shadows forth a truth too little known, and, when known, too readily forgotten – a truth embodied in these memorable words of the apostle, "God forbid that I should glory save in the cross of our Lord Jesus Christ, whereby the world is crucified unto me, and I unto the world."

We are all far too prone to accept the cross as the ground

of escape from all the consequences of our sins, and of full acceptance with God, and, at the same time, refuse it as the ground of our complete separation from the world. True it is, thanks and praise be to our God, the solid ground of our deliverance from guilt and consequent condemnation; but it is more than this. It has severed us, for ever, from all that pertains to this world, through which we are passing. Are my sins put away? Yes; blessed be the God of all grace! According to what? According to the perfection of Christ's atoning sacrifice as estimated by God Himself. Well then, such, precisely, is the measure of our deliverance from this present evil world – from its fashions, its maxims, its habits, its principles. The believer has absolutely nothing in common with this world, in so far as he enters into the spirit and power of the cross of the Lord Jesus Christ. That cross has dislodged him from everything here below, and made him a pilgrim and a stranger in this world. The truly devoted heart sees the dark shadow of the cross looming over all the glitter and glare, the pomp and fashion of this world. Paul saw this, and the sight of it caused him to esteem the world, in its very highest aspect, in its most attractive forms, in its brightest glories, as dross.

Such was the estimate formed of this world by one who had been brought up at the feet of Gamaliel. "The world is crucified unto me," said he, "and I unto the world." Such was Paul, and such should every Christian be – a stranger on earth, a citizen of heaven, and this, not merely in sentiment or theory, but in downright fact and reality; for, as surely as our deliverance from hell is more than a mere sentiment or theory, so surely is our separation from this present evil age. The one is as positive and as real as the other.

But here let us ask, Why is not this great practical truth more pressed home upon the hearts of evangelical Christians at the present moment? Why are we so slow to urge upon one another the separating power of the cross of Christ? If my heart loves Jesus, I shall not seek a place, a portion, or a name where He found only a malefactor's cross. This, dear reader, is the simple way to look at the matter. Do you really love Christ? Has your heart been touched and attracted by His wondrous love to you? If so, remember that He was cast out by this world. Yes, Jesus was, and still is, an outcast from this world. There is no change. The world is the world still; and be it remembered, that one of Satan's special devices is to lead people to accept salvation from Christ, while, at the same time, they refuse to be identified with Him in His rejection – to avail themselves of the atoning work of the cross, while abiding comfortably in the world that is stained with the guilt of nailing Christ thereto. In other words, he leads people to think and to say that the offence of the cross has ceased; that the world of the nineteenth century is totally different from the world of the first; that if the Lord Jesus were on earth now He would meet with very different treatment from that which He received then; that it is not now a pagan world, but a Christian one, and this makes a material and a fundamental difference; that now it is quite right for a Christian to accept of citizenship in this world, to have a name, a place, and a portion here, seeing it is not the same world at all, as that which nailed the Son of God to Calvary's cursed tree.

Now we feel it incumbent on us to press upon all who read these lines that this is, in very deed, a lie of the arch-enemy of souls. The world is not changed. It may have changed its dress, but it has not changed its nature, its spirit, its principles. It hates Jesus as cordially as when the cry went forth, "Away with him! Crucify him!" There is really no change. If only we try the world by the same grand test, we shall find it to be the same evil, God-hating, Christ-rejecting world as ever. And what is that test? Christ crucified. May this solemn truth be engraved on our hearts! May we realise and manifest its formative power! May it detach us more completely from all that belongs to the world! May we be enabled to understand more fully the truth presented in the ashes of the red heifer! Then shall our separation from the world, and our dedication to Christ, be more intense and real. The Lord, in His exceeding goodness, grant that thus it may be, with all His people, in this day of hollow, worldly, half-and-half profession!

The water of separation

Let us now consider, for a moment, how the ashes were to be applied.

"He that toucheth the dead body of any man shall be unclean seven days. He shall purify himself with it on the third day, and on the seventh day he shall be clean; but if he purify not himself the third day, then the seventh day he shall not be clean. Whosoever toucheth the dead body of any man that is dead, and purifieth not himself, defileth the tabernacle of the Lord; and that soul shall be cut off from Israel: because the water of separation was not sprinkled upon him, he shall be unclean; his uncleanness is yet upon him."

It is a solemn thing to have to do with God – to walk with Him, from day to day, in the midst of a defiled and defiling scene. He cannot tolerate any uncleanness upon those with whom He deigns to walk, and in whom He dwells. He can pardon and blot out; He can heal, cleanse, and restore; but He cannot sanction unjudged evil, or suffer it upon His people. It would be a denial of His very name and nature were He to do so. This, while deeply solemn, is truly blessed. It is our joy to have to do with One whose presence demands and secures holiness. We are passing through a world in which we are surrounded with defiling influences. True, defilement is not now contracted by touching "a dead body, or a bone of a man, or a grave." These things were, as we know, types of things moral and spiritual with which we are in danger of coming in contact every day and every hour. We doubt not but those who have much to do with the things of this world are most painfully sensible of the immense difficulty of escaping with unsoiled hands. Hence the need of holy diligence in all our habits and associations, lest we contract defilement, and interrupt our communion with God. He must have us in a condition worthy of Himself. "Be ye holy, for I am holy."

But the anxious reader, whose whole soul breathes after holiness, may eagerly inquire, "What, then, are we to do, if it be true that we are thus surrounded, on all hands, with defiling influences, and if we are so prone to contract that defilement? Furthermore, if it is impossible to have fellowship with God, with unclean hands and a condemning conscience, what are we to do?" First of all, then, we should say, be watchful. Wait much and earnestly on God. He is faithful and gracious – a prayer-hearing and a prayer-answering God – a liberal and an unupbraiding Giver. "He giveth *more* grace." This is, positively, a blank cheque which faith can fill up to any amount. Is it the real purpose of your soul to get on, to advance in the divine life, to grow in personal holiness? Then beware how you continue, for a single hour, in contact with what soils your hands and wounds your conscience, grieves the Holy Ghost, and mars your communion. Be decided. Be whole-hearted. Give up, at once, the unclean thing, whatever it be, habit, or association, or anything else. Cost what it may, give it up. Entail what loss it may, abandon it. No worldly gain, no earthly advantage, could compensate for the loss of a pure conscience, an uncondemning heart, and the light of your Father's countenance. Are you not convinced of this? If so, seek grace to carry out your conviction.

But it may be further asked, "What is to be done when defilement is actually contracted? How is the defilement to be removed?" Hear the reply in the figurative language of Numbers 19. "And for an unclean person, they shall take of the *ashes* of the burnt heifer of purification for sin, and running water shall be put thereto in a vessel. And a clean person shall take hyssop and dip it in the water, and sprinkle it upon the tent, and upon all the vessels, and upon the persons that were there, and upon him that touched a bone, or one slain, or one dead, or a grave. And the clean person shall sprinkle upon the unclean on the third day, and on the seventh day; and on the seventh day he shall purify himself, and wash his clothes, and bathe himself in water, and shall be clean at even."

The reader will remark that, in the twelfth and eighteenth verses, there is a double action set forth. There is the action of the third day, and the action of the seventh day. Both were essentially necessary to remove the ceremonial defilement caused by contact with the varied forms of death above specified. Now, what did this double action typify? What is it that, in our spiritual history, answers thereto? We believe it to be this. When we, through lack of watchfulness and spiritual energy, touch the unclean thing and get defiled, we may be ignorant of it; but God knows all about it. He cares for us, and is looking after us; not, blessed be His name, as an angry judge, or stern censor, but as a loving father, who will never impute anything to us, because it was all, long ago, imputed to the One who died in our stead. But, though He will never impute it to us, He will make us feel it deeply and keenly. He will be a faithful reprover of the unclean thing; and He can reprove all the more powerfully simply because He will never reckon it against us. The Holy Spirit brings our sin to remembrance, and this causes unutterable anguish of heart. This anguish may continue for some time. It may be moments, days, months, or years. We once met with a young Christian, who was rendered miserable, for three years, by having gone with some worldly friends on an excursion. This convicting operation of the Holy Ghost we believe to be shadowed forth by the action of the third day. He first brings our sin to remembrance; and then He graciously brings to our remembrance, and applies to our souls, through the written word, the value of the death of Christ as that which has already met the defilement which we so easily contract. This answers to the action of the seventh day – removes the defilement and restores our communion.

And, be it carefully remembered, that we can never get rid of defilement in any other way. We may seek to forget, to slur over, to heal the wound slightly, to make little of the matter, to let time obliterate it from the tablet of memory. It will never do. Nay, it is most dangerous work. There are few things more disastrous than trifling with conscience or the claims of holiness. And it is as foolish as it is dangerous; for God has, in His grace, made full provision for the removal of the uncleanness which His holiness detects and condemns.

But the uncleanness must be removed, else communion is impossible. "If I wash thee not, thou hast no part *with* me." The suspension of a believer's communion is what answers to the cutting off of a member from the congregation of Israel. The Christian can never be cut off from Christ; but his communion can be interrupted by a single sinful thought, and that sinful thought must be judged and confessed, and the soil of it removed, ere the communion can be restored. It is well to remember this. It is a serious thing to trifle with sin. We may rest assured we cannot possibly have fellowship with God and walk in defilement. To think so, is to blaspheme the very name, the very nature, the very throne and majesty of God. No, dear reader, we must keep a clean conscience, and maintain the holiness of God, else we shall, very soon, make shipwreck of faith and break down altogether. May the Lord keep us walking softly and tenderly, watchfully and prayerfully, until we have laid aside our bodies of sin and death, and entered upon that bright and blessed world above, where sin, death, and defilement are unknown.

The holiness and the grace of God

In studying the ordinances and ceremonies of the Levitical economy, nothing is more striking than the jealous care with which the God of Israel watched over His people, in order that they might be preserved from every defiling influence. By day and by night, awake and asleep, at home and abroad, in the bosom of the family and in the solitary walk, His eyes were upon them. He looked after their food, their raiment, their domestic habits and arrangements. He carefully instructed them as to what they might and what they might not eat; what they might and what they might not wear. He even set forth, distinctly, His mind as to the very touching and handling of things. In short, He surrounded them with barriers amply sufficient, had they only attended to them, to resist the whole tide of defilement to which they were exposed on every side.

In all this, we read, in unmistakable characters, the

holiness of God; but we read also, as distinctly, the grace of God. If divine holiness could not suffer defilement upon the people, divine grace made ample provision for the removal thereof. This provision is set forth in our chapter under two forms, namely, the blood of atonement, and the water of separation. Precious provision! a provision illustrating, at once, the holiness and the grace of God. Did we not know the ample provisions of divine grace, the lofty claims of divine holiness would be perfectly overwhelming; but being assured of the former, we can heartily rejoice in the latter. Could we desire to see the standard of divine holiness lowered a single hair's breadth? Far be the thought. How could we, or why should we, seeing that divine grace has fully provided what divine holiness demands? An Israelite of old might shudder as he hearkened to such words as these, "He that toucheth the dead body of any man shall be unclean seven days." And again, "Whosoever toucheth the dead body of any man that is dead, and purifieth not himself, defileth the tabernacle of the Lord; and that soul shall be cut off from Israel." Such words might indeed terrify his heart. He might feel led to exclaim, "What am I to do? How can I ever get on? It seems perfectly impossible for me to escape defilement." But, then, what of the ashes of the burnt heifer? What of the water of separation? What could these mean? They set forth the memorial of the sacrificial death of Christ, applied to the heart by the power of the Spirit of God. "He shall purify himself with it the third day, and on the seventh day he shall be clean; but if he purify not himself the third day, then the seventh day he shall not be clean." If we contract defilement, even though it be through negligence, that defilement must be removed, ere our communion can be restored. But we cannot get rid of the soil by any effort of our own. It can only be by the use of God's gracious provision, even the water of purification. An Israelite could no more remove by his own efforts the defilement caused by the touch of a dead body, than he could have broken Pharaoh's yoke, or delivered himself from the lash of Pharaoh's taskmasters.

And let the reader observe that it was not a question of offering a fresh sacrifice, nor yet of a fresh application of the blood. It is of special importance that this should be distinctly seen and understood. The death of Christ cannot be repeated. "Christ being raised from the dead, dieth no more; death hath no more dominion over him, For in that he died, he died unto sin once; but in that he liveth, He liveth unto God." We stand, by the grace of God, in the full credit and value of the death of Christ; but, inasmuch as we are surrounded, on all sides, by temptations and snares; and as we have, within us, such capabilities and tendencies; and, further, seeing we have a powerful adversary who is ever on the watch to ensnare us, and lead us off the path of truth and purity, we could not get on for a single moment, were it not for the gracious way in which our God has provided for all our exigencies, in the precious death and all prevailing advocacy of our Lord Jesus Christ. It is not merely that the blood of Jesus Christ has washed away all our sins, and reconciled us to a holy God, but "We have an advocate with the Father, Jesus Christ the righteous." "He ever liveth to make intercession for us," and "He is able to save them to the uttermost that come unto God by him." He is ever in the presence of God for us. He represents us there, and maintains us in the divine integrity of the place and relationship in which His atoning death has set us. Our case can never, by any possibility, fall through, in the hands of such an Advocate. He must cease to live, ere the very feeblest of His saints can perish. We are identified with Him and He with us.

Now, then, Christian reader, what should be the practical effect of all this grace upon our hearts and lives? When we think of the death, and of the burning – of the blood, and of the ashes – of the atoning sacrifice, and the interceding Priest and Advocate, what influence should it exert upon our souls? How should it act upon our consciences? Should it lead us to think little of sin? Should it cause us to walk carelessly and indifferently? Should it have the effect of making us light and frivolous in our ways? Alas! for the heart that can think so.

We may rest assured of this, that the man who can draw a plea, from the rich provisions of divine grace, for lightness of conduct or levity of spirit, knows very little, if indeed he knows anything at all, of the true nature or proper influence of grace and its provisions. Could we imagine, for a moment, that the ashes of the heifer or the water of separation would have had the effect of making an Israelite careless as to his walk? Assuredly not. On the contrary, the very fact of such careful provision being made, by the goodness of God, against defilement, would make him feel what a serious thing it was to contract it. Such, at least, would be the proper effect of the provisions of divine grace. The heap of ashes, laid up in a clean place, gave forth a double testimony; it testified of the goodness of God; and it testified of the hatefulness of sin. It declared that God could not suffer uncleanness upon His people; but it declared also that He had provided the means of removing it. It is utterly impossible that the blessed doctrine of the sprinkled blood, of the ashes, and of the water of separation, can be understood and enjoyed, without its producing a holy horror of sin in all its defiling forms. And we may further assert that no one who has ever felt the anguish of a defiled conscience could lightly contract defilement. A pure conscience is far too precious a treasure to be lightly parted with; and a defiled conscience is far too heavy a burden to be lightly taken up. But, blessed be the God of all grace, He has met all our need, in His own perfect way; and, He has met it, too, not to make us careless, but to make us watchful. "My little children, these things write I unto you, that ye sin not." But then he adds, "If any man sin, we have an advocate with the Father, Jesus Christ the righteous. And he is the propitiation for our sins; and not for ours only, but for the whole world." 1 John.

The one who attended to the impurity

But we must draw this section to a close, and shall merely add a word on the closing verses of our chapter. "And it shall be a perpetual statute unto them, that he that sprinkleth the water of separation shall wash his clothes; and he that toucheth the water of separation shall be unclean until even. And whatsoever the unclean person toucheth shall be unclean, and the soul that toucheth it shall be unclean until even" (chap. 19:21, 22). In verse 18, we are taught that it needed a clean person to sprinkle the unclean; and in verse 21, we are taught that the act of sprinkling another defiled oneself.

Putting both these together, we learn, as another has said, "That any one who has to do with the sin of another, though it be in the way of duty, to cleanse it, is defiled; not as the guilty person, it is true, but we cannot touch sin without being defiled." And we learn also that, in order to lead another into the enjoyment of the cleansing virtue of Christ's work, I must be in the enjoyment of that cleansing work myself. It is well to remember this. Those who applied the water of separation to others had to use that water for themselves. May our souls enter into this! May we ever abide in the sense of the perfect cleanness into which the death of Christ introduces us, and in which His priestly work maintains us! And oh! let us never forget that *contact with evil defiles.* It was so under the Mosaic economy, and it is so now.

---

[16] "The camp", in the above passage, refers primarily to Judaism; but it has a very pointed moral application to every system of religion set up by man, and governed by the spirit and principles of this present evil world.

Chapter 20

NEARING THE END OF THE WILDERNESS JOURNEY

The death of Miriam

"Then came the children of Israel, even the whole congregation, into the desert of Zin, in the first month: and the people abode in Kadesh; and Miriam died there, and was buried there." Verse 1.

The chapter which now opens before us furnishes a very remarkable record of wilderness life and experience. In it, we see Moses, the servant of God, passing through some of the most trying scenes of his eventful life. First of all, Miriam dies. The one whose voice was heard, amid the brilliant scenes of Exodus 15 chanting a hymn of victory, passes away, and her ashes are deposited in the wilderness of Kadesh. The timbrel is laid aside. The voice of song is hushed in the silence of death. She can no longer lead in the dance. She had sung sweetly, in her day; she had, very blessedly, seized the key note of that magnificent song of praise sung on the resurrection side of the Red Sea. Her chorus embodied the great central truth of redemption. "Sing ye to the Lord, for he hath triumphed gloriously: the horse and his rider hath he thrown into the sea." This was, truly, a lofty strain. It was the suited utterance for the joyous occasion.

But now the prophetess passes off the scene, and the voice of melody is exchanged for the voice of murmuring. Wilderness life is becoming irksome. The trials of the desert put nature to the test; they bring out what is in the heart. Forty years' toil and travail make a great change in people.

It is very rare indeed to find a case in which the verdure and freshness of spiritual life are kept up, much less augmented, throughout all the stages of Christian life and warfare. It ought not to be such a rarity. It ought to be the very reverse, inasmuch as it is in the actual details, the stern realities of our path through this world, that we prove what God is. He, blessed be His name, takes occasion from the very trials of the way to make Himself known to us in all the sweetness and tenderness of love that knows no change. His loving kindness and tender mercy never fail. Nothing can exhaust those springs which are in the living God. He will be what He is, spite of all our naughtiness. God will be God, let man prove himself ever so faithless and faulty.

This is our comfort, our joy, and the source of our strength. We have to do with the living God. What a reality! Come what may, He will prove Himself equal to every emergency – amply sufficient "for exigence of every hour." His patient grace can bear with our manifold infirmities, failures, and shortcomings; and His strength is made perfect in our utter weakness. His faithfulness never fails. His mercy is from everlasting to everlasting. Friends fail or pass away. Links of fond friendship are snapped in this cold, heartless world. Fellow-labourers part company. Miriams and Aarons die; but God remaineth. Here lies the deep secret of all true and solid blessedness. If we have the hand and the heart of the living God with us, we need not fear. If we can say, "The Lord is my shepherd," we can, assuredly add, "we shall not want."

The striving at Meribah

Still there are the scenes of sorrow and trial in the desert; and we have to go through them. Thus it was with Israel, in the chapter before us. They were called to meet the keen blasts of the wilderness, and they met them with accents of impatience and discontent. "And there was no water for the congregation: and they gathered themselves together against Moses and against Aaron. And the people chode with Moses, and spake, saying, Would God that we had died when our brethren died before the Lord! And why have ye brought up the congregation of the Lord into this wilderness, that we and our cattle should die there? And wherefore have ye made us to come up out of Egypt, to bring us unto this evil place? It is no place of seed, or of figs, or of vines, or of pomegranates; neither is there any water to drink." Verses 2-5.

This was a deeply trying moment to the spirit of Moses. We can form no conception of what it must have been to encounter six hundred thousand murmurers, and to be obliged to listen to their bitter invectives, and to hear himself charged with all the misfortunes which their own unbelief had conjured up before them. All this was no ordinary trial of patience; and, most assuredly, *we* need not marvel if that dear and honoured servant found the occasion too much for him. "And Moses and Aaron went from the presence of the assembly unto the door of the tabernacle of the congregation, and they fell upon their faces: and the glory of the Lord appeared unto them." Verse 6.

It is deeply touching to find Moses, again and again, on his face before God. It was a sweet relief, to make his escape from a tumultuous host, and betake himself to the only One whose resources were adequate to meet such an occasion. "They fell upon their faces: and the glory of the Lord appeared unto them." They do not appear, on this occasion, to have attempted any reply to the people; "they went from the presence of the assembly" and cast themselves upon the living God. They could not possibly have done better. Who but the God of all grace could meet the ten thousand necessities of wilderness life? Well had Moses said, at the very beginning, "If thy presence go not with us, carry us not up hence." Assuredly, he was right and wise in so expressing himself. The divine presence was the *only* answer to the demand of such a congregation. But that presence *was* an all-sufficient answer. God's treasury is absolutely inexhaustible. He can never fail a trusting heart. Let us remember this. God delights to be used. He never grows weary of ministering to the need of His people. If this were ever kept in the remembrance of the thoughts of our hearts, we should hear less of the accents of impatience and discontent, and more of the sweet language of thankfulness and praise. But, as we have had frequent occasion to remark, desert life tests every one. It proves what is in us; and, thanks be to God, it brings out what is in *Him* for us.

Striking the rock in error

"And the Lord spake unto Moses, saying, Take *the* rod, and gather thou the assembly together, thou and Aaron thy brother, and speak ye unto the rock before their eyes; and it shall give forth his water, and thou shalt bring forth to them water out of the rock: so thou shalt give the congregation and their beasts drink. And Moses took *the* rod from before the Lord as he commanded him. And Moses and Aaron gathered the congregation together before the rock; and he said unto them, Hear now, ye rebels; must we fetch you water out of this rock? And Moses lifted up his hand, and with *his* rod he smote the rock twice: and the water came out abundantly; and the congregation drank, and their beasts also." Verse 7-11.

Two objects, in the foregoing quotation, demand the reader's attention, namely, "The Rock," and "The Rod." They both present Christ, most blessedly, to the soul; but in two distinct aspects. In 1 Corinthians 10:4, we read, "They drank of that spiritual Rock that followed them: and that Rock was Christ." This is plain and positive. It leaves no room whatever for the exercise of the imagination. "That Rock was Christ" – Christ smitten for us.

Then, as regards "the rod," we must remember that it was not the rod of Moses – the rod of authority – the rod of power. This would not suit the occasion before us. It had done its work. It had smitten the rock once, and that was enough. This we learn from Exodus 17, where we read, "The Lord said unto Moses, Go on before the people, and take with thee of the elders of Israel; and *thy* rod, *wherewith thou smotest the river* (see Ex. 7:20), take in thine hand and go. Behold, I will stand before thee there upon the rock in Horeb; and thou shalt smite the rock, and there shall come water out of it, that the people may drink. And Moses did so in the sight of the elders of Israel."

Here we have a type of Christ smitten for us, by the hand of God, in judgment. The reader will note the expression, "Thy rod wherewith thou smotest the river." Why the river? Why should this particular stroke of the rod be referred to? Exodus 7:20 furnishes the reply. "And he (Moses) lifted up the rod, and smote the waters that were in the river, in the sight of Pharaoh, and in the sight of his servants; and all the waters that were in the river *were turned to blood."* It was the rod which turned the water into blood that was to smite "that Rock which was Christ" in order that streams of life and refreshment might flow for us.

Now, this smiting could only take place once. It is never to be repeated. "Knowing that Christ, being raised from the dead, dieth no more; death hath no more dominion over him. For in that he died, he died unto sin *once*: but in that he liveth, he liveth unto God" (Rom. 6:9, 10). "But now *once* in the end of the world hath he appeared to put away sin by the sacrifice of himself . . . so Christ was *once* offered to bear the sins of many" (Heb. 9:26, 27). "For Christ also hath *once* suffered for sins, the just for the unjust, that he might bring us to God." 1 Peter 3:18.

There can be no repetition of the death of Christ; and hence Moses was wrong in smiting the rock twice with *his* rod – wrong in smiting it at all. He was commanded to take "*the rod*" – Aaron's rod – the priestly rod, and speak to the rock. The atoning work is done, and now our great High Priest has passed into the heavens, there to appear in the presence of God for us, and the streams of spiritual refreshment flow to us, on the ground of accomplished redemption, and in connection with Christ's priestly ministry, of which Aaron's budding rod is the exquisite figure.

Hence, then, it was a grave mistake for Moses to smite the rock a second time – a mistake to use his rod in the matter at all. To have smitten with Aaron's rod would, as we can easily understand, have spoiled its lovely blossom. A word would have sufficed, in connection with the rod of priesthood – the rod of grace. Moses failed to see this – failed to glorify God. He spoke unadvisedly with his lips; and as a consequence he was prohibited going over Jordan. His rod could not take the people over – for what could mere authority do with a murmuring host – and he was not suffered to go over himself because he failed to sanctify Jehovah in the eyes of the congregation.

But Jehovah took care of His own glory. He sanctified Himself before the people; and, notwithstanding their rebellious murmurings, and Moses' sad mistake and failure, the congregation of the Lord received a gushing stream from the smitten rock.

Nor was this all. It was not merely that grace triumphed in furnishing Israel's murmuring hosts with drink; but even in reference to Moses himself, it shines out most brilliantly, as we may see in Deuteronomy 34. It was grace that brought Moses to the top of Pisgah and shewed him the land of Canaan from thence. It was grace that led Jehovah to provide a grave for His servant and bury him therein. It was better to see the land of Canaan, in company with God, than to enter it in company with Israel. And yet we must not forget that Moses was prevented entering the land because of the unadvised speaking. God, in government, kept Moses out of Canaan. God, in grace, brought Moses up to Pisgah. These two facts, in the history of Moses, illustrate, very forcibly, the distinction between grace and government – a subject of the deepest interest, and of great practical value. Grace pardons and blesses; but government takes its course. Let us ever remember this. "Whatsoever a man soweth that shall he also reap." This principle runs through all the ways of God in government, and nothing can be more solemn; nevertheless "grace reigns through righteousness, unto eternal life, by Jesus Christ our Lord." All praise to Him who is at once, the fountain and the channel of this grace!

Messengers to the king of Edom

From verses 14-20 of our chapter, we have the correspondence between Moses and the king of Edom. It is instructive and interesting to notice the style of each, and to compare it with the history given in Genesis 32, 33. Esau had a serious grudge against Jacob; and albeit, through the direct interposition of God, he was not suffered to touch a hair of his brother's head, still, on the other hand, Israel must not meddle with Esau's possessions. Jacob had supplanted Esau; and Israel must not molest Edom. "Command thou the people, saying, Ye are to pass through the coast of your brethren the children of Esau, which dwell in Seir; and they shall be afraid of you: take ye good heed unto yourselves therefore. Meddle not with them; for I will not give you of their land, no, not so much as a foot breadth, because I have given mount Seir unto Esau for a possession. Ye shall buy meat of them for money, that ye may eat; and ye shall also buy water of them for money, that ye may drink. (Deut. 2:4-6.) Thus we see that the same God who would not suffer Esau to touch Jacob, in Genesis 33, now will not suffer Israel to touch Edom, in Numbers 20.

The death of Aaron

The closing paragraph of Numbers 20 is deeply touching. We shall not quote it, but the reader should refer to it, and compare it carefully with the scene in Exodus 4:1-17. Moses had deemed Aaron's companionship indispensable; but he afterwards found him to be a sore thorn in his side, and here he is compelled to strip him of his robes and see him gathered to his fathers. All this is very admonitory, in whatever way we view it, whether as regards Moses or Aaron. We have already referred to this instructive piece of history, and therefore we shall not dwell upon it here; but may the good Lord engrave its solemn lesson deeply upon the tablets of our hearts!

Chapter 21

THE BRAZEN SERPENT

Israel loathes the manna

This chapter brings prominently before us the familiar and beautiful ordinance of the brazen serpent – that great evangelical type. "And they journeyed from mount Hor by the way of the Red sea, to compass the land of Edom: and the soul of the people was much discouraged because of the way. And the people spake against God, and against Moses, Wherefore have ye brought us up out of Egypt to die in the wilderness? for there is no bread, neither is there any water; and our soul loatheth this light bread." Verses 4, 5.

Alas! alas! it is the same sad story, over and over again – "The murmurs of the wilderness." It was all well enough to escape out of Egypt, when the terrific judgments of God were falling upon it in rapid succession. At such a moment, there was but little attraction in the flesh pots, the leeks, the onions, and the garlick, when they stood connected with the heavy plagues sent forth from the hand of an offended God. But now the plagues are forgotten, and the flesh pots alone remembered. "Would to God we had died at the hand of the Lord in the land of Egypt, when we sat by the flesh pots, and when we did eat bread to the full."

What language! Man would rather sit by the flesh pots, in a land of death and darkness, than walk with God through the wilderness, and eat bread from heaven. The Lord Himself had brought His glory down into connection with the very sand of the desert, because His redeemed were there. He had come down to bear with all their provocation – to "suffer their manners in the wilderness." All this grace and exceeding condescension might well have called forth in them a spirit of grateful and humble subjection. But no; the very earliest appearance of trial was sufficient to elicit from them the cry, "Would to God we had died in the land of Egypt!"

However, they were very speedily made to taste the bitter fruits of their murmuring spirit. "The Lord sent fiery serpents among the people, and they bit the people; and much people of Israel died" (ver. 6). The serpent was the *source* of their discontent; and their condition, when bitten of the serpents, was well calculated to reveal to them the true *character* of their discontent. If the Lord's people will not walk happily and contentedly with Him, they must taste the power of the serpent – alas! a terrible power, in whatever way it may be experienced.

The serpents' bite brought Israel to a sense of their sin. "Therefore the people came to Moses, and said, We have sinned, for we have spoken against the Lord, and against thee: pray unto the Lord, that he take away the serpents from us." Verse 7.

Here, then, was the moment for divine grace to display itself. Man's need has ever been the occasion for the display of God's grace and mercy. The moment Israel could say, "We have sinned," there was no further hindrance. God could act, and this was enough. When Israel murmured, the serpents' bite was the answer. When Israel confessed, God's grace was the answer. In the one case, the serpent was the instrument of their wretchedness; in the other, it was the instrument of their restoration and blessing. "And the Lord said unto Moses, make thee a fiery serpent, and set it upon a pole: and it shall come to pass, that every one that is bitten, when he looketh upon it, shall live" (ver. 8). The very image of that which had done the mischief was set up to be the channel through which divine grace might flow down, in rich abundance, to poor wounded sinners. Striking and beautiful type of Christ on the cross!

The love of God

It is a very common error to view the Lord Jesus rather as the averter of God's wrath, than as the channel of His love. That He endured the wrath of God against sin is most preciously true. But there is more than this. He has come down into this wretched world to die upon the cursed tree, in order that, by dying, He might open up the everlasting springs of the love of God to the heart of poor rebellious man. This makes a vast difference in the presentation of God's nature and character to the sinner, which is of the very last importance. Nothing can ever bring a sinner back to a state of true happiness and holiness, but his being fully established in the faith and enjoyment of the love of God. The very first effort of the serpent, when, in the garden of Eden, he assailed the creature, was to shake his confidence in the kindness and love of God, and thus produce discontent with the place in which God had set him. Man's fall was the result – the immediate result of his doubting the love of God. Man's recovery must flow from his belief of that love; and it is the Son of God himself who says, "God so loved the world, that he gave his only begotten Son, that whosoever believeth in him should not perish, but have everlasting life." John 3:16.

Now, it is in close connection with the foregoing statement that our Lord expressly teaches that He was the Antitype of the brazen serpent. As the Son of God sent forth from the Father, He was, most assuredly, the gift and expression of God's love to a perishing world. But He was also to be lifted up upon the cross in atonement for sin, for *only* thus could divine love meet the necessities of the dying sinner. "As Moses lifted up the serpent in the wilderness, even so *must* the Son of man be lifted up; that whosoever believeth in him should not perish, but have eternal life." The whole human family have felt the serpent's deadly sting; but the God of all grace has found a remedy in the One who was lifted up on the cursed tree; and now, by the Holy Ghost sent down from heaven, He calls on all those who feel themselves bitten, to look to Jesus for life and peace. Christ is God's great ordinance, and through Him a full, free, present, and eternal salvation is proclaimed to the sinner – a salvation so complete, so well based, so consistent with all the attributes of the divine character and all the claims of the throne of God, that Satan cannot raise a single question about it. Resurrection is the divine vindication of the work of the cross, and the glory of Him who died thereon, so that the believer may enjoy the most profound repose in reference to sin. God is well pleased in Jesus; and, inasmuch as He views all believers in Him, He is well pleased in them also.

Faith which lays hold of salvation

And, be it noted, faith is the instrument whereby the sinner lays hold of Christ's salvation. The wounded Israelite had simply to *look and live* – look, not at himself – not at his wounds – not at others around him, but, directly and exclusively, to God's remedy. If he refused or neglected to look to that, there was nothing for him but death. He was called to fix his earnest gaze upon God's remedy, which was so placed that all might see it. There was no possible use in looking anywhere else, for the word was, *"Every one* that is bitten, *when* he looketh upon *it* shall live." The bitten Israelite was shut up to the brazen serpent; for the brazen serpent was God's exclusive remedy for the bitten Israelite. To look anywhere else was to get nothing; to look at God's provision was to get life.

Thus it is now. The sinner is called simply to look to Jesus. He is not told to look to ordinances – to look to churches – to look to men or angels. There is no help in any of these, and therefore he is not called to look to them, but exclusively to Jesus, whose death and resurrection form the eternal foundation of the believer's peace and hope. God assures him that "Whosoever believeth in him shall not perish, but have everlasting life." This should fully satisfy the heart and conscience. God is satisfied, and so ought we to be. To raise doubt is to deny the record of God. If an Israelite had said, "How do I know that looking to that serpent of brass will restore me?" or if he had begun to dwell upon the greatness and hopeless nature of his malady, and to reason upon the apparent uselessness of looking up to God's ordinance; in short, if anything, no matter what, had prevented his looking to the brazen serpent, it would have involved a positive rejection of God, and death would have been the inevitable result.

Thus, in the case of the sinner, the moment he is enabled to cast a look of faith to Jesus, his sins vanish. The blood of Jesus, like a mighty cleansing stream, flows over his conscience, washes away every stain, and leaves him without spot or wrinkle, or any such thing; and all this, too, in the very light of the holiness of God, where not one speck of sin can be tolerated.

But, ere closing our meditation on the brazen serpent, it may be well just to observe what we may call the intense individuality which marked the bitten Israelite's look at the serpent. Each one had to look for himself. No one could look for another. It was a personal question. No one could be saved by proxy. There was life in a look; but the look must be given. There needed to be a personal link – direct individual contact with God's remedy.

Thus it was then, and thus it is now. We must have to do with Jesus for ourselves. The Church cannot save us – no order of priests or ministers can save us. There must be the personal link with the Saviour, else there is no life. "It came to pass, that if a serpent had bitten *any man,* when *he* beheld the serpent of brass he lived." This was God's order then; and this is His order now, for "*As* Moses lifted up the serpent in the wilderness, even *so* must the Son of man be lifted up." Let us remember the two little words "*as*" and "*so,*" for they apply to every particular in the type and the antitype. Faith is an individual thing; repentance is an individual thing; salvation is an individual thing. Let us never forget this. True, there is, in Christianity, union and communion; but we must have to do with Christ for ourselves, and we must walk with God for ourselves. We can neither get life nor live by the faith of another. There is, we repeat with emphasis, an intense individuality in every stage of the Christian's life and practical career.

We shall not dwell further upon the familiar type of "The serpent of brass;" but we pray God to enable the reader to meditate upon it for himself, and to make a direct personal application of the precious truth unfolded in one of the most striking figures of Old Testament times. May he be led to gaze, with a more profound and soul-subduing faith, upon the cross, and to drink into his inmost soul the precious mystery there presented. May he not be satisfied with merely getting life by a look at that cross, but seek to enter, more and more, into its deep and marvellous meaning, and thus be more devotedly knit to Him who, when there was no other way of escape possible, did voluntarily surrender Himself to be bruised on that cursed tree for us and for our salvation.

And from there they came to Beer

We shall close our remarks on Numbers 21 by calling the reader's attention to verses 16-18. "And from thence they went to Beer: that is the well whereof the Lord spake unto Moses, Gather the people together and I will give them water. Then Israel sang this song, Spring up, O well; sing ye unto it. The princes digged the well, the nobles of the people digged it, by the direction of the lawgiver, with their staves."

This is a remarkable passage coming in at such a moment and in such a connection. The murmurings are hushed – the people are nearing the borders of the promised land – the effects of the serpents' bite have passed away, and now, without any rod, without any smiting, the people are supplied with refreshment. What though the Amorites, Moabites, and Ammonites are about them; what though the power of Sihon stands in the way; God can open a well for His people and give them a song in spite of all. Oh! what a God is our

God! How blessed it is to trace His actings and ways with His people in all these wilderness scenes! May we learn to trust Him more implicitly, and to walk with Him, from day to day, in holy and happy subjection! This is the true path of peace and blessing.

Chapters 22-24

BALAAM

The covetous prophet

These three chapters form a distinct section of our book – a truly marvellous section, abounding in rich and varied instruction. In it we have presented to us, first, the covetous prophet; and, secondly, his sublime prophecies. There is something peculiarly awful in the case of Balaam. He evidently loved money – no uncommon love, alas! in our own day. Balak's gold and silver proved a very tempting bait to the wretched man – a bait too tempting to be resisted. Satan knew his man, and the price at which he could be purchased.

If Balaam's heart had been right with God, he would have made very short work with Balak's message; indeed it would not have cost him a moment's consideration to send a reply. But Balaam's heart was all wrong, and we see him, in chapter 22 in the melancholy condition of one acted upon by conflicting feelings. His heart was bent upon going, because it was bent upon the silver and gold; but, at the same time, there was a sort of reference to God – an appearance of religiousness put on as a cloak to cover his covetous practices. He longed for the money; but he would fain lay hold of it after a religious fashion. Miserable man! Most miserable! His name stands on the page of inspiration as the expression of one very dark and awful stage of man's downward history. "Woe unto them," says Jude, "for they have gone in the way of Cain, and ran greedily after *the error of Balaam for reward* and perished in the gainsaying of Core." Peter, too, presents Balaam as a prominent figure in one of the very darkest pictures of fallen humanity – a model on which some of the vilest characters are formed. He speaks of those "having eyes full of adultery, and that cannot cease from sin; beguiling unstable souls; an heart they have exercised with covetous practices; cursed children: which have forsaken the right way, and are gone astray, following the way of Balaam the son of Bosor, *who loved the wages of unrighteousness;* but was rebuked for his iniquity: the dumb ass speaking with man's voice forbad the madness of the prophet." 2 Peter 2:14-16.

These passages are solemnly conclusive as to the true character and spirit of Balaam. His heart was set upon money – "he loved the wages of unrighteousness," and his history has been written by the pen of the Holy Ghost, as an awful warning to all professors to beware of covetousness which is idolatry. We shall not dwell further upon the sad story. The reader may pause for a few moments, and gaze upon the picture presented in Numbers 22. He may study the two prominent figures, the crafty king, and the covetous self-willed prophet; and we doubt not he will rise up from the study with a deepened sense of the evil of covetousness, the great moral danger of setting the heart's affections upon this world's riches, and the deep blessedness of having the fear of God before our eyes.

Can Balaam curse Israel?

We shall now proceed to examine those marvellous prophecies delivered by Balaam in the audience of Balak, king of the Moabites.

It is profoundly interesting to witness the scene enacted on the high places of Baal, to mark the grand question at stake, to listen to the speakers, to be admitted behind the scenes on such a momentous occasion. How little did Israel know or imagine what was going on between Jehovah and the enemy. It may be they were murmuring in their tents at the very moment in the which God was setting forth their perfection by the tongue of the covetous prophet. Balak would fain have Israel cursed; but, blessed be God, He will not suffer any one to curse His people. He may have to deal with them Himself, in secret, about many things; but He will not suffer another to move his tongue against them. He may have to expose them to themselves; but He will not allow a stranger to expose them.

This is a point of deepest interest. The great question is not so much what the enemy may think of God's people, or what they may think about themselves, or what they may think of one another. The real – the all-important question is, What does God think about them? He knows exactly all that concerns them; all that they are; all that they have done; all that is in them. Everything stands clearly revealed to His all penetrating eye. The deepest secrets of the heart, of the nature, and of the life, are all known to Him. Neither angels, men, nor devils know us as God knows us. God knows us perfectly; and it is with Him we have to do, and we can say, in the triumphant language of the apostle, "If God be for us, who can be against us? (Rom. 8)

The difference between standing and state

God sees us, thinks of us, speaks about us, acts towards us, according to what He Himself has made us, and wrought for us – according to the perfection of His own work. "Beholders many faults may find;" but, as regards our standing, our God sees us only in the comeliness of Christ; we are perfect in Him. When God looks at His people, He beholds in them His own workmanship; and it is to the glory of His holy name, and to the praise of His salvation, that not a blemish should be seen on those who are His – those whom He, in sovereign grace, has made His own. His character, His name, His glory, and the perfection of His work are all involved in the standing of those with whom He has linked Himself.

Hence, therefore, the moment any enemy or accuser enters the scene, Jehovah places Himself in front to receive and answer the accusation; and His answer is always founded, not upon what His people are in themselves, but upon what

He has made them through the perfection of His own work. His glory is linked with them, and, in vindicating them, He maintains His own glory. He places Himself between them and every accusing tongue. His glory demands that they should be presented in all the comeliness which He has put upon them. If the enemy comes to curse and accuse, Jehovah answers him by pouring forth the rich current of His everlasting complacency in those whom He has chosen for Himself, and whom He has made fit to be in His presence for ever.

All this is strikingly illustrated in the third chapter of the prophet Zechariah. There, too, the enemy presents himself to resist the representative of the people of God. How does God answer him? Simply by cleansing, clothing, and crowning the one whom Satan would fain curse and accuse, so that Satan has not a word to say. He is silenced for ever. The filthy garments are gone, and he that was a brand is become a *mitred* priest – he who was only fit for the flames of hell is now fitted to walk up and down in the courts of the Lord.

So also when we turn to the Book of Canticles we see the same thing. There the Bridegroom, in contemplating the bride, declares to her, "Thou art *all fair,* my love; there is *no spot* in thee" (chap. 4:7). She, in speaking of herself, can only exclaim *"I am black"* (chap. 1:5, 6). So also in John 13 the Lord Jesus looks at His disciples, and pronounces them "Clean every whit;" although, in a few hours afterwards, one of them was to curse and swear that he did not know Him. So vast is the difference between what we are in ourselves and what we are in Christ – between our positive standing and our possible state.

Should this glorious truth as to the perfection of our standing make us careless as to our practical state? Far away be the monstrous thought! Nay, the knowledge of our absolutely settled and perfect position in Christ is the very thing which the Holy Ghost makes use of in order to raise the standard of practice. Hearken to those powerful words from the pen of the inspired apostle, "If ye then be risen with Christ, seek those things which are above, where Christ sitteth on the right hand of God. Set your affection on things above, not on things on the earth. For ye are dead, and your life is hid with Christ in God. When Christ, our life, shall appear, then shall ye also appear with him in glory. Mortify *therefore* your members," &c. (Col. 3:1 – 5). We must never measure the standing by the state, but always judge the state by the standing. To lower the standing because of the state, is to give the death-blow to all progress in practical Christianity.

The foregoing line of truth is most forcibly illustrated in Balaam's four parables. To speak after the manner of men, we never should have had such a glorious view of Israel, as seen in "The vision of the Almighty" – "from the top of the rocks" – by one "having his eyes open," had not Balak sought to curse them. Jehovah, blessed be His name, can, very speedily, open a man's eyes to the true state of the case, in reference to the standing of His people, and His judgment respecting them. He claims the privilege of setting forth *His* thoughts about them. Balak and Balaam with "all the princes of Moab" may assemble to hear Israel cursed and defied; they may "build seven altars," and "offer a bullock and a lamb on every altar;" Balak's silver and gold may glitter under the covetous gaze of the false prophet; but not all the powers of earth and hell, men and devils combined, in their dark and terrible array, can evoke a single breath of curse or accusation against the Israel of God. As well might the enemy have sought to point out a flaw in that fair creation which God had pronounced "very good," as to fasten an accusation upon the redeemed of the Lord. Oh! no; they shine in all the comeliness which He has put upon them, and all that is needed, in order to see them thus, is to mount to "the top of the rocks" – to have "the eyes open" to look at them from His point of view, so that we may see them in "the vision of the Almighty."

Having thus taken a general survey of the contents of these remarkable chapters, we shall briefly glance at each of the four parables in particular. We shall find a distinct point in each – a distinct feature in the character and condition of the people, as seen in "The vision of the Almighty."

Balaam's first prophecy

In the first of Balaam's wonderful parables, we have the marked separation of God's people from all the nations, most distinctly set forth. "How shall I curse, whom God hath not cursed? or how shall I defy, whom the Lord hath not defied? For from the top of the rocks I see him, and from the hills I behold him: lo, the people shall dwell alone, and shall not be reckoned among the nations. Who can count the dust of Jacob, and the number of the fourth part of Israel? Let me die the death of the righteous, and let my last end be like his."[17]

Here we have Israel singled out, and partitioned off to be a separated and peculiar people – a people who, according to the divine thought concerning them, were never, at any time, on any ground, or for any object whatsoever, to be mingled with or reckoned amongst the nations. "The people shall dwell *alone*." This is distinct and emphatic. It is true of the literal seed of Abraham, and true of all believers now. Immense practical results flow out of this great principle. God's people are to be separated unto Him, not on the ground of being better than others, but simply on the ground of what God is, and of what He would ever have His people to be. We shall not pursue this point further just now; but the reader would do well to examine it thoroughly in the light of the divine word. *"The people shall dwell alone, and shall not be reckoned among the nations."* Numbers 23:8, 9.

The second prophecy

But if Jehovah, in His sovereign grace, is pleased to link Himself with a people; if He calls them out to be a separate people, in the world – to "dwell alone," and shine for Him in the midst of those who are still "sitting in darkness and the shadow of death," He can only have them in such a condition as suits Himself. He must make them such as He would have them to be – such as shall be to the praise of His great and glorious name. Hence, in the second parable, the prophet is made to tell out, not merely the negative, but the positive condition of the people. "And he took up his parable and said, Rise up, Balak, and hear; hearken unto me, thou son of Zippor: God is not a man, that he should lie; neither the son of man, that he should repent: hath he said, and shall he not do it? or hath he spoken, and shall he not make it good? Behold, I have received commandment to bless; and *he hath blessed;* and I *cannot* reverse it. He hath not beheld iniquity in Jacob, neither hath he seen perverseness in Israel: the Lord his God is with him, and the shout of a king is among them. God brought them out of Egypt; he hath as it were the strength of an unicorn. Surely there is no enchantment against Jacob, neither is there any divination against Israel: according to this time it shall be said of Jacob and of Israel, What hath *God wrought* [not What hath Israel wrought!] Behold, the people shall rise up as a great lion, and lift up himself as a young lion: he shall not lie down until he eat of the prey, and drink the blood of the slain." Chap. 23:18-24.

Here we find ourselves on truly elevated ground, and on ground as solid as it is elevated. This is, in truth "The top of the rocks" – the pure air and wide range of "the hills," where the people of God are seen only in "the vision of the Almighty" – seen as He sees them, without spot or wrinkle or any such thing – all their deformities hidden from view – all His comeliness seen upon them.

In this very sublime parable, Israel's blessedness and security are made to depend, not on themselves, but upon the truth and faithfulness of Jehovah. "God is not a man that he should lie; neither the son of man that he should repent." This places Israel upon safe ground. God must be true to Himself. Is there any power that can possibly prevent Him from fulfilling His word and oath? Surely not. "*He hath blessed;* and I cannot reverse it." God *will* not, and Satan *can* not reverse the blessing.

Thus all is settled. "It is ordered in all things and sure." In the previous parable, it was, "God hath *not cursed.*" Here it is, "He *hath blessed.*" There is very manifest advance. As

Balak conducts the money-loving prophet from place to place, Jehovah takes occasion to bring out fresh features of beauty in His people, and fresh points of security in their position. Thus it is not merely that they are a separated people dwelling alone; but they are a justified people, having the Lord their God *with* them, and the shout of a king *among* them. "He hath not beheld iniquity in Jacob, neither hath he seen perverseness in Israel." The enemy may say, "There is iniquity and perverseness there all the while." Yes, but who can make Jehovah behold it, when He Himself has been pleased to blot it all out as a thick cloud for His name's sake? If He has cast it behind His back, who can bring it before His face "It is God that justifieth; who is he that condemneth?" God sees His people so thoroughly delivered from all that could be against them, that He can take up His abode in their midst, and cause His voice to be heard amongst them.

Well, therefore may we exclaim "What hath God wrought!" It is not "What hath Israel wrought!" Balak and Balaam would have found plenty to do in the way of cursing, had Israel's work been in question. The Lord be praised, it is on what He hath wrought that His people stand, and their foundation is as stable as the throne of God. "If God be for us, who can be against us?" If God stands right between us and every foe, what have we to *fear?* If He undertakes, on our behalf, to answer every accuser, then, assuredly, perfect peace is our portion.

The third prophecy

However, the king of Moab still fondly hoped and sedulously sought to gain his end. And, doubtless, Balaam did the same, for they were leagued together against the Israel of God, thus reminding us forcibly of the beast and the false prophet, who are yet to arise and play an awfully solemn part in connection with Israel's future, as presented on the apocalyptic page.

"And when Balaam saw that it pleased the Lord to bless Israel, he went not, as at other times, to seek for enchantments [what a dreadful disclosure is here!] but he set his face toward the wilderness. And Balaam lifted up his eyes, and he saw Israel abiding in His tents, according to their tribes; and the Spirit of God came upon him. And he took up his parable, and said, Balaam the son of Beor hath said, *and the man whose eyes are open* hath said, he hath said, which heard *the words of God,* which saw *the vision of the Almighty,* falling into a trance, but having his eyes open: How goodly are thy tents, O Jacob, and thy tabernacles, O Israel! As the valleys are they spread forth, as gardens by the river's side, as the trees of lign aloes which the Lord hath planted, and as cedar trees beside the waters. He shall pour the water out of his buckets, and his seed shall be in many waters, and his king shall be higher than Agag, and his kingdom shall be exalted. God brought him forth out of Egypt; he hath, as it were, the strength of an unicorn: he shall *eat up the nations* his enemies [terrible announcement for Balak!] and shall break their bones, and pierce them through with his arrows. He couched, he lay down as a lion, and as a great lion: who shall stir him up? Blessed is he that blesseth thee, and cursed is he that curseth thee." Numbers 24:1-9.

"Higher and higher yet" is surely the motto here. We may well shout "Excelsior," as we mount up to the top of the rocks, and hearken to those brilliant utterances which the false prophet was forced to give out. It was better and better for Israel – worse and worse for Balak. He had to stand by and not only hear Israel "blessed," but hear himself "cursed" for seeking to curse them.

But let us particularly notice the rich grace that shines in this third parable. "How goodly are thy tents, O Jacob, and thy tabernacles, O Israel!" If one had gone down to examine those tents and tabernacles, in "the vision" of man they might have appeared "Black as the tents of Kedar." But, looked at in "the vision of the Almighty," they were "goodly," and whoever did not see them thus needed to have *"his eyes opened."* If I am looking at the people of God "from the top of the rocks," I shall see them as God sees them, and that is as clothed with all the comeliness of Christ – complete in Him – accepted in the Beloved. This is what will enable me to get on with them, to walk with them, to have fellowship with them, to rise above their points and angles, blots and blemishes, failures and infirmities.[18] If I do not contemplate them from this lofty – this divine ground, I shall be sure to fix my eye on some little flaw or other, which will completely mar my communion, and alienate my affections.

In Israel's case, we shall see, in the very next chapter, what terrible evil they fell into. Did this alter Jehovah's judgment? Surely not. "He is not the son of man that he should repent." He judged and chastened them for their evil, because He is holy, and can never sanction, in His people, anything that is contrary to His nature. But He could never reverse His judgment respecting them. He knew all about them. He knew what they were and what they would do; but yet He said, "I have not beheld iniquity in Jacob, neither have I seen perverseness in Israel. How goodly are thy tents, O Jacob, and thy tabernacles, O Israel!" Was this making light of their evil? The thought were blasphemy. He could chasten them for their sins; but the moment an enemy comes forth to curse or accuse, He stands in front of His people and says, "I see no iniquity" – "How goodly are their tents"

Reader, dost thou think that such views of divine grace will minister to a spirit of Antinomianism? Far be the thought! We may rest assured we are never further away from the region of that terrible evil than when we are breathing the pure and holy atmosphere of "the top of the rocks" – that high ground from whence God's people are viewed, not as they are in themselves, but as they are in Christ – not according to the thoughts of man, but according to the thoughts of God. And, furthermore, we may say that the only true and effectual mode of raising the standard of moral conduct is to abide in the faith of this most precious and tranquillizing truth, that God sees us perfect in Christ.

But we must take one more glance at our third parable. Not only are Israel's tents seen to be goodly in the eyes of Jehovah, but the people themselves are presented to us as abiding fast by those ancient sources of grace and living ministry which are found in God. "As the valleys are they spread forth, as gardens by the river's side, as the trees of lign aloes which the Lord hath planted, and as cedar trees beside the waters." How exquisite! How perfectly beautiful! And only to think that we are indebted to the godless confederacy between Balak and Balaam for those sublime utterances!

But there is more than this. Not only is Israel seen drinking at those everlasting well-springs of grace and salvation, but, as must ever be the case, as a channel of blessing to others. "He shall pour the water out of his buckets." It is the fixed purpose of God that Israel's twelve tribes shall yet be a medium of rich blessing to all the ends of the earth. This we learn from such scriptures as Ezekiel 47 and Zechariah 14, on which we do not now attempt to dwell; we merely refer to them as showing the marvellous fullness and beauty of these glorious parables. The reader may meditate, with much spiritual profit, upon these and kindred scriptures; but let him carefully guard against the fatal system falsely called spiritualizing, which, in fact, consists mainly in applying to the professing church all the special blessings of the house of Israel, while, to the latter, are left only the curses of a broken law. We may rest assured that God will not sanction any such system as this. Israel is beloved for the fathers' sakes; and "the gifts and calling of God are without repentance." Romans 11.

The fourth prophecy

We shall close this section by a brief reference to Balaam's last parable. Balak, having heard such a glowing testimony to Israel's future, and the overthrow of all their enemies, was not only sorely disappointed, but greatly enraged; "And Balak's anger was kindled against Balaam, and he smote his hands together: and Balak said unto Balaam, I called thee to curse mine enemies, and, behold, thou hast altogether blessed them these three times. Therefore now flee thou to thy place: I thought to promote thee unto *great honour;* but, lo, the Lord hath kept thee back from honour. And Balaam said unto Balak, Spake I not also to thy messengers which thou sentest unto me, saying, If Balak would give me his house full of silver and gold [the very thing his poor heart craved intensely], I *cannot* go beyond the commandment of the Lord, to do either good or bad of mine own mind; but what the Lord saith, that will I speak. And now, behold, I go unto my people: come therefore, and I will advertise thee what *this people* shall do to *thy people* in the latter days. [This was coming to close quarters.] And he took up his parable, and said, Balaam the son of Beor hath said, and the man whose eyes are open hath said: he hath said, which heard the words of God, and knew the knowledge of the most High, which saw the vision of the Almighty, falling into a trance, but having his eyes open: I shall see him, but not now: I shall behold him, but not nigh: [tremendous fact for Balaam!] there shall come a Star out of Jacob, and a Sceptre shall rise out of Israel, and shall smite the corners of Moab, and destroy all the children of Sheth." Verse 10-17.

This gives great completeness to the subject of these parables. The top-stone is here laid on the magnificent superstructure. It is, in good truth, grace and glory. In the first parable we see the absolute separation of the people; in the second, their perfect justification; in the third, their moral beauty and fruitfulness; and, now, in the fourth, we stand on the very summit of the hills – on the loftiest crag of the rocks, and survey the wide plains of glory in all their length and breadth, stretching away into a boundless future. We see the Lion of the tribe of Judah crouching; we hear his roar; we see Him seizing upon all his enemies, and crushing them to atoms. The Star of Jacob rises to set no more. The true David ascends the throne of His father, Israel is pre-eminent in the earth, and all his enemies are covered with shame and everlasting contempt.

It is impossible to conceive anything more magnificent than these parables; and they are all the more remarkable as coming at the very close of Israel's desert wanderings, during which they had given such ample proof of what they were – of what materials they were made – and what their capabilities and tendencies were. But God was above all, and nothing changeth His affection. Whom He loves, and as He loves, He loves to the end; and hence the league between the typical "beast and false prophet" proved abortive. Israel was blessed of God and not to be cursed of any. "And Balaam rose up, and went, and returned to his place: and Balak also went his way."

---

[17] Poor, wretched Balaam! Miserable man! He would fain die the death of the righteous. Many there are who would say the same; but they forget that the way "to die the death of the righteous" is to possess and exhibit the *life* of the righteous. Many – alas! how many – would like to die the death who do not live the life. Many would like to possess Balak's silver and gold, and yet be enrolled amongst the Israel of God. Vain thought! Fatal delusion! We cannot serve God and Mammon.

[18] The statement in the text does not, by any means, touch the question of discipline in the house of God. We are bound to judge moral evil and doctrinal error. 1 Cor. 5:12, 13.

Chapter 25

FORNICATION WITH THE DAUGHTERS OF MOAB

Israel joins himself to Baal-Peor

Here a new scene opens upon our view. We have been on the top of Pisgah, hearkening to God's testimony respecting Israel, and there all was bright and fair, without a cloud, without a spot. But now we find ourselves in the plains of Moab, and all is changed. There, we had to do with God and His thoughts. Here, we have to do with the people and their joys. What a contrast! It reminds us of the opening and the close of 2 Corinthians 12. In the former, we have the *positive standing* of the Christian; in the latter, the *possible state* into which he may fall if not watchful. That shows us "a man in Christ" capable of being caught up into paradise, at any moment. This shows us saints of God capable of plunging into all manner of sin and folly.

Thus it is with Israel, as seen from "The top of the rocks," in "The vision of the Almighty," and Israel as seen in the plains of Moab. In the one case, we have their perfect standing; in the other, their imperfect state. Balaam's parables give us God's estimate of the former; the javelin of Phinehas, His judgment upon the latter. God will never reverse His decision as to what His people are as to standing; but He must judge and chasten them when their ways comport not with that standing. It is His gracious will that their state should correspond with their standing. But here is, alas! where failure comes in. Nature is allowed to act in various ways, and our God is constrained to take down the rod of discipline, in order that the evil thing which we have suffered to manifest itself may be crushed and subdued.

The energetic action of Phinehas

Thus it is in Numbers 25. Balaam, having failed in his attempt to curse Israel, succeeds in seducing them, by his wiles, to commit sin, hoping whereby to gain his end. "And Israel joined himself unto Baal-peor: and the anger of the Lord was kindled against Israel. And the Lord said unto Moses, Take all the heads of the people, and hang them up before the Lord against the sun, that the fierce anger of the Lord may be turned away from Israel." (Ver. 3, 4.) Then we have the striking record of the zeal and faithfulness of Phinehas: "And the Lord spake unto Moses, saying, Phinehas, the son of Eleazar, the son of Aaron the priest, hath turned my wrath away from the children of Israel, while he was zealous for my sake among them, that I consumed not the children of Israel in my jealousy. Wherefore say, Behold, I give unto him my covenant of peace: and he shall have it, and his seed after him, even the covenant of an everlasting priesthood; because he was zealous for his God, and made an atonement for the children of Israel." Verse 10-13.

God's glory and Israel's good were the objects that ruled the conduct of the faithful Phinehas on this occasion. It was a critical moment. He felt there was a demand for the most stern action. It was no time for false tenderness. There are moments in the history of God's people in the which tenderness to man becomes unfaithfulness to God; and it is of the utmost importance to be able to discern such moments. The prompt acting of Phinehas saved the whole congregation, glorified Jehovah in the midst of His people, and completely frustrated the enemy's design. Balaam fell among the judged Midianites; but Phinehas became the possessor of an everlasting priesthood.

Thus much as to the solemn instruction contained in this brief section of our book, May we profit by it. May God's Spirit give us such an abiding sense of the perfection of our standing in Christ, that our practical ways may be more in accordance with it!

Chapter 26

A NEW NUMBERING

Six hundred thousand men fallen in the wilderness

This, though one of the longest chapters in our book, does not call for much in the way of remark or exposition. In it we have the record of the second numbering of the people, as they were about to enter upon the promised land. How sad to think that, out of the six hundred thousand men of war which were numbered, at the first, only two remain – Joshua and Caleb! All the rest lay mouldering in the dust, buried beneath the sand of the desert, all passed away. The two men of simple faith remained to have their faith rewarded. As for the men of unbelief, the inspired apostle tells us "Their carcasses fell in the wilderness."

How solemn! How full of instruction and admonition for us! Unbelief kept the first generation from entering the land of Canaan, and caused them to die in the wilderness. This is the fact on which the Holy Ghost grounds one of the most searching warnings and exhortations anywhere to be found in the compass of the inspired volume. Let us hear it! "Wherefore . . . take heed, brethren, lest there be in any of you an evil heart of unbelief, in departing from the living God. But exhort one another daily while it is called To day; lest any of you be hardened through the deceitfulness of sin. For we are made partakers of Christ, if we hold the beginning of our confidence steadfast unto the end; while it is said, To day, if ye will hear his voice, harden not your hearts, as in the provocation. For some, when they had heard, did provoke: howbeit not all that came out of Egypt by Moses. But with whom was he grieved forty years? was it not with them that had sinned, whose carcasses fell in the wilderness? And to whom sware he that they should not enter into his rest, but to them that believed not? So we see that they could not enter in because of unbelief. Let us therefore fear, lest a promise being left us of entering into his rest, any of you should seem to come short of it. For unto us was the gospel preached, as well as unto them: but the word preached did not profit them, not being mixed with faith in them that heard." Hebrews 3:7 – 4:1, 2.

The word of God mixed with faith

Here lies the great practical secret. The word of God mixed with faith. Precious mixture! the only thing that can really profit any one. We may hear a great deal; we may talk a great deal; we may profess a great deal; but we may rest assured that the measure of real spiritual power – power to surmount difficulties – power to overcome the world – power to get on – power to possess ourselves of all that God has bestowed upon us – the measure of this power is simply the measure in which God's word is mixed with faith. That word is settled for ever in heaven; and if it is fixed in our hearts, by faith, there is a divine link connecting us with heaven and all that belongs to it; and, in proportion as our hearts are thus livingly linked with heaven and the Christ who is there, shall we be practically separated from this present world, and lifted above its influence. Faith takes possession of all that God has given. It enters into that within the veil; it endures as seeing Him who is invisible; it occupies itself with the unseen and eternal, not with the seen and the temporal. Men think possession sure; faith knows nothing sure but God and His word. Faith takes God's word and locks it up in the very innermost chamber of the heart, and there it remains as hid treasure – the only thing that deserves to be called treasure. The happy possessor of this treasure is rendered thoroughly independent of the world. He may be poor as regards the riches of this perishing scene; but if only he is rich in faith, he is the possessor of untold wealth – "durable riches and righteousness" – "the unsearchable riches of Christ."

Reader, these are not the pencillings of fancy – the mere visions of the imagination. No; they are substantial verities – divine realities, which you may now enjoy in all their preciousness. If you will only take God at His word – only believe what He says because He says it – for this is faith – then verily you have this treasure, which renders its possessor entirely independent of this scene where men live only by the sight of their eyes. The men of this world speak of *"the positive"* and *"the real,"* meaning thereby what they can see and experience; in other words, the things of time and sense – the tangible – the palpable. Faith knows nothing positive, nothing real, but the word of the living God.

Now it was the lack of this blessed faith that kept Israel out of Canaan, and caused six hundred thousand carcasses to fall in the wilderness. And it is the lack of this faith that keeps thousands of God's people in bondage and darkness, when they ought to be walking in liberty and light – that keeps them in depression and gloom, when they ought to be walking in the joy and strength of God's full salvation – that keeps them in fear of judgment, when they ought to be walking in the hope of glory – that keeps them in doubt as to whether they shall escape the sword of the destroyer in Egypt, when they ought to be feasting on the old corn of the land of Canaan.

Oh! that God's people would consider these things in the secret of His presence and in the light of His word! Then indeed they would better know and more fully appreciate the fair inheritance which faith finds in the eternal word of God – they would more clearly apprehend the things which are freely given to us of God in the Son of His love. May the Lord send out His light and His truth, and lead His people into the fullness of their portion in Christ, so that they may take their true place, and yield a true testimony for Him, while waiting for His glorious advent.

Chapter 27

THE DAUGHTERS OF ZELOPHEHAD

God responds to faith

The conduct of the daughters of Zelophehad, as recorded in the opening section of this chapter, presents a striking and beautiful contrast to the unbelief on which we have just been commenting. They, most assuredly, belonged not to the generation of those who are ever ready to abandon divine ground, lower the divine standard, and forego the privileges conferred by divine grace. No; those five noble women had no sympathy with such. They were determined, through grace, to plant the foot of faith on the very highest ground, and, with holy yet bold decision, to make their own of that which God had given. Let us read the refreshing record.

"Then came the daughters of Zelophehad, the son of Hepher, the son of Gilead, the son of Machir, the son of Manasseh, of the families of Manasseh the son of Joseph: and these are the names of his daughters, Mahlah, Noah, and Hoglah, and Milcah, and Tirzah, and they stood before Moses, and before Eleazar the priest, and before the princes and all the congregation, by the door of the tabernacle of the congregation, saying, Our father died in the wilderness, and he was not in the company of them that gathered themselves together against the Lord, in the company of Korah; but died in his own sin, and had no sons. Why should the name of our father be done away from among his family because he hath no son? Give unto us, therefore, a possession among the brethren of our father." Verses 1-4.

This is uncommonly fine. It does the heart good to read such words as these at a time like the present, when so little is made of the proper standing and portion of God's people, and when so many are content to go on from day to day, and year to year, without caring even to inquire into the things which are freely given to them of God. Nothing is more sad than to see the carelessness, the utter indifference, with which many professing Christians treat such great and all important questions as the standing, walk, and hope of the believer and the Church of God. It is not, by any means, our purpose to go into these questions here. We have done so repeatedly in the other volumes of the series of "Notes." We merely desire to call the reader's attention to the fact, that it is at once sinning against our own rich mercies, and dishonouring the Lord, when we evince a spirit of indifferentism in reference to any one point of divine revelation as to the position and portion of the Church, or of the individual believer. If God, in the aboundings of His grace, has been pleased to bestow upon us precious privileges, as Christians, ought we not to seek earnestly to know what these privileges are? Ought we not to seek to make them our own, in the artless simplicity of faith? Is it treating our God and His revelation worthily, to be indifferent as to whether we are servants or sons – as to whether we have the Holy Ghost dwelling in us or not – as to whether we are under law or under grace – whether ours is a heavenly or an earthly calling?

Surely not. If there be one thing plainer than another in scripture, it is this, that God delights in those who appreciate and enjoy the provision of His love – those who find their joy in Himself. The inspired volume teems with evidence on this point. Look at the case now before us in our chapter. Here were those daughters of Joseph – for such we must call them – bereaved of their father – helpless and desolate, as viewed from nature's standpoint. Death had snapped the apparent link which connected them with the proper inheritance of God's people. What then? Were they content to give up? – to fold their arms, in cold indifference? Was it nothing to them whether or not they were to have a place and a portion with the Israel of God? Ah! no, reader; these illustrious women exhibit something totally different from all this – something which we may well study and seek to imitate – something which, we are bold to say, refreshed the heart of God. They felt sure there was a portion for them in the land of promise, of which neither death nor anything that happened in the wilderness could ever deprive them. "Why should the name of our father be done away from among his people because he hath no son?" Could death – could failure of male issue – could anything – frustrate the goodness of God? Impossible. "Give unto us, therefore, a possession among the brethren of our father."

Noble words! words that went right up to the throne and to the heart of the God of Israel. It was a most powerful testimony delivered in the ears of the whole congregation. Moses was taken aback. Here was something beyond the range of the lawgiver. Moses was a servant, and a blessed and honoured servant too. But, again and again, in the course of this marvellous Book of Numbers, this wilderness volume, questions arise with which he is unable to deal, as for example, the defiled men in chapter 9, and the daughters of Zelophehad in the section before us.

"And Moses brought their cause before the Lord. And the Lord spake unto Moses, saying, *The daughters of Zelophehad speak right: thou shalt surely give them a possession of an inheritance among their father's brethren; and thou shalt cause the inheritance of their father to pass unto them.*" Verses 5-7.

Here was a glorious triumph, in the presence of the whole assembly. A bold and simple faith is always sure to be rewarded. It glorifies God, and God honours it. Need we travel from section to section, and from page to page of the holy volume to prove this? Need we turn to the Abrahams, the Hannahs, the Deborahs, the Rahabs, the Ruths of Old Testament times? or to the Marys, the Elizabeths, the centurions, and the Syro-phoenicians of The New Testament times? Wherever we turn, we learn the same great practical truth that God delights in a bold and simple faith – a faith that artlessly seizes and tenaciously holds all that He has given

– that positively refuses, even in the very face of nature's weakness and death, to surrender a single hair's breadth of the divinely given inheritance. What though Zelophehad's bones lay mouldering in the dust of the wilderness; what though no male issue appeared to sustain his name? faith could rise above all these things, and count on God's faithfulness to make good all that His word had promised.

"The daughters of Zelophehad speak right." They always do so. Their words are words of faith, and, as such, are always right in the judgment of God. It is a terrible thing to limit "the Holy One of Israel." He delights to be trusted and used. It is utterly impossible for faith to overdraw its account in God's bank. God could no more disappoint faith than He could deny Himself. He can never say to faith, "You have miscalculated; you take too lofty – too bold a stand; go lower down, and lessen your expectations." Ah! no; the only thing in all this world that truly delights and refreshes the heart of God is the faith that can simply trust him; and we may rest assured of this, that the faith that can trust Him is also the faith that can love Him, and serve Him, and praise Him.

Hence, then, we are deeply indebted to the daughters of Zelophehad. They teach us a lesson of inestimable value. And more than this, their acting gave occasion to the unfolding of a fresh truth which was to form the basis of a divine rule for all future generations. The Lord commanded Moses, saying, "If a man die, and have no son, then ye shall cause his inheritance to pass unto his daughter."

Here we have a great principle laid down, in reference to the question of inheritance, of which, humanly speaking, we should have heard nothing had it not been for the faith and faithful conduct of these remarkable women. If they had listened to the voice of timidity and unbelief – if they had refused to come forward, before the whole congregation in the assertion of the claims of faith; then, not only would they have lost their own inheritance and blessing, but all future daughters of Israel, in a like position, would have been deprived of their portion likewise. Whereas, on the contrary, by acting in the precious energy of faith, they preserved their inheritance; they got the blessing; they received testimony from God; their names shine on the page of inspiration; and their conduct furnished, by divine authority, a precedent for all future generations.

That the inheritance remove not from tribe to tribe

Thus much as to the marvellous results of faith. But then we must remember that there is moral danger arising out of the very dignity and elevation which faith confers on those who, through grace, are enabled to exercise it; and this danger must be carefully guarded against. This is strikingly illustrated in the further history of the daughters of Zelophehad, as recorded in the last chapter of our book. "And the chief fathers of the families of the children of Gilead, the son of Machir, the son of Manasseh, of the families of the sons of Joseph, came near, and spake before Moses, and before the princes, the chief fathers of the children of Israel: and they said, The Lord commanded my lord to give the land for an inheritance by lot to the children of Israel: and my lord was commanded by the Lord to give the inheritance of Zelophehad our brother unto his daughters. And if they be married to any of the sons of the other tribes of the children of Israel, then shall their inheritance be taken from the inheritance of our fathers, and shall be put to the inheritance of the tribe whereunto they were received: so shall it be taken from the lot of our inheritance. And when the jubilee of the children of Israel shall be, then shall their inheritance be put unto the inheritance of the tribe whereunto they are received: so shall their inheritance be taken away from the inheritance of the tribe of our fathers. And Moses commanded the children of Israel according to the word of the Lord, saying, "The tribe of the sons of Joseph hath said well." Numbers 36:1-5.

The "fathers" of the house of Joseph must be heard as well as the "daughters." The faith of the latter was most lovely; but there was just a danger lest, in the elevation to which that faith had raised them, they might forget the claims of others, and remove the landmarks which guarded the inheritance of their fathers. This had to be thought of and provided for. It was natural to suppose that the daughters of Zelophehad would marry; and moreover it was possible they might form an alliance outside the boundaries of their tribe; and thus in the year of jubilee – that grand adjusting institution – instead of adjustment, there would be confusion, and a permanent breach in the inheritance of Manasseh. This would never do; and therefore the wisdom of those ancient fathers is very apparent. We need to be guarded on every side, in order that the integrity of faith and the testimony may be duly maintained. We are not to carry things with a high hand and a strong will, though we have ever such strong faith, but be ever ready to yield ourselves to the adjusting power of the whole truth of God.

"This is the thing which the Lord doth command concerning the daughters of Zelophehad, saying, Let them marry to whom they think best, only to the family of the tribe of their father shall they marry; so shall not the inheritance of the children of Israel remove from tribe to tribe; for every one of the children of Israel shall keep himself to the inheritance of the tribe of his fathers . . . Even as the Lord commanded Moses, so did the daughters of Zelophehad; for they [the five daughters] were married unto their father's brothers' sons. And they were married into the families of the sons of Manasseh, the son of Joseph; and their inheritance remained in the tribe of the family of their father." Verses 6-12.

Thus all is settled. The activities of faith are governed by the truth of God, and individual claims are adjusted in harmony with the true interests of all; while, at the same time, the glory of God is so fully maintained, that at the time of the jubilee, instead of any confusion in the landmarks of Israel, the integrity of the inheritance is secured according to the divine grant.

Nothing can be more instructive than this entire history of the daughters of Zelophehad. May we really profit by it!

Moses approaches the end

The closing paragraph of our chapter is full of deep solemnity. The governmental dealings of God are displayed before our eyes in a manner eminently calculated to impress the heart. "The Lord said unto Moses, Get thee up into this mount Abarim and see the land which I have given unto the children of Israel. And when thou hast seen it, thou also shalt be gathered unto thy people, as Aaron thy brother was gathered. For ye rebelled against my commandment in the desert of Zin, in the strife of the congregation, to sanctify me at the water before their eyes: that is the water of Meribah in Kadesh, in the wilderness of Zin." Verses 12-14.

Moses must not go over Jordan. It is not only that he cannot officially bring the people over, but he cannot even go himself. Such was the enactment of the government of God. But, on the other hand, we see grace shining out, with uncommon lustre, in the fact that Moses is conducted, by God's own hand, to the top of Pisgah, and from thence he sees the land of promise, in all its magnificence, not merely as Israel afterwards possessed it, but as God had originally given it.

Now, this was the fruit of grace, and it comes out more fully in the close of Deuteronomy, where we are also told that God buried His dear servant. This is wonderful. Indeed there is nothing like it in the history of the saints of God. We do not dwell upon this subject here, having done so elsewhere;[19] but it is full of the deepest interest. Moses spake unadvisedly with his lips, and for that he was forbidden to cross the Jordan. This was God in *government*. But Moses was taken up to Pisgah, there, in company with Jehovah, to get a full view of the inheritance; and then Jehovah made a grave for His servant and buried him therein. This was God in *grace* – marvellous, matchless grace! – grace that has ever made the eater yield meat and the strong sweetness. How precious to be the subjects of such grace! May our souls rejoice in it more and more, in the eternal fountain whence it emanates, and in the channel through which it flows!

We shall close this section by a brief reference to the lovely unselfishness of Moses in the matter of appointing a successor. That blessed man of God was ever characterised by a most exquisite spirit of self-surrender – that rare and admirable grace. We never find him seeking his own things; on the contrary, again and again, when opportunity was afforded him of building up his own fame and fortune, he proved, very distinctly, that the glory of God and the good of His people so occupied and filled his heart that there was no room for a single selfish consideration.

Thus it is in the closing scene of our chapter. When Moses hears that he is not to go over Jordan, instead of being occupied in regrets as to himself, he only thinks of the interests of the congregation. "And Moses spake unto the Lord saying, Let the Lord, the God of the spirits of all flesh, set a man over the congregation, which may go out before them, and which may go in before them, and which may lead them out, and which may bring them in; that the congregation of the Lord be not as sheep which have no shepherd."

What unselfish breathings are here. How grateful they must have proved to the heart of that One who so loved and cared for His people! Provided that Israel's need were met Moses was content. If only the work was done he cared not who did it. As to himself, his interest, and his destinies, he could calmly leave all in the hand of God. He would take care of him, but oh! his loving heart yearns over the beloved people of God; and the very moment he sees Joshua ordained as their leader, he is ready to depart and be at rest forever. Blessed servant! Happy man! Would there were even a few amongst us characterised, in some small degree, by his excellent spirit of self-abnegation, and jealous care for God's glory and His people's good. But alas! alas! we have to repeat, with deepening emphasis, the words of the apostle, "All seek their own, not the things that are Jesus Christ's." O Lord, stir up all our hearts to desire a more earnest consecration of ourselves, in spirit, soul, and body, to thy blessed service! May we, in good truth, learn to live, not unto ourselves, but unto Him who died for us – who came from heaven to earth about our sins; and is gone back from earth to heaven about our infirmities; and who is coming again for our eternal salvation and glory.

---

[19] See an article entitled "Grace and Government" in "Things New and Old," Vol., 4. p. 111. G, Morrish.

THE CONTINUAL BURNT OFFERING AND THE PERIODIC BURNT OFFERINGS

The most precious sacrifices to God

These two chapters must be read together; they form a distinct section of our book – a section pregnant with interest and instruction. The second verse of chapter 28 gives us a condensed statement of the contents of the entire section. "And the Lord spake unto Moses, saying, Command the children of Israel, and say unto them, My offering, and my bread for my sacrifices made by fire, for a sweet savour unto me, shall ye observe to offer unto me in their due season."

In these words the reader is furnished with a key with which to unlock the whole of this portion of the Book of Numbers. It is as distinct and simple as possible. "*My* offering," "*My* bread," "*My* sacrifices," *"A sweet savour unto me."* All this is strongly marked. We may learn here, without an effort, that the grand leading thought is Christ to Godward. It is not so much Christ as meeting our need – though surely He does most blessedly meet that – as Christ feeding and delighting the heart of God. It is God's bread – a truly wonderful expression, and one little thought of or understood. We are all sadly prone to look at Christ merely as the procuring cause of our salvation, the One through whom we are forgiven and saved from hell, the channel through which all blessing flows to us. He is all this, blessed for ever be His Name. He is the Author of eternal salvation to all them that obey Him. He bore our sins in His own body on the tree. He died, the just for the unjust, to bring us to God. He saves us from our sins, from their present power, and from their future consequences.

All this is true; and, consequently, throughout the whole of the two chapters which lie open before us, and in each distinct paragraph, we have the sin offering introduced. (See chap. 28:15, 22, 30; chap. 29:5, 11, 16, 19, 22, 25, 28, 31, 34, 38.) Thirteen times over is mention made of the sin offering of atonement; and yet, for all that, it remains true and obvious that sin or atonement for sin is not, by any means, the great prominent subject. There is no mention of it in the verse which we have quoted for the reader, although that verse plainly gives a summary of the contents of the two chapters; nor is there any allusion to it until we reach the fifteenth verse.

Need we say that the sin offering is essential inasmuch as man is in question, and man is a sinner? It would be impossible to treat of the subject of man's approach to God, his worship, or his communion, without introducing the atoning death of Christ as the necessary foundation. This the whole heart confesses with supreme delight. The mystery of Christ's precious sacrifice shall be the wellspring of our souls throughout the everlasting ages.

But shall we be deemed Socinian in our thoughts if we assert that there is something in Christ and in His precious death beyond the bearing of our sins and the meeting of our necessities? We trust not. Can any one read Numbers 28 and 29 and not see this? Look at one simple fact which might strike the mind of a child. There are seventy-one verses in the entire section; and, out of these, thirteen allude to the sin offering, and the remaining fifty-eight are occupied with sweet savour offerings.

In a word then, the special theme here is God's delight in Christ. Morning and evening, day by day, week after week, from one new moon to another, from the opening to the close of the year, it is Christ in His fragrance and preciousness to Godward. True it is – thanks be to God, and to Jesus Christ His Son – our sin is atoned for, judged, and put away for ever – our trespasses forgiven and guilt cancelled. But above and beyond this, the heart of God is fed, refreshed, and delighted by Christ. What was the morning and evening lamb? Was it a sin offering or a burnt offering? Hear the reply in God's own words: "And thou shalt say unto them, This is the offering made by fire which ye shall offer unto the Lord; two lambs of the first year without spot day by day, for a *continual burnt offering*. The one lamb shalt thou offer in the morning, and the other lamb shalt thou offer at even; and a tenth part of an ephah of flour for a meat offering, mingled with the fourth part of an hin of beaten oil. It is a continual burnt offering, which was ordained in Mount Sinai, for a sweet savour, a sacrifice made by fire unto the Lord."

Again; what were the two lambs for the Sabbath? a sin offering or a burnt offering? "This is *the burnt offering* of every sabbath." It was to be double, because the Sabbath was a type of the rest that remaineth for God's people, when there will be a twofold appreciation of Christ. But the character of the offering is as plain as possible. It was Christ to Godward. This is the special point in the burnt offering. The sin offering is Christ to usward. In this, it is a question of the hatefulness of sin; in that, it is a question of the preciousness and excellency of Christ.

So also, at the beginnings of their months (ver. 11), in the feast of the Passover and unleavened bread (ver. 16-25), in the feast of firstfruits (ver. 26-31), in the feast of trumpets (chap. 29:1-6), in the feast of tabernacles (ver. 7-38). In a word, throughout the entire range of feasts, the leading idea is Christ as a sweet savour. The sin offering is never lacking; but the sweet savour offerings get *the* prominent place, as is evident to the most cursory reader. We do not think it possible for any one to read this remarkable portion of scripture and not observe the contrast between the place of the sin offering and that of the burnt offering. The former is only spoken of as "one kid of the goats," whereas the latter comes before us in the form of "fourteen lambs," "thirteen bullocks" and such like. Such is the large place which the sweet savour offerings get in this scripture.

Christian worship

But why dwell upon this? Why insist upon it? Simply to show to the Christian reader the true character of the worship God looks for, and in which He delights. God delights in Christ; and it should be our constant aim, to present to God that in which He delights. Christ should ever be the material of our worship; and He will be, in proportion as we are led by the Spirit of God. How often, alas! it is otherwise with us the heart call tell. Both in the assembly and in the closet, how often is the tone low, and the spirit dull and heavy. We are occupied with self instead of with Christ; and the Holy Ghost, instead of being able to do His own proper work, which is to take of the things of Christ and show them unto us, is obliged to occupy us with ourselves, in self-judgment, because our ways have not been right.

All this is to be deeply deplored. It demands our serious attention both as assemblies and as individuals – in our public reunions and in our private devotions. Why is the tone of our public meetings frequently so low? Why such feebleness, such barrenness, such wandering? Why are the hymns and prayers so wide of the mark? Why is there so little that really deserves the name of worship? Why is there such restlessness and aimless activity? Why is there so little in our midst to refresh the heart of God? so little that He can really speak of as "*His* bread, for *his* sacrifices made by fire, for a sweet savour unto him?" We are occupied with self and its surroundings – our wants, our weakness, our trials and difficulties; and we leave God without the bread of His sacrifice. We actually rob Him of His due, and of that which His loving heart desires.

Is it that we can ignore our trials, our difficulties, and our wants? No; but we can commit them to Him. He tells us to cast *all* our care upon Him, in the sweet and tranquillizing assurance that He careth for us. He invites us to cast our burdens upon Him, in the assurance that He will sustain us. He is mindful of us. Is not this enough! Ought we not to be sufficiently at leisure from ourselves, when we assemble in His presence, to be able to present to Him something besides our own things? He has provided for us. He has made all right for us. Our sins and our sorrows have all been divinely met. And most surely we cannot suppose that such things are the food of God's sacrifice. He has made them His care, blessed be His name; but they cannot be said to be His food.

Christian reader, ought we not to think of these things? – think of them, in reference both to the assembly and the closet? – for the same remarks apply both to the one and the other. Ought we not to cultivate such a condition of soul as would enable us to present to God that which He is pleased to call "His bread?" The truth is we want more entire and habitual occupation of heart with Christ as a sweet savour to God. It is not that we should value the sin offering less; far be the thought! But let us remember that there is something more in our precious Lord Jesus Christ than the pardon of our sins and the salvation of our souls. What do the burnt offering, the meat offering, and the drink offering set forth? Christ as a sweet savour – Christ the food of God's offering – the joy of His heart. Need we say it is one and the same Christ? Need we insist upon it that it is the same One who was made a curse for us that is a sweet savour to God? Surely, surely every Christian owns this. But are we not prone to confine our thoughts of Christ to what *He did for us,* to the virtual exclusion of what *He is to God?* It is this we have to mourn over and judge – this we must seek to have corrected; and we cannot but think that a careful study of Numbers 28, 29 would prove a very excellent corrective. May God, by His Spirit, use it to this end!

Having, in our "Notes on Leviticus," offered to the reader what God has given to us in the way of light on the sacrifices and feasts, we do not feel led to dwell upon them here. That little volume can be had of the publisher, and the reader will find in chapters 1 – 8 and chapter 33 what may interest and help him in reference to the subjects treated of in the two chapters on which we have been dwelling.

Chapter 30

THE VOWS

This brief section has what we may term a dispensational bearing. It applies specially to Israel, and treats of the question of vows and bonds. The man and the woman stand in marked contrast, in relation to this subject. "If a man vow a vow unto the Lord, or swear an oath to bind his soul with a bond; he shall not break his word, he shall do according to all that proceedeth out of his mouth." Verse 2.

In reference to the woman, the case was different. "If a woman also vow a vow unto the Lord, and bind herself by a bond, being in her father's house in her youth; and her father hear her vow, and her bond wherewith she hath bound her soul, and her father shall hold his peace at her: then all her vows shall stand, and every word wherewith she hath bound her soul shall stand. But if her father disallow her in the day that he heareth; not any of her vows, or of her bonds wherewith she hath bound her soul, shall stand: and the Lord shall forgive her, because her father disallowed her" (ver. 3-5). The same thing applied in the case of a wife. Her husband could either confirm or disannul all her vows and bonds.

Such was the law with regard to vows. There was no relief for the man. He was bound to go right through with whatever had proceeded out of his mouth. Whatever he undertook to do, he was solemnly and irreversibly held to it. There was no back door, as we say – no way of getting out of it.

Now we know who, in perfect grace, took this position, and voluntarily bound Himself to accomplish the will of God, whatever that will might be. We know who it is that says, "I will pay my vows unto the Lord now in the presence of all his people." "The man Christ Jesus," who, having taken the vows upon Him, discharged them perfectly to the glory of God, and the eternal blessing of His people. There was no escape for Him. We hear Him exclaiming, in the deep anguish of His soul, in the garden of Gethsemane, "If it be possible, let this cup pass from me." But it was not possible. He had undertaken the work of man's salvation, and He had to go through the deep and dark waters of death, judgment, and wrath; and perfectly meet all the consequences of man's condition. He had a baptism to be baptised with, and was straitened until it was accomplished. In other words, He had to die in order that, by death, He might open the pent-up flood gates, and allow the mighty tide of divine and everlasting love to flow down to His people. All praise and adoration be to His peerless name for ever!

Thus much as to the man and his vows and bonds. In the case of the woman, whether as the daughter or the wife, we have the nation of Israel, and that in two ways, namely, under government and under grace; Looked at from a governmental point of view, Jehovah, who is at once the Father and the Husband, has held his peace at her, so that her vows and bonds are allowed to stand; and she is, to this day, suffering the consequences, and made to feel the force of those words, "Better that thou shouldest not vow, than that thou shouldest vow and not pay."

But, on the other hand, as viewed from the blessed standpoint of grace, the Father and the Husband has taken all upon Himself, so that she shall be forgiven and brought into the fulness of blessing by and by, not on the ground of accomplished vows and ratified bonds, but on the ground of sovereign grace and mercy, through the blood of the everlasting covenant. How precious to find Christ everywhere! He is the centre and foundation, the beginning and the end, of all the ways of God. May our hearts be ever filled with Him! May our lips and lives speak His praise! May we, constrained by His love, live to His glory all our days upon earth, and then go home to be with Himself for ever, to go no more out!

We have here given what we believe to be the primary

thought of this chapter. That it may be applied, in a secondary way, to individuals, we do not, by any means, question; and further, that, like all scripture, it has been written for our learning, we most thankfully own. It must ever be the delight of the devout Christian to study all the ways of God, whether in grace or government – His ways with Israel – His ways with the Church – His ways with all – His ways with each. Oh! to pursue this study with an enlarged heart and an enlightened understanding!

Chapter 31

JEHOVAH'S VENGEANCE ON MIDIAN

We have here the closing scene of Moses' *official* life; as in Deuteronomy 34 we have the closing scene of his *personal* history. "And the Lord spake unto Moses, saying, Avenge the children of Israel of the Midianites; afterward shalt thou be gathered unto thy people. And Moses spake unto the people, saying, Arm some of yourselves unto the war, and let them go against the Midianites, and avenge the Lord of Midian. Of every tribe a thousand, throughout all the tribes of Israel, shall ye send to the war. So there were delivered out of the thousands of Israel, a thousand of every tribe, twelve thousand armed for war. And Moses sent them to the war, a thousand of every tribe, them and *Phinehas the son of Eleazar the priest*, to the war, *with the holy instruments,* and the trumpets to blow in his hand. And they warred against the Midianites, as the Lord commanded Moses; *and they slew all the males.* Verses 3-7.

This is a very remarkable passage. The Lord says to Moses, *"Avenge the children of Israel* of the Midianites." And Moses says to Israel, *"Avenge the Lord* of Midian." The people had been ensnared by the wiles of the daughters of Midian, through the evil influence of Balaam the son of Peor; and they are now called upon to clear themselves thoroughly from all the defilement which, through want of watchfulness, they had contracted. The sword is to be brought upon the Midianites; and all the spoil is to be made to pass either through the fire of judgment or through the water of purification. Not one jot or tittle of the evil thing is to be suffered to pass unjudged.

Now, this war was what we may call abnormal. By right, the people ought not to have had any occasion to encounter it at all. It was not one of the wars of Canaan. It was simply the result of their own unfaithfulness – the fruit of their own unhallowed commerce with the uncircumcised. Hence, although Joshua, the son of Nun, had been duly appointed to succeed Moses, as leader of the congregation, we find no mention whatever of him in connection with this war. On the contrary, it is to Phinehas, the son of Eleazar the priest, that the conduct of this expedition is committed; and he enters upon it "with the holy instruments and the trumpets."

All this is strongly marked. *The priest* is the prominent person; and *the holy instruments,* the prominent instrumentality. It is a question of wiping away the stain caused by their unholy association with the enemy; and therefore, instead of a general officer with sword and spear, it is a priest with holy instruments that appears in the foreground. True, the sword is here; but it is not the prominent thing. It is the priest with the vessels of the sanctuary; and that priest the selfsame man who first executed judgment upon that very evil which has here to be avenged.

The moral of all this is, at once, plain and practical. The Midianites furnish a type of that peculiar kind of influence which the world exerts over the hearts of the people of God – the fascinating and ensnaring power of the world used by Satan to hinder our entrance upon our proper heavenly portion. Israel should have had nothing to do with these Midianites; but having, in an evil hour – an unguarded moment – been betrayed into association with them, nothing remains but war and utter extermination.

So with us, as Christians. Our proper business is to pass through the world, as pilgrims and strangers; having nothing to do with it, save to be the patient witnesses of the grace of Christ, and thus shine as lights in the midst of the surrounding moral gloom. But, alas! we fail to maintain this rigid separation; we suffer ourselves to be betrayed into alliance with the world, and, in consequence, we get involved in trouble and conflict which does not properly belong to us at all. War with Midian formed no part of Israel's proper work. They had to thank themselves for it. But God is gracious; and hence, through a special application of priestly ministry, they were enabled, not only to conquer the Midianites, but to carry away much spoil. God, in His infinite goodness, brings good out of evil. He will cause the eater to yield meat, and the strong sweetness. His grace shines out, with exceeding brightness, in the scene before us, inasmuch as He actually deigns to accept a portion of the spoils taken from the Midianites. But the evil had to be thoroughly judged. "Every male" had to be put to death – all in whom there was the energy of the evil had to be completely exterminated; and finally the fire of judgment and the water of purification had to do their work on the spoil, ere God or His people could touch an atom of it.

What holy lessons are here! May we apply our hearts to them! May we be enabled to pursue a path of more intense separation, and to press on our heavenly road as those whose portion and whose home is on high! God, in His mercy grant it!

Chapter 32

TWO AND A HALF TRIBES ON THE EAST OF JORDAN

A lack of faith and energy

The fact recorded in this chapter has given rise to considerable discussion. Various have been the opinions advanced in reference to the conduct of the two tribes and a half. Were they right or were they wrong in choosing their inheritance on the wilderness side of Jordan? This is the question. Was their acting in this matter, the expression of power or of weakness? How are we to form a sound judgment in this case?

In the first place, where was Israel's proper portion – their divinely destined inheritance? Most surely, on the other side of Jordan, in the land of Canaan. Well, then, ought not this fact to have sufficed? Would or could a really true heart – a heart that thought, and felt, and judged with God – have entertained the idea of selecting a portion other than that which God had allotted and bestowed? Impossible. Hence, then, we need not to go further, in order to have a divine judgment on this subject. It was a mistake, a failure, a stopping short of the divine mark, on the part of Reuben and Gad, and the half tribe of Manasseh, to choose any boundary line short of the river Jordan. They were governed, in their conduct, by worldly and selfish considerations – by the sight of their eyes – by carnal motives. They surveyed "the land of Jazer and the land of Gilead," and they estimated it entirely according to their own interests, and without any reference to the judgment and will of God. Had they been simply looking to God, the question of settling down short of the river Jordan would never have been raised at all.

But when people are not simple, not true-hearted, they get into circumstances which give rise to all sorts of questions. It is a great matter to be enabled, by Divine grace, to pursue a line of action, and to tread a path so unequivocal as that no question can be raised. It is our holy and happy privilege so to carry ourselves as that no complication may ever arise. The secret of so doing is to walk with God, and thus to have our conduct wholly governed by His word.

But that Reuben and Gad were not thus governed, is manifest from the entire history. They were half-and-half men; men of mixed principles; mere borderers; men that sought their own things, and not the things of God. Had these latter engrossed their hearts, nothing would have induced them to take up their position short of the true boundary line.

It is very evident that Moses had no sympathy with their proposal. It was a judgment upon his conduct that he was not allowed to go over. His heart was in the promised land; and he longed to go thither in person. How could he then approve of the conduct of men who were not only prepared, but actually desirous, to take up their abode somewhere else? Faith can never be satisfied with anything short of the true position and portion of God's people. A single eye can only see – a faithful heart only desire – the inheritance given of God.

Hence, therefore, Moses at once condemned the proposition of Reuben and Gad. True, he afterwards relaxed his judgment and gave his consent. Their promise to cross the Jordan, ready armed, before their brethren, drew from Moses a kind of assent. It seemed an extraordinary manifestation of unselfishness and energy to leave all their loved ones behind, and cross the Jordan, only to fight for their brethren. But where had they left those loved ones? They had left them short of the divine mark. They had deprived them of a place and a portion in the true land of promise – that inheritance of the which God had spoken to Abraham, Isaac, and Jacob.

And for what? Just to get good pasture for their cattle. For an object like this did the two tribes and a half abandon their place within the true limits of the Israel of God.

Further consequences

And now let us look at the consequences of this line of action. Let the reader turn to Joshua 22. Here we have the first sorrowful effect of the equivocal conduct of Reuben and Gad. They must needs build an altar – "a great altar to see to" lest in time to come their brethren might disown them. What does all this prove? It proves that they were all wrong in taking up their position on this side of Jordan. And only mark the effect upon the whole assembly – the disturbing, alarming effect of this altar. At the first blush, it wore the aspect of actual rebellion. "And when the children of Israel heard of it, *the whole congregation of the children of Israel* gathered themselves together at Shiloh, to go up to war against them. And *the children of Israel* sent unto *the children of Reuben*, and to the children of Gad, and to the half tribe of Manasseh,[20] into the land of Gilead, Phinehas the son of Eleazar the priest, and with him ten princes, of each chief house a prince throughout all the tribes of Israel; and each one was an head of the house of their fathers among the thousands of Israel. And they came unto the children of Reuben, and to the children of Gad, and to the half tribe of Manasseh, unto the land of Gilead, and they spake with them, saying, Thus saith *the whole congregation of the Lord* [Did not the two and a half belong to it?] what trespass is this that ye have committed against the God of Israel, to turn away this day from following the Lord, in that ye have builded you an altar, that ye might rebel this day against the Lord? Is the iniquity of Peor too little for us, from which we are not cleansed until this day, although there was a plague in the congregation of the Lord, but that ye must turn away this day from following the Lord? and it will be, seeing ye rebel to-day against the Lord, that to-morrow he will be wroth with the whole congregation of Israel. Notwithstanding, if the land of *your possession* be unclean, then pass ye over unto *the land of the possession of the Lord,* wherein the Lord's tabernacle dwelleth, [what burning words!] and take possession among us: but rebel not against the Lord, nor rebel against us, in building you an altar beside the altar of the Lord our God." Joshua 22:12-19.

Now all this serious misunderstanding, all this trouble and alarm, was the result of failure on the part of Reuben and Gad. True, they are able to explain themselves and satisfy their brethren, in reference to the altar. But then there would have been no need of the altar, no demand for explanation, no cause of alarm, had they not taken up an equivocal position.

Here was the source of all the mischief; and it is important for the Christian reader to seize this point with clearness, and to deduce from it the great practical lesson which it is designed to teach. It can hardly be questioned, by any thoughtful, spiritually minded person who fully weighs all the evidence in the case, that the two tribes and a half were wrong in stopping short of the Jordan, in taking up their position. This seems to us unquestionable, seen on the ground of what has already come before us; and if further proof were needed, it is furnished by the fact that they were the very first to fall into the enemy's hands. See 1 Kings 22:3.

But it may be that the reader is disposed to ask, "What has all this to say to us? Has this piece of history any voice, any instruction for us?" Unquestionably. It sounds in our ears, with accents of deep solemnity, "Beware of falling short of your proper position – your proper portion – of being content with the things which belong to this world – of taking any stand short of death and resurrection – the true, the spiritual Jordan."[21]

Such, we conceive, is the teaching of this portion of our book. It is a grand point to be whole-hearted, decided, and unequivocal in taking our stand for Christ. Serious damage is done to the cause of God and the testimony of Christ, by those who profess to be Christians denying their heavenly calling and character, and acting as though they were citizens of this world. This is a powerful engine in the hands of Satan. An undecided, half-and-half Christian is more inconsistent than an open out-and-out worldling or infidel. The unreality of professors is more injurious by far to the cause of God than all the forms of moral pravity put together. This may seem a strong statement; but it is too true. Christian professors who are only mere borderers – men of mixed principles – persons of doubtful deportment – these are the men who most seriously damage the blessed cause, and promote the designs of the enemy of Christ. What we want, just now, is a band of whole-hearted, thorough-going, unmistakable witnesses for Jesus Christ – men who shall declare plainly that they seek a country – earnest, unworldly men.

These are the men for the present crisis. What can be more deplorable, more saddening and discouraging, than to find those who make a lofty profession, who talk loudly of death and resurrection, who boast of their high doctrines and heavenly privileges, but whose walk and ways give the lie to their words? They love the world and the things of the world. They love money and are eager to grasp and hoard as much as possible.

Beloved Christian reader, let us see to these things. Let us honestly judge ourselves as in the very presence of God, and put away from us everything, no matter what, that tends to hinder the complete devotion of ourselves in spirit and soul and body to Him who loved us and gave Himself for us. May we, to use the language of Joshua 22 so carry ourselves as not to need any altar to see to, nor anything to declare where we belong to, where we worship, whose we are and whom we serve. Thus shall everything about us be transparent and unquestionable, our testimony shall be distinct, and the sound of our trumpet certain. Our peace, too, shall flow like an even river, and the entire bent of our course and character shall be to the praise of Him whose name is called upon us. May the good Lord stir up the hearts of His people, in this day of hateful indifferentism, lukewarmness, and easy-going profession, to more genuine self-surrender, true consecration to the cause of Christ, and unshaken faith in the living God! Will the reader join us in pleading for all this?

---

[20] As though the two tribes and a half were actually detached from the nation of Israel.

[21] No doubt there are many sincere Christians who do not see the heavenly calling and position of the Church – who do not enter into the special character of truth taught in the Epistle to the Ephesians – who are, nevertheless, according to their light, earnest, devoted, and true-hearted; but we feel persuaded that such persons lose incalculable blessing in their own souls, and fall very short of the true Christian testimony.

Chapters 33 & 34

THE JOURNEYINGS OF ISRAEL IN THE WILDERNESS

The first of these sections gives us a wonderfully minute description of the desert wanderings of the people of God. It is impossible to read it without being deeply moved by the tender love and care of God so signally displayed throughout the whole. To think of His deigning to keep such a record of the journeyings of His poor people, from the moment they marched out of Egypt until they crossed the Jordan – from the land of death and darkness to the land flowing with milk and honey. "He knoweth thy walking through this great wilderness: these forty years the Lord thy God hath been with thee; thou hast lacked nothing." He went before them, every step of the way; He travelled over every stage of the wilderness; in all their afflictions He was afflicted. He took care of them like a tender nurse. He suffered not their garments to wax old, or their feet to swell, for these forty years; and here He retraces the entire way by which His hand had led them, carefully noting down each successive stage of that marvellous pilgrimage, and every spot in the desert at which they had halted. What a journey! What a travelling companion!

It is very consolatory to the heart of the poor, weary pilgrim to be assured that every stage of his wilderness journey is marked out by the infinite love and unerring wisdom of God. He is leading His people by a right way, home to Himself; and there is not a single circumstance in their lot, or a single ingredient in their cup, which is not carefully ordered by Himself, with direct reference to their present profit and their everlasting felicity. Let it only be our care to walk with Him, day by day, in simple confidence, casting all our care upon Him, and leaving ourselves and all our belongings absolutely in His hands. This is the true source of peace and blessedness, all the journey through. And then, when our desert wanderings are over – when the last stage of the wilderness has been trodden, He will take us home to be with Himself for ever.

> "There with what joy reviewing
> Past conflicts, dangers, fears–
> Thy hand our foes subduing,
> And drying all our tears–
> Our hearts with rapture burning,
> The path we shall retrace,
> Where now our souls are learning,
> The riches of Thy grace."

The boundaries of Israel's inheritance

Chapter 34 gives the boundaries of the inheritance, as drawn by the hand of Jehovah. The selfsame hand which had guided their wanderings here fixes the bounds of their habitation. Alas! they never took possession of the land as given of God. He gave them the whole land, and gave it for ever. They took but a part, and that for a time. But, blessed be God, the moment is approaching when the seed of Abraham shall enter upon the full and everlasting possession of that fair inheritance, from which they are for the present excluded. Jehovah will assuredly accomplish all His promises, and lead His people into all the blessings secured to them in the everlasting covenant – that covenant which has been ratified by the blood of the Lamb. Not one jot or tittle shall fail of all that He has spoken. His promises are all Yea and Amen in Christ Jesus, who is the same yesterday, to-day, and for ever. All praise to the Father, and unto the Son, and to the Holy Spirit!

THE CITIES OF REFUGE

The Levites' cities

The opening lines of this most interesting chapter set before us the gracious provision which Jehovah made for His servants the Levites. Each of the tribes of Israel was privileged – that we say not bound – to furnish the Levites with a certain number of cities with their suburbs, according to their ability. "All the cities which ye shall give to the Levites shall be forty and eight cities: them shall ye give with their suburbs. And the cities which ye shall give shall be of the possession of the children of Israel: from them that have many ye shall give many; but from them that have few ye shall give few: every one shall give of his cities unto the Levites, according to his inheritance which he inheriteth." Verses 7, 8.

The Lord's servants were wholly cast upon Him for their portion. They had no inheritance or possession save in Himself. Blessed inheritance! Precious portion! None like it, in the judgment of faith. Blessed are all those who can truly say to the Lord, "Thou art the portion of my cup, and the lot of my inheritance." God took care of His dependent servants, and permitted the whole congregation of Israel to taste the hallowed privilege – for such it most assuredly was – of being co-workers with Him in providing for those who had willingly devoted themselves to His work, abandoning all besides.

Six cities of refuge

Thus, then, we learn that, out of the twelve tribes of Israel, forty and eight cities, with their suburbs, were to be given over to the Levites; and out of these again, the Levites had the privilege of furnishing six cities to be a refuge for the poor manslayer. Most lovely provision! Lovely in its origin! Lovely in its object!

The cities of refuge were situated, three on the eastern and three on the western side of Jordan. Whether Reuben and Gad were right or wrong in settling east of that significant boundary, God in His mercy would not leave the slayer without a refuge from the avenger of blood. On the contrary, like Himself, He ordained that those cities which were designed as a merciful provision for the slayer should be so situated that wherever there was need of a shelter that shelter might be near at hand. There was always a city within reach of any who might be exposed to the sword of the avenger. This was worthy of our God. If any slayer happened to fall into the hands of the avenger of blood, it was not for want of a refuge near at hand, but because he had failed to avail himself of it. All necessary provision was made; the cities were named, and well defined, and publicly known. Everything was made as plain, as simple, and as easy as possible. Such was God's gracious way.

No doubt, the slayer was responsible to put forth all his energy to reach the sacred precincts; and, no doubt, he would. It is not at all likely that any one would be so blind or so infatuated as to fold his arms, in cool indifference, and say, "If I am fated to escape, I shall escape, my efforts are not needed. If I am not fated to escape, I cannot escape, my efforts are of no use." We cannot fancy a manslayer using such silly language, or being guilty of such blind fatuity as this. He knew too well that if the avenger could but lay his hand upon him, all such notions would be of small account. There was but the one thing to be done, and that was to escape for his life – to flee from impending judgment – to find his safe abode within the gates of the city of refuge. Once there, he could breathe freely. No evil could overtake him there. The moment he crossed the threshold of the gate, he was as safe as God's provision could make him. If a hair of his head could be touched, within the bounds of the city, it could but be a dishonour and a reproach upon the ordinance of God. True, he had to keep close. He dared not venture outside the gate. Within, he was perfectly safe. Without, he was thoroughly exposed. He could not even visit his friends. He was an exile from his father's house. He was a prisoner of hope. Absent from the home of his heart's affections, he waited for the death of the high priest, which was to set him perfectly free and restore him, once more, to his inheritance and to his people.

Israel guilty of murder

Now, we believe that this beautiful ordinance had special reference to Israel. They have killed the Prince of life; but the question is, As which are they viewed by God, as the murderer or as the slayer? If the former, there is no refuge, no hope. No murderer could be sheltered within the city of refuge. Here is the law of the case, as stated in Joshua 20, "The Lord also spake unto Joshua, saying, Speak to the children of Israel, saying, Appoint out for you cities of refuge, whereof I spake unto you by the hand of Moses: that the slayer that killeth any person unawares and unwittingly may flee thither: and they shall be your refuge from the avenger of blood. And when he that doth flee unto one of those cities shall stand at the entering of the gate of the city, and shall declare his cause in the ears of the elders of that city, they shall take him into the city unto them, and give him a place, that he may dwell among them. And if the avenger of blood pursue after him, then they shall not deliver the slayer up into his hand; *because he smote his neighbour unwittingly,* and hated him not beforetime, And he shall dwell in that city, until he stand before the congregation for judgment, and until the death of the high priest that shall be in those days: then shall the slayer return, and come unto his own city, and unto his own house, unto the city from whence he fled." Verses 1-6.

But with respect to the murderer; the law was rigid and unbending: "The murderer shall surely be put to death. The revenger of blood himself shall slay the murderer, when he meeteth him." Numbers 35.

Israel, then, through the marvellous grace of God, will be treated as a slayer and not as a murderer. "Father, forgive them, for they know not what they do." These potent words ascended to the ear and to the heart of the God of Israel. They were heard and answered; nor are we to suppose that the answer was exhausted in its application on the day of Pentecost. No; it still holds good, and its efficacy will be illustrated in the future history of the house of Israel. That people are now under God's keeping. They are exiles from the land and the home of their fathers. But the time is coming when they shall be restored to their own land, not by the death of the high priest – blessed be His deathless name! He can never die – but He will leave His present position, and come forth, in a new character, as the Royal Priest, to sit upon His throne. Then shall the exile return to his long-lost home, and his forfeited inheritance. But not till then, else it would be ignoring the fact that they killed the Prince of life, which were impossible. The manslayer must remain out of his possession until the appointed time; but he is not to be treated as a murderer, because he did it unwittingly. "I obtained mercy" – says the Apostle Paul, speaking as a pattern to Israel – "because I did it ignorantly in unbelief." "And now, brethren," says Peter, "I wot that through ignorance ye did it, as did also your rulers."

These passages, together with the precious intercession of the slain One, do, in the most distinct manner, place Israel on the ground of the manslayer, and not on the ground of the murderer. God has provided a refuge and a shelter for His much-loved people, and in due time they shall return to their long-lost dwellings, in that land which Jehovah gave as a gift to Abraham his friend for ever.

The application to the sinner

Such we believe to be the true interpretation of the ordinance of the city of refuge. Were we to view it as bearing upon the case of a sinner taking refuge in Christ, it could only be in a very exceptional way, inasmuch as we should find ourselves surrounded, on all hands, by points of contrast rather than by points of similarity. For in the first place, the manslayer, in the city of refuge, was not exempt from judgment, as we learn from Joshua 20:6. But for the believer in Jesus there is and can be no judgment, for the simplest of all reasons, that Christ has borne the judgment instead.

Again, there was a possibility of the slayer's falling into the hands of the avenger, if he ventured outside the gates of the city. The believer in Jesus can never perish; he is as safe as the Saviour himself.

Finally, as regards the slayer, it was a question of temporal safety and life in this world. As regards the believer in Jesus, it is a question of eternal salvation and life everlasting in the world to come. In fact, in almost every particular, it is striking contrast rather than similarity.

One grand point there is common to both, and that is, the point of exposure to imminent danger and the urgent need of fleeing for refuge. If it would have been wild folly on the part of the slayer to linger or hesitate for a moment, until he found himself safely lodged in the city of refuge, it is surely still wilder folly, yea, the very height of madness, on the part of the sinner, to linger or hesitate in coming to Christ. The avenger might perhaps fail to lay hold on the slayer even though he were not in the city; but judgment *must* overtake the sinner out of Christ. There is no possibility of escape, if there is the thickness of a gold leaf between the soul and Christ. Solemn thought! May it have its due weight in the heart of the reader who is yet in his sins! May he find no rest – not one moment's rest – until he has fled for refuge to lay hold of the hope set before him in the gospel. Judgment impends sure, certain, solemn judgment. It is not only that the avenger may come, but judgment must come upon all who are out of Christ.

Oh! unconverted, thoughtless, careless reader – should this volume fall into the hands of such – hear the warning voice! Flee for thy life! Tarry not, we entreat thee! Delay is madness. Every moment is precious. You know not the hour in the which you may be cut down, and consigned to that place in the which a single ray of hope, not even the faintest glimmer, can ever visit you – the place of eternal night, eternal woe, eternal torment – the place of a deathless worm and an unquenchable flame. Beloved friend, do let us entreat thee, in these few closing lines of our volume, to come now, just as thou art, to Jesus, who stands with open arms and loving heart, ready to receive thee, to shelter, to save, and to bless, according to all the love of His heart, and the perfect efficacy of His name and His sacrifice. May God the Holy Spirit, by His own resistless energy, lead thee, just now, to come. "Come unto me," says the loving Lord and Saviour, "all ye that labour and are heavy laden and I will give you rest." Precious words! May they fall, with divine power, upon many a weary heart!

Here we close our meditations upon this marvellous section of the volume of God[22]; and, in doing so, we are impressed with a profound sense of the depth and richness of the mine to which we have sought to conduct the reader, and also of the excessive feebleness and poverty of the suggestions which we have been enabled to offer. However, our confidence is in the living God, that He will, by His Holy Spirit, lead the heart and mind of the Christian reader into the enjoyment of His own precious truth, and thus fit him, more and more, for His service in these last evil days, that the name of our Lord Jesus Christ may be magnified, and His truth maintained in living power. May God, in His abounding mercy, grant this, for Jesus Christ's sake!

C. H. M.

---

[22] Chapter 36 has been referred to in our meditation on chapter 27.

CONTENTS

Preface 5

Chapters 1 & 2
Pedigree and banners 9
   The Book of Numbers in the Pentateuch 9
   Belonging to the people of God 14
   Wisdom is justified of all her children 17
   Knowing one's pedigree 19
   Being ready for battle 20
   Three types of conflict 21
   The order of the camp of Israel 24
   A question to the reader 28

Chapters 3 & 4
Israel in the wilderness, a picture of the Church in this world 31
   God in the midst of His people 31
   The all-sufficiency of God faced with the needs of the people in the wilderness 32
   The assembly separated from this world 35
   In the midst of a Christianity in ruin 38
   What is of God endures 40
   Warriors, workers and worshippers 43
   The families of the Levites and their service 44
   The purification of the Levites 46
   "Who is on the Lord's side?" 48
   The covenant with Levi 52
   The consecration of the Levites 55
   The service of the Levites 59
   To each his work 61

Three classes of Levite	62
Subjection to the God-given order	64
The value of everything that is connected to Christ	68
The service of the Kohathites	70

Chapter 5
Uncleanness outside the camp 77

A picture of discipline in the assembly	77
The example of Achan	79
To judge or not to judge?	80
The unity of the body of Christ	81
The holiness of the house of God	84
Confession and reparation	87
Restitution	88
The tender conscience	88
Infidelity and jealousy	91

Chapter 6
The Nazarite 93

The institution of the Nazarite	93
The perfect Nazarite	94
Separation from the joys of this world	95
Renouncement of our personal dignity	97
No contact with a dead body	99
Communion with God	99
The example of Samson	100
Divine resources	102
Removal and return	104
The end of the Nazarite's time of consecration	106
There is no Church in the Old Testament	108
The final benediction on the people of Israel	111

Chapter 7
The offerings of Israel's princes 115

The wagons	115
The offerings for the dedication of the altar	116

Chapter 8
The light of the candlestick ... 120
The place of this teaching ... 120
A light which reflected on the candlestick itself ... 123

Chapter 9
The Passover in the desert ... 128
A problem ... 129
The Passover in the second month ... 131
Grace in no way lowers the divine standard ... 132
Negligence in respect of the Passover ... 135
The value of the Lord's Supper ... 137
Attentive to the movements of the cloud ... 140
Slavery and liberty ... 142
God's will and ours ... 144

Chapter 10
How God guides His people ... 148
The two silver trumpets ... 148
Dependence and submission ... 150
God occupies Himself with the details of our lives ... 152
The camp of Israel ready to move ... 154
The ark in front of the people ... 155

Chapter 11
The murmurings, the manna and the quails ... 158
Man and his failures ... 158
Will the bread from heaven be enough for us? ... 160
The bad elements in the midst of God's people ... 163
Moses discouraged ... 165
Forgetting the divine resources ... 167
The seventy elders of Israel ... 169
God's response to unbelief ... 170
The Spirit on the seventy elders ... 171
Eldad and Medad prophesy in the camp ... 174
The quails ... 175

Chapter 12
Miriam struck with leprosy 177
   The wife of Moses, a type of the Church 177
   Calumny against a servant of God 178
   Miriam's seven days outside the camp 181

Chapter 13
Sending out the spies to Canaan 183
   The origin of this expedition 183
   The result of the exploration 187

Chapter 14
Kadesh: the refusal to enter the land of Canaan 191
   Discouragement and unbelief 191
   A march back 193
   Joshua and Caleb, two faithful witnesses 194
   God ready to execute judgment 196
   Moses' intercession 197
   Grace and government 199
   The typical significance of the entry into Canaan 202
   Faith and unbelief 205
   Confidence in their own strength 207
   Submission to the consequences of their faults 209

Chapter 15
Various instructions 212
   When you have entered 212
   A picture of Israel restored 217
   Sins of ignorance and presumptuous sins 219
   Profaning the Sabbath 224
   A fringe and a riband of blue 225

Chapter 16
The rebellion of Korah, Dathan and Abiram 227
   Jealousy 227
   Moses' attitude 232
   Ministers and priests 236

The judgment of God	238
The next day	241

Chapters 17 & 18
The priesthood — 244
The rod that budded	244
A witness to the grace of God	248
Priesthood and ministry	251
Misplaced fear	256
The Levites, servants of Aaron	257
Workers subject to their head	259
The priestly service	261
Eating the sin offering	264
The heave offerings	265
The redemption of the firstborn	268
No earthly heritage for the Levites	268

Chapter 19
The red heifer — 271
A picture of the perfection of Christ	271
Christ as victim and then as priest	273
Outside the camp	276
Purification by the blood of Christ	279
The ashes of the heifer	285
The water of separation	290
The holiness and the grace of God	293
The one who attended to the impurity	296

Chapter 20
Nearing the end of the wilderness journey — 298
The death of Miriam	298
The striving at Meribah	299
Striking the rock in error	301
Messengers to the king of Edom	304
The death of Aaron	304

Chapter 21
The brazen serpent 305
   Israel loathes the manna 305
   The love of God 307
   Faith which lays hold of salvation 308
   And from there they came to Beer 310

Chapters 22-24
Balaam 312
   The covetous prophet 312
   Can Balaam curse Israel? 313
   The difference between standing and state 314
   Balaam's first prophecy 317
   The second prophecy 317
   The third prophecy 319
   The fourth prophecy 322

Chapter 25
Fornication with the daughters of Moab 325
   Israel joins himself to Baal-Peor 325
   The energetic action of Phinehas 326

Chapter 26
A new numbering 328
   Six hundred thousand men fallen in the wilderness 328
   The word of God mixed with faith 329

Chapter 27
The daughters of Zelophehad 331
   God responds to faith 331
   That the inheritance remove not from tribe to tribe 335
   Moses approaches the end 337

Chapters 28 & 29
The continual burnt offering and the periodic burnt offerings 340
   The most precious sacrifices to God 340

Christian worship 343

Chapter 30
The vows 345

Chapter 31
Jehovah's vengeance on Midian 348

Chapter 32
Two and a half tribes on the east of Jordan 351
    A lack of faith and energy 351
    Further consequences 353

Chapters 33 & 34
The journeyings of Israel in the wilderness 357
    The boundaries of Israel's inheritance 358

Chapter 35
The cities of refuge 359
    The Levites' cities 359
    Six cities of refuge 359
    Israel guilty of murder 361
    The application to the sinner 363